Chasing
Tarzan

Chasing Tarzan

Catherine Forster

E. L. Marker
Salt Lake City

Published by E.L. Marker, an imprint of WiDo Publishing

WiDo Publishing
Salt Lake City, Utah
widopublishing.com

Cover design by Steven Novak and Catherine Forster
Book design by Marny K. Parkin

ISBN 978-1-947966-61-1

To my mother, Ruth,
my daughters Kyra and Megan,
and Mum.

Contents

Artist Note

CHASING TARZAN BEGAN AS A SERIES OF DRAWINGS. INITIALLY, I WAS unsure of their purpose. But when I married words with the drawings, the project found its home in memoir. Memory is fickle, but it defines who we are. It's not fact, but it can reveal truth.

I am the second child of eight children. We grew up together, lived under the same roof, shared vacations, watched fireworks together on the Fourth of July, and hunted Easter eggs—my dad's home movies reveal we'd done so—but we did not have the same childhood.

This book is an excavation of my childhood. I've changed the names of some individuals and, in a few cases, identifying places because I believe everyone should tell their own story.

This one is mine.

Part One
Tarzan

Chapter One
Avoiding Cracks

I WAS BAREFOOT IN THE FRONT YARD, MY TOES WARMED BY A sunbaked sidewalk. Ants bled from its cracks. I poked them with a stick and watched them recoil, flee, and come right back, some carrying bounty. I was three years old, alone (except for the ants), and ever so careful not to step on the cracks. My big brother, Steve, told me that even one teeny step on a crack would break my mother's back.

"Does everyone forage for food, or do some stay home and clean up?" I conversed with the ants, deliberating on colony jobs. Like most of my conversations, this one took place in my head. I moved on in search of new creatures. Avoiding the cracks, I hopped, skipped, and twirled my way down the block, eyeing trees, bugs, and birds. It was nice being alone with the bugs and birds: no crying babies or adults saying, "Do this or do that." I hummed a tune from church and walked past gardens chock full of flowers, yards clipped clean, and yards overgrown with dandelions. I was tempted to pick the flowers, but I knew not to. Instead, I picked the dandelions bordering the sidewalk.

A woman in a yellow dress called out to me, asking me what I was up to. I was not in her yard, but I was smelling one of her roses. Standing on her porch, she asked me where I lived and where my mother was. Her husband came outside. Tall and frowning, he stood next to her and watched me, silent. I stepped away from her roses, then I told them my name and that I lived down the street. Unbeknownst to me, I'd been walking for hours, blissfully drifting; I was nowhere near my house. Her husband brought out the phone book, found my last name, and called the number. I don't remember what he said over the phone, but his wife's face plumped up like she'd eaten a tasty treat.

"Sit here," she said, pointing to the bottom step, "until your mother comes."

Mom arrived. "Hello, so sorry to bother you," she sputtered, addressing the cross-armed twosome. She grabbed my arm and pulled me up. The adults chatted, but I don't remember what they said. I remember studying Mom's face and the tone of her voice—she used her out-of-the-house-friendly voice—knowing both revealed more than the words coming out of her mouth. She was hopping mad. When we got home, she let loose, adopting her you-are-bad voice. I was wide-eyed and confused. What was all the fuss about? Why was she so mad? I was just on a walk, a very fine walk, and I wanted to go back outside for another. Whatever I'd done, it must have happened in front of the neighbors.

"—might be Dad's customers. Don't ever do that again." I nodded my head like big people expected, all the while wondering what *that* was.

Sometime later, maybe days or even weeks later, it's hard to know for sure, I watched her face as she berated me once again. Then, too, I was unable to comprehend her rage. Again, I was paralyzed by it, afraid to pull away.

I was playing in the backyard, immersed in an imaginary adventure. I had to pee, but I didn't want to stop and go inside. I waited too long and wet myself. Knowing I was bound to get into trouble, I slipped inside to change, but Mom spotted my soiled shorts and the pee dribbling down my legs. Her face scrunched up, turning ugly, and she yelled. I have no memory of what she said, but her voice hit me like a thunderclap. I nearly fell down. She barreled toward me. I froze, expecting the worst but not knowing what that might be. She cupped her hands under my arms, carried me into the bedroom, and tossed me onto the bed. My head snapped forward, and I bit my tongue, but I didn't cry—dared not to.

"I have enough diapers to change!" she yelled, pulling off my pants and wiping me down as if I were a baby. She put training pants on me, or maybe a diaper; I don't remember, but it wasn't my underwear. Her mouth moved, but I didn't hear her. Her eyes frightened me. They said, *I don't want you.*

In that moment, she may not have wanted me or Steve or Tom. I was too young to understand that it might not have been me she was seeing or yelling at. The rage behind her eyes could have been meant for Dad, who was gone, away on business. Maybe she hated the new town, the prying neighbors, the stacks upon stacks of laundry, the spit-up on her clothes, the absence of friends, and the loneliness. She was twenty-three with a bundle of babes, and she was one hundred fifty-six miles from home.

I was too young to know what her eyes meant.

I didn't cry or fight back; I didn't say I was sorry. Steve would never have stayed on that bed. But I just lay there, watching. It seemed the safest thing to do. When she was done, I slid off the bed and ducked outside. My tummy churned, and my head ached. I wanted to hide, to make the day go away—to make me go away. I didn't understand what was happening or what had happened, and I didn't have a word for it. In time, I would know it as *shame*.

Years later, I'd ache for a time when I could meander and talk to ants if I wanted to without having to watch my back. These early memories would later trigger questions and clog my thoughts like leaves in a gutter. *Why did I lie still doing nothing? Why didn't I cry? Or protest? Or attempt to crawl away? I just watched her like I was one of those ants crawling out from under the cracks.*

Chapter Two

On the Move

"EYES FRONT!" SISTER MARY CLARE ROARED.

I was seven and in second grade, though I was kind of in first grade, too. My classroom at Immaculate Conception combined first and second grades. Sister Mary Clare taught both, over sixty students, and maintained order by means of a booming voice box, a well-used pointer, and a knotted rope she didn't hesitate to deploy as a whip. Mom and Dad didn't seem to mind the two-grade structure. We were Catholics; there was never a question about our attending Immaculate Conception, the school associated with our church, which were both linked by the parking lot.

Convinced Sister Mary Clare's words were meant for me—she always knew when my mind wandered—I gave her my full attention, but it didn't last long. It rarely did.

It was 1962, my last day in school, my last day in Augusta, Georgia. I'd already lived in four towns, two states, and six houses that I could remember. Steve and I were born in Tacoma, Washington. From there we moved to Yakima, on the east side of the state, where Tom and Mary were born. Two years later we headed northwest, crossing the Cascade Mountains and the Olympic Mountain range to Port Angeles, a small fishing village and harbor on the Strait of Juan de Fuca. We could see Canada across the strait. Barely six months after unpacking (Mom hated the town; Dad hated the store), we moved to Augusta, where Barry James and Joseph were born. Tomorrow we were heading back to Washington State, the home of the world's largest lumber mill and the giant lumberjack, my favorite childhood hero, Paul Bunyan.

I was far too antsy to sit still. I tried focusing on my ABCs, but Paul Bunyan and his trusted sidekick, a blue ox, beckoned.

With her ever-present pointer in her right hand, Sister dashed to the blackboard, her robes fluttering like black sheets on a line. I imagined her soaring upward, banging her head on the classroom ceiling, and then the force of the collision dispatching her back to the floor.

The pointer circled round and round above Sister's head. My eyes pursued it until they crossed. Without warning, the pointer morphed into a colossal axe, and Sister turned into Paul Bunyan, the axe swinging high above his head. The giant Bunyan sliced through a mighty cedar with his axe, relieving it of its branches just as I might prune a stick for a marshmallow roast. He tossed the log in the air, cast me a wide smile paired with a wink, and, ever so gently, strapped the log to the back of Babe, his blue ox companion. Ground crunching under his massive boots, Paul hunted for the next tree, one with a similar girth to the first. I followed, hopping from footprint to footprint. It took me several hops just to cross the hollow stamp of his heel. Panting and out of breath, I struggled to keep up.

I tried to hold on to the crunch-crunch of his giant footsteps, but the sound faded, eclipsed by the splat of Sister's shoes on the classroom floor. She pointed at a letter hanging over the blackboard, the one stuck in the middle of the alphabet.

"Sounds like *mmm*," Sister said, writing big M and its companion, little m, on the blackboard.

M was better looking than the others, stronger and in command, a soldier ready for battle. M was number thirteen of twenty-six letters; how would I learn the other thirteen? I desperately wanted to take this M with me. I wanted to rip it off the wall and stuff it under my sweater, believing that my new teacher somehow required it to teach me the rest of the alphabet.

Sister didn't announce my departure or that I wouldn't be in class tomorrow. She didn't say goodbye either, but I didn't care. I wouldn't miss her: she scared me. She was pee-in-your-pants scary. One time in the classroom, I did pee my pants. Mom was furious, but I couldn't help it. My offense was asking whether I could go to the bathroom when it wasn't break time. Sister wouldn't allow me, but I couldn't wait. I froze as pee ran down my legs and into and over my shoes. My fellow classmates gasped. Sister's face went purple. Her cheeks quadrupled in size, stretching the wimple framing her face. She came after me, soaring down the aisle. Thinking she was going to flatten me, I closed my eyes and waited, but the blow never came. Instead, I was made to clean up my sinful puddle while my classmates watched. Sister's incensed roar ricocheted off the blackboard and the back of the room. "Godliness, discipline, and control are the path to heaven," she lectured. Concluding, she said, "School is not for babies." Wishing I could magically vanish, I rolled my body into a tiny ball and scrubbed.

I was glad to see the back of her. I was unaware that in less than a year's time, I'd long to return; unknowing that my nighttime prayers would become consumed with pleas for my father to be transferred back. Sister's tyranny was no match for the relentless bullying awaiting me; her antics were lame compared to my future foe's dirty tricks.

"Catherine. Give me a word beginning with *M*."

I shook off images of Sister's gargoyle face and answered, "Monster?"

Sister spelled out *monster* on the board, and for once the chalk didn't squeak. She had an affection for pressing hard.

I liked this letter. It rolled off my tongue in waves.

M is for move, monster, mother, and Mars.

Class ended without fanfare. I stared at big *M* and little *m*, mouthed goodbye, and left. Embedding the handsome pair in my brain, I repeated them over and over again, whispering their unique hum. I didn't have their cardboard likenesses, but I took them with me.

All was a bustle when I got home from school. Dad was strapping suitcases to the top of the station wagon. Steve and I peeked through the car windows. A crib minus its legs consumed all the space in the back seat. The crib was lodged tight, end to end and side to side. Dad left the front gate unhinged so Mom could reach around and tend to the baby. Brand new and tiny, Joseph Benedict slept with his butt up in the air. He made soft, gurgling sounds and cried like a duck. Like a lot of families in our Catholic church, there was always a new baby or one on the way. Families of six, eight, or more were common. Joseph was number six of an eventual eight.

My father didn't spend a lot of time at home. He spent most of his time in a car or roaming the aisles of our local department store. Whenever I revealed the number of houses we had lived in, our new neighbors always assumed we were a military family. Not so. Dad worked in retail. He was renowned for his salesmanship—an honest Harold Hill—there wasn't an item in the store he couldn't move. He worked for a big department store retailer, which consisted of multiple chains. I assumed the company transferred Dad every two years or so, but I was wrong. Dad initiated our moves, seeking bigger challenges and higher positions: working his way up the ladder, as he liked to say. The first chain Dad worked in was *Peoples,* a small department store selling everything but only in limited quantities. Dad was the assistant store manager for *Peoples* in Tacoma, Yakima, and Port Angeles. Then when we moved to Augusta, he joined the *Bon Marche,* a larger and more upscale chain. It was a big store, but he was still an assistant manager. He was determined to score a store manager position when we moved back to Washington.

He was gone a lot. As head buyer, he went to every seasonal market where companies from around the world would present their offerings, from clothes to washing machines. He also flew to Seattle to attend head office meetings. I had a shoebox full of tiny hotel soaps wrapped in delicate paper that I never opened. The miniature souvenirs were too special. He saved them for me—only me.

Dad's face lit up when he announced our coming move. "A new adventure," he promised, "traveling coast to coast, from the Atlantic to the Pacific. We'll cross the mighty Mississippi, climb over mountains, traverse deserts, pass through miles and miles of this country's most magnificent farmlands, ranches, oil fields . . ." When I got home from school, I ached for a fresh batch of tales, but he was too busy securing suitcases and boxes.

I turned my attention to the inside of the car. Blankets covered the far back end of the station wagon. The cargo space was half the size of my bed and would be our—Steve, Tom, Mary, Barry James, and my—turf. We each had a pillow and our own blanket. Coloring books and crayons; decks of cards, real ones and Old Maid; toddler toys; and a doll for Mary lined the perimeter. No comic books: Dad's orders. Steve got carsick.

Where was Chatty Cathy, my favorite doll?

Mom was inside, holding on to her last moments of sanity before getting into the car with our unruly brood. Dad tested the ropes, rearranged

Station-wagon Hotel

the suitcases, grunted, shoved, and pulled. Between grunts and without looking up, he told me to fetch Mom. Maybe my doll was inside.

I met Mom on the way to the house. She walked slowly, delaying getting into the car. "I heard," she said.

Running through the empty house, I checked for my doll. Chatty Cathy wasn't there. We'd already thrown out everything we weren't taking. As big as Barry James—too big to carry along in the car—Chatty Cathy was put in the keeper pile, designated for the moving van. Mom must have packed her.

"All aboard," Dad said, his voice cheerful and circus-ringmaster lively. "California or bust." He was overdoing it, compensating for Mom's awkward silence. She looked straight ahead and climbed into the passenger seat without saying a word. Mom was glad to move. She hated Augusta, the heat, the bugs, and the snakes. She had friends here but missed home—Tacoma and a town ten miles south, Puyallup, Washington, where she grew up—and she wasn't keen to spend four days cooped up in a car with five kids and a newborn. We traveled by train the first time around, when there were only four of us kids. Our party of six had shared one cabin. The journey was a happy one. I turned five on that adventure. There was no cake, but I remember sitting on the top bunk opening presents, the world flying by outside the window. This time we were driving because we couldn't afford the train.

Our destination was not California, despite Dad's hurrah and our appeals for Mickey Mouse from the back of the station wagon. There would be no detours to Disneyland or panning for gold. We didn't have a final destination. Dad's new posting was still up in the air. We were on our way to Tacoma, where my grandparents lived. Dad would figure out the next steps when we got there. Mom preferred something more definite. She may have been thinking about Port Angeles, where we had stayed only six months, loathing another twice-in-a-matter-of-months move.

The drive across the country sounded magical to me, crossing nine states like pioneers, but in a station wagon. I was a pretty good packer and unpacker, and I couldn't wait.

The moving van had already left. I worried about our things and Chatty Cathy. I knew nothing about Dad's dicey job situation, but I did know we lacked an address. I imagined Chatty Cathy, our sofa, my bed, our toys, all being tossed about on a vacant lot, wind blowing loose items away. Where would the movers unpack our stuff? I caught airborne toys in my head while Dad laid down the rules.

"Prepare yourselves," he said, referring to our four-day trip. "No stopping, except to go to the bathroom, and I'm not stopping every two minutes. You'll have to hold it until everyone needs to go. Am I clear?" He eyed us older kids, waiting until we nodded in agreement.

Steve, at eight years old, was only eleven months older than me. Steve and I looked alike: spitting images of Dad. To Steve's chagrin, people often confused us for twins. We were the same height and had red curly hair and abundant freckles, though my hair was a different shade of red than Steve's. Dad's hair used to be dark red like Steve's, but most of the red had now vanished. My hair was the shade of a Halloween pumpkin.

Steve climbed in first, then me. I claimed the corner abutting the back seat, sitting as far away from him as was possible. It was a knee-jerk reaction. *Ornery* was the descriptor adults gave to Steve. Mom often said, "If you want him to do something, tell him the opposite." Lately, deciphering his intentions was increasingly impossible. Did he want to play or harass? Keeping my distance seemed like the best option.

Our uneasy relationship, a reluctant marriage of playmates and antagonists, was inevitable, a competition ensured since the day I was brought home and Mom nursed me and gave him a bottle. As toddlers, we shared a playpen, an arena he could control when Mom wasn't looking. He'd round up toys, even ones he didn't want. Later, we played on our backyard swing set, played hide-and-go-seek, and tossed a ball. He'd play nice at first, but then he'd aim for my body and throw harder than I could catch. When Tom was old enough, about three, we became a twosome, forging an alliance to counter Steve's growing tendencies to strike.

Tom was my best buddy. At age five, two years younger than me, he was easy to be around. He presented one face, one I could always count on. Tom took after Mom. He had curly blond hair, blue eyes, and skin that would tan and wasn't covered in freckles. He climbed in and took the rear corner closest to me. Dad lifted Mary, a miniature version of Mom, into the car and plopped Barry James, redheaded and soon to be two, on my lap. Barry James was named after Dad, so we coupled his first and middle names to prevent confusion. What's more, he was born in the South where double names were common, like Kenny Ray, the kid next door.

Joey was in Mom's lap, awake, so we didn't have to be quiet. When he slept, our mouths had to be zipped. Glancing at Mary, I imagined her pretty little mouth suddenly disappearing, replaced by a large silver zipper. She was three and a half years old. I envied her blonde hair, her blue eyes, her unfreckled skin, and how Mom's friends cooed over her. "What a peach, pretty as a picture, a picture of you, Ruth." Dad was a good-looking man, but he was a man. I didn't want a man's nose or face. I wanted Mom's. Mary caught me gawking, and the zipper disappeared.

"Alabama, Mississippi, Louisiana, New Mexico, Texas, Arizona, California, Oregon, Washington, here we come," Dad said, signaling the beginning of our adventure. "We'll be better traveled than most Americans. Most people, period." He waved a free hand above his head as if he were twirling a Fourth of July sparkler. Dad's face was always trickier to read than Mom's, but I was dead sure he was not keen on this venture. He was trying too hard.

Mom rolled her eyes—she was allowed to. We weren't, so we cheered.

Tom and I weren't happy to leave Lennit Loop, our street in Augusta, or our buddy Kenny Ray for all the reasons Mom hated Augusta. For us, the heat was a gift, allowing us to play outside all year, mostly barefoot. Running in Augusta's heavy air was like pushing through a wall and was especially exhilarating when it rained. We collected frogs, bugs, and snakes. The snakes turned Mom sheet white. Once, a monstrous water moccasin slithered up alongside our house. Mom screamed so loud that the neighbors came running out of their houses. Kenny Ray's dad shot it dead with his shotgun. On top of all that, we had our very own mysterious woods right at the back of the house. Mom forbade us to enter, fearing snakes, gators, wild boar, and hillbillies. Dad said illegal moonshine operations could be running deep in the woods and that it would be dangerous to run into one. Steve ducked inside the woods anyway when Mom wasn't looking. I nudged dangerously close to the edge, peering in for predators and hillbillies toting guns. I never saw either, except in my daydreams.

Lennit Loop was a real-life adventure park (at least I thought so), yet I was goosebumps excited just thinking about traveling across the country. The night before we left, I dreamed of meeting Davy Crockett and Jim Bowie at the Alamo. I was wearing Davy's raccoon hat and learning how to throw a Bowie knife. Daring feats, imminent peril, and the camaraderie of fighting alongside a noted hero from TV land consumed my fantasy world. Princesses were not invited—too boring. I loved pretty dresses and how they swayed when the prince and princess danced, but princesses just didn't have the stature or dangerous life of someone like Davy Crockett.

Dad slipped into the driver's seat and turned on the ignition. Kenny Ray knocked on the window. "Tom, Tom," he yelled. He was grimacing, his big eyes narrowing. Kenny Ray was short for his age and was a wired ball of muscle. He could never stand still; he was jumping while he hammered on the window.

Busy organizing my space, I hadn't noticed he was still there, standing guard by the car. He waved frantically, as if fearing we'd already forgotten him. We waved back and kept waving as the car pulled out, circled the Loop, and turned onto the main road. Tom kept looking, searching. Spit welled up in my mouth. I swallowed hard, realizing we would never see Kenny Ray again. I turned away and placed my cheek on Barry James's soft curls. I looked up again and stared out the window, trying to hold on to Augusta by recording its sunset clay and those evenings spent frogging with Kenny Ray, playing hide-and-seek, and catching fireflies at the edge of the woods.

Our first bathroom stop was the Alabama state line, four hours away. We didn't make it.

"Ew, yuck! Barry James pooped! I'm gonna be sick," Steve yelled. Gagging, the rest of us joined in, pleading, "Open a window! Open a window!"

"Hold on, hold on," Dad said, looking for a place to stop.

Dad pulled into a gas station, Mom changed Barry James, we dashed to the bathroom, did our business, then climbed back into the car and headed off—a procedure repeated time and time again over the course of our grueling trip. Tom and I played cards. We taught Mary how to play Snap. Steve kicked and punched anyone who touched him. The baby cried, then Barry James cried. He wanted Mom. Mary pretended to soothe her doll, rocking it and murmuring, "Shh, shh." Mary needed a cuddle, too, but none would come. Mom couldn't reach us all the way in the back even if she wanted to.

"Catherine, see to Barry James!" she yelled.

"I am!" I yelled back.

I bounced him, cuddled him, and gave him something to chew. Tom attempted to distract him with tickles, but the poking made him cry harder. I bounced him some more. Barry James wanted Mom. I could only bounce and coo. Eventually, he dozed off.

Tom and I played Old Maid. I played one-handed.

"Old Maid! . . . Bingo. You're so ugly. Nobody's gonna marry you," Steve snarled.

I ignored him but wondered, was I too ugly to be a bride?

"I heard that!" Dad yelled, momentarily shutting Steve up.

My arm ached with Barry James's weight, but I dared not lay him down, fearing his resumed wails. It was hot and sweaty, and my legs were cramped, yet I shrunk deeper into my corner and away from Steve. We all did, as much as possible in our bitty box. He pretended to stretch, legs searching until they reached a mark, then he'd threaten, "I said don't touch me." Tom fought back, Mary cringed, but I pretended he wasn't there. Complaining would only further agitate Mom. I didn't want to be the one to set her off.

"Enough back there!" Dad shouted, but his threats were empty. He couldn't reach Steve.

Hours passed, each like the others. My arm was long past numb.

"Alabama!" Dad said, pointing to a sign overhead.

I can't say whether we made it to the state line within his four-hour target, but I do remember thinking we ought to be in Texas by now.

Dad stopped on the side of the road and lowered the tailgate. We jumped out, elated to stand up and move. My body welcomed unbending. Mom deployed the tailgate as a table and made peanut butter and jelly sandwiches. Cheap, easy, and reasonably nutritious, the sandwich was a family staple. I hated peanut butter. I hated how it stuck to the rim of my mouth, I hated its poop-like texture and color, and I didn't like jelly. I preferred jam: strawberry, raspberry, blackberry—any kind of berry but grape.

Mom moved quickly, like a factory assembly line; there was no time for special orders. Twenty minutes later, we were curled up again. Resuming our positions, we began a game of I Spy. It was fun for the first half hour, before Steve got bored.

"I spy an oink-oink."

No one responded. He made a Jerry Lewis face, implying we should find him funny. Steve oinked and pointed at me, laughing. He smashed the tip of his nose, making a pig face, a common ploy. So common, I figured his nose would grow upward. I should've been numb to it by now, but it landed as viscerally as ever. It always would. My nose was no uglier than Steve's—we had the same one—but when he grew up,

I assumed he'd be handsome like Dad. Mom's nose was dainty, and so were all the ladies' noses in her magazines and on TV. Mine wouldn't be, or so I thought, imagining Dad's nose on Mom's face.

I stared out the window, waiting for Dad to shut him up. But no relief came. There was only silence from the front. *Maybe Dad didn't hear him.*

"I spy . . . oink, oink." Steve doubled down.

"My turn. I spy something yellow," Tom said, attempting to recover the game and a civil mood. "Out the window, for real. Come on," he prodded. I appreciated the effort, and his courage defying Steve, but I didn't want to play anymore. I stared out the window and counted telephone poles.

M is for mean, maid, monkey, and menace.

Black and white monkeys appeared outside my window. Orangutans, chimpanzees, and baby baboons swung from telephone pole to telephone pole. Joining them, I pivoted around an orangutan and overtook a chimpanzee on my way to the front of the line. They cried and screeched, and so did I, but we didn't wake the baby. Darkness fell. I cuddled Barry James as if he were my very own baby monkey, and then I drifted off to sleep.

On day two, Mississippi water crept over our wheels. The highway was closed due to flooding, so Dad took a detour, but it didn't work. Water surrounded the car. We were in the middle of a river—a brand-new river.

Mom freaked out. "Get us out of here!"

Frightened by Mom's voice, Mary started whimpering.

"It's okay, the car floats," I whispered.

We all knew to be quiet, so quiet we heard only water and Mom's fear. Augusta floods brought snakes and alligators to Lennit Loop. Snakes swam up storm water drains and even up toilets. We heard many a tale and watched TV reports of snakes biting unsuspecting folks while sitting on their toilets. I always turned on the light, looked before sitting, and peed fast, imagining snakes swimming toward my bottom. Last summer, a giant water moccasin had to be removed from a neighbor's porch. I don't remember whether we watched from our front window or saw it on TV, but agents from Wildlife Control, wearing tan uniforms and carrying long sticks with wire-looped ends, gingerly approached the six-foot-long serpent, deftly snared the monster, and dropped it in a bag. This giant fared better than the snake who clashed with Kenny Ray's dad. Mom cried with abandon and wouldn't come out of her bedroom for hours.

Mom covered her eyes. I desperately wanted to see something swimming in the murky water. Anticipating an exciting find, I searched for snakes and alligators and imagined the car floating away like Noah's ark. Diving into the water, Bowie knife in hand, I wrestled a giant gator threatening baby Joey and Barry James. Swirling in the turgid water, I buried the knife deep into the gator's gut, just like Tarzan, obliterating the menace.

"Family survives flash flood, an adventure to remember!" Dad quipped, driving out of the water onto a damp but clear road.

"It's not funny," Mom shot back, firing Dad an icy look. Her cheeks were wet with tears. She turned away, but I knew her face was stony and close to crumbling. Staring at the back of her head, I willed her to turn around and smile, even if it wasn't a real smile. I hated when she fell apart; I hated seeing her weak. I wanted her to wrestle snakes, to gut 'em and serve 'em for dinner.

By the time we reached Texas, Tom, Mary, and I adopted Steve's urge to punch, kick, and push all who crossed our invisible boundaries. We'd mastered fighting in silence so as to not wake the baby or drive Mom crazy.

In the mornings, after nursing, Mom drove while Dad slept. He required quiet, too. We played a lot of cards and I Spy, fought covertly, pouted, and stared out the window. A day passed, then a restless night and more peanut butter and jelly sandwiches. I changed Barry James when his diaper was full of pee, a tricky procedure in a moving car. The diaper pin slipped in easiest with a little oil obtained by drawing the pin along my scalp—a trick Mom taught me—but a dangerous one during a bumpy ride. I placed my fingers under the diaper, protecting Barry James's skin and pricking my own every time the car jerked. After a changing, I'd rub my scalp and suck my sore fingers.

We stopped to rinse poop and soiled items in gas station bathrooms, but otherwise we kept to the road. Louisiana's lush landscape faded, replaced with dry red soil like the Georgia clay stains on our clothes. By now, I'd spent hours staring out the window, watching lone houses, farms, and towns cruise by. But somehow, I'd missed when the lush greens had turned to desert dust.

All of a sudden, Dad pulled off the highway even though it was too soon for a bathroom break and no one was begging to stop.

"Who wants to go to Mexico?" Dad asked playfully, despite our obvious fatigue.

Mom and Joey stayed with the car. I watched her pace like a caged animal despite her freedom from the confines of the car. She wanted to be done with our adventure. But we, on the other hand, couldn't wait to join Dad.

"I want to go," Tom said. "Me too, me too!" we chimed in, raising our hands and jumping in the air. I waved Barry James's arms, too.

We lined up behind Dad. He stopped at a bridge with a guardhouse and two guards. They held rifles and wore green uniforms with short sleeves and pants tucked into shiny black boots. It was hot. I pondered the state of their toes. *Bet they're sweating.* Dad chatted with one of the guards. We did our best stand-at-attention pose behind him, knowing better than to talk or fidget. The guard cocked his head, motioning us toward the gate. When the barrier rose, we filed through, serious-like, as we did in church.

"That's the Rio Grande we're crossing," Dad said.

I looked over the side. It was muddy and not very impressive. I'd imagined it bigger. In one of Dad's favorite movies, John Wayne's horse nearly drowned in the Rio Grande. Its paltry state had me questioning John Wayne's stature—but only for a second.

"You are officially out of the United States and in a foreign country!"

Dad's enthusiasm shattered our timidity. Cheering, we raised our fists in the air. Free of our confining box, our muscles and lungs cut loose, we raced back and forth across the bridge. "I'm in Mexico . . . I'm in Texas!" we shouted.

I yelled, "*M* is for Mexico!"

Dad picked Barry James up, swung him high, and belted, "An adventure to tell your grandkids someday!" With eyes the size of whopper marbles, Barry James looked as if he wasn't sure whether to cry or laugh.

Mexico was our last memorable adventure. Steve, Tom, and I were ready for another exploit, a reason to escape what had become our above-ground dungeon, but Dad didn't stop driving. He was in a race to end this folly before Mom lost it.

Chapter Three
Final Stretch

ANOTHER MISERABLE DAY PASSED BEFORE WE REACHED TACOMA. Dad found a small rent-by-the-month house. I don't remember what it looked like, but it was virtually empty: there was only a kitchen table. Why unpack if we might move on a day's notice? Dad spent his days in Seattle, negotiating his next position. Out of four possible choices, he landed the manager position for the Bon Marche in Longview, Washington, a mill town on the Columbia River, fifty-five miles from the Pacific Coast.

I wasn't to see Longview just yet. We moved in stages. Dad decided it would be more efficient to farm out some of us kids until he and Mom found a house in Longview and moved in. I stayed with Grandma Lu and Grandpa Mel, Dad's parents. No one remembers where Steve, Tom, and Mary went. When I asked my mother years later, she could only guess: "Someone probably stayed with my mother; she could only handle one."

Mom's parents were a lot older than Dad's parents. Her mother, Grandma Quinn, had lived alone since Grandpa Quinn died when I was an infant. Mom was Grandma's last surprise (Mom's four siblings were grown and married, some with children, when she was born). Steve remembers getting into trouble for fighting with cousins on Mom's side, so he most likely stayed with Aunt Eileen.

I remember every inch of my grandparents' farm: their grand red farmhouse, hay-packed barn, riotous chicken coop, expansive vegetable garden, and five acres of pasture, plus the goats, a couple cows, my aunt's horse, and Grandma's dog, a gray terrier named Lucy. It was not a working farm, since my grandpa was a barber, but to me, it was farm life.

My Tacoma bedroom was bathroom-sized: tiny and cozy. The bed was short and half the width of a regular kid's bed, and the slanted ceiling was wallpapered with mini flowers. Standing on the bed, I could touch the tiny flowers and both walls. I loved it. It was sweet to have the room all to myself—no sharing, no Steve—but I did miss Tom. There was no one to play with. Grandma had lots of frilly dolls, but they weren't toys. She had a lot of toys that weren't toys. Mostly, I stayed outside. Grandma smiled more when I did. She'd had a lot of kids (four girls and two boys), but she didn't like having young ones around anymore, so I made myself scarce. I crawled through the tiny door of Grandpa's henhouse and played with the chickens. At first, they protested, scurrying about in a frenzy, but they got used to me.

I spent evenings in the living room with Grandpa. He was tall and lean with an open, quiet but friendly face. He was movie-star handsome in a Gregory Peck kind of way. He always had room on his lap for me. Dad took after Grandma. He was sturdily built and shorter than Grandpa; Dad had a rounder face than him, too, and no one would ever call Dad quiet.

During the week, I went to Visitation, the Benedictine school Dad had attended when he was a boy. I arrived in my Georgia uniform. There was no point in buying a new uniform for my in-between school since I was only going to be in Tacoma for a short while. The Benedictine nuns wore a strange getup with odd wimples. These nuns looked nothing like the Sisters in Augusta. Sister Teresa's head balanced on a stiff collar, reminiscent of the bead-coiled necks of Burmese women in Dad's *National Geographic* magazine. I knew I wasn't supposed to stare, but I couldn't help it. Sister spoke. I watched her neck. *How does she swallow?*

Second grade was different here, too. They'd finished the alphabet and were reading. Sister didn't think I'd be in Tacoma long enough to teach me to read, so she gave me a math book and told me to work on my sums. I sat in the back, doing addition and subtraction, and worried about the letters after *M*. The rest of the class took turns reading. I was near the top of my class in Georgia and proud of it, but now I was on the bottom and didn't like it one bit.

"Why can't you read?" a girl whispered, her breath hot on the back of my neck.

"She's slow?" a snotty-nosed boy chipped in. He sat to my right.

I informed all three, "My school didn't do reading in second grade."

"Catherine, we don't talk in class! Maybe such behavior is okay down south, but not here. Come to the front."

Sister grabbed a paddle from her desk. She grabbed my hand. I pulled it away. Incensed, she seized my shoulder and turned me around so my back was to her. The swishing sound of her robes warned me that the paddle was headed my way. I jumped forward, and she missed. Grabbing my arm, she tried again. I started to run. Entangled, we spun in circles as Sister screamed for me to stop, her paddle pummeling my legs and bottom. I heard muffled giggles and gasps; my classmates were unsure how to respond. Breathless and with sweat beading across her brow, she marched me to the back of the room, pulled a desk away from the other rows, retrieved my math book, and slapped it down in front of me. No one dared breathe, but several kids stole a look my way. Mortified and humiliated, I stared at the book, my mind racing. *How had I become the bad kid?*

After a month at the farm, I finally arrived in our new house in Longview. The house had two floors instead of one, and it was on a straight street, not a loop. My new school was only a block from the house. We had a small backyard instead of woods, and at the end of our street was a lake. Mom called it a slough.

Our backyard had one tree, and it was infested with caterpillars. The tree looked like a monster spider had attacked it, spinning it into a colossal silk tent. Up close, the caterpillars wiggled under the mesh. Fascinated, I'd watch them, cloaked behind the web, carry on their business. Their teeny feet and wormy bodies were creepier than the cockroaches that scurried across our old kitchen floor in Augusta. During the night, the caterpillars visited me, invading my dreams. I pushed and poked and screamed, but I couldn't escape the silk mesh and caterpillar claws— nightmare claws bigger than my own hands.

We also had slugs: big, fat, gooey slugs. Disgusting slugs. Stepping on them was the worst; snot-slimy guts would ooze between my toes. *Yuck.* And the town stunk. When the wind blew in from the mills, a stench like rotten eggs mixed with rank farts and something vile growing in the fridge consumed the air. On bad days, I didn't dare breathe through my nose, or I'd risk losing my breakfast.

We didn't go frogging. I hadn't seen a frog since Augusta. Instead, Steve and I fished. Mom wouldn't let Tom go; she said he was too little. I liked sitting on the bank watching our bobbers, willing them to bounce, waiting for a catfish to strike. But we had to throw the fish back. Mom wouldn't have them in the house. She said they were dirty just like the water. I suspected the catfish whiskers reminded her of the cockroaches.

Images of my days at Visitation (me spinning to avoid the paddle) unnerved me as I dressed for my new school, St. Rose. I hoped the nuns at St. Rose would be nice. I wore my Augusta uniform. Mom said she'd buy our St. Rose uniforms for the new school year. It was May, and there was barely a month left of the school year. "A waste to buy them now," Mom claimed. Wearing my foreign uniform, I would stand out in the classroom and on the playground, just as I did at Visitation.

I gingerly walked up to my second-grade teacher, Sister Brendan, and handed her the piece of paper scribbled with notes about me. I don't know what it said, but she handed me a math book. My classmates could read, like the ones in Tacoma, so there was no point in teaching me; it was too late in the year. Despite being several chapters ahead in math, everyone thought I was slow, but I knew not to answer the why-can't-you-read questions in class. I pretended to do my numbers while Sister wrote words on the board and sounded them out.

"C . . . A . . . T."

Sister tapped *C* with her pointer, and my classmates shouted, "C." I looked up at *T*. It was seven letters after *M*. Working through the alphabet, I was determined to learn my letters. I would master reading even if I had to teach myself. I copied *T* onto the corner of my math assignment. My eyes were down and my pencil was tracing *T* when the chuckles started. I looked up to riotous laughter and a commotion on the other side of the room. A boy in the third seat from the window was hiding under his chair. Sister Brendan was not happy. She grabbed her pointer and walked toward the boy's desk. Her face was purple, reminiscent of Sister Mary Clare.

"Hunter, get up *now!*" she yelled.

I winced.

He crawled under another desk and into the aisle, jumped to his feet, and started running. My classmates squealed. Some jumped up on their seats to get a better look. The room erupted into chaos: Sister yelling, kids laughing, and chairs banging.

Shocked, I watched. *This would never happen in Augusta.*

Sister waved the stick again and again, hitting desks, the floor, and the blackboard. She found her mark once, poorly swiping the boy's clothes but not his body. He raced up and down the aisles. With robes flying, Sister dashed close behind, occasionally snagging a desk or almost smothering a student. Finally, she caught him . . . or he let her catch him. They were both out of breath and oddly triumphant.

She didn't send him to the principal's office or to the rectory to be reprimanded by the priest. He got only one swat, a meager one, with the pointer. Swaggering back to his seat, he took the long way around, parading for the kids who were encouraging his mischief. The spectacle was mystifying, though it appeared to be run-of-the-mill entertainment for this party of seven-year-olds. The boy and Sister seemed to be enjoying themselves despite displaying their own versions of outrage.

He weaved his way to my row. Stopping at my desk, he glared, waiting for something I didn't know, then sneered, "What are *you* looking at?"

Giggles erupted nearby. Perplexed by him and the circus he provoked, I was caught off guard and didn't know how to respond. Tongue-tied and frozen to my seat, I prayed he'd move on.

"I said, *what* are you looking at?"

I stared at him. Said nothing. Did nothing.

"Hunter! Sit down, *now!*" Sister's voice thundered. I felt the floor shake, but he was unmoved.

He glowered and walked on. Back in his seat, he looked my way and made a face, as if forewarning that he was not finished with me.

I turned away and tried to solve a math problem. It was a distraction that didn't quiet my unease: there was something creepy about the way the boy's eyes bored into me.

I had only just arrived in this place. My clothes were finally placed in their dresser, and my favorite doll was out of its box and on my bed. Dad promised our adventure would continue here, but I had an uneasy feeling that this wasn't a good place to unpack.

Chapter Four

Cottage Cheese

FIVE MONTHS AFTER WE MOVED IN, MY INTRODUCTORY MONTH at St. Rose was long over but not forgotten. The first day of third grade was approaching fast. The caterpillars decamped, quitting our yard, leaving a mottled tree behind. All summer long I waited for butterflies, envisioning a cloud of them consuming our yard. I was disappointed when the wormy beasts disappeared and winged silhouettes did not engulf our yard. A few delicate wings fluttered by, but I wasn't sure they were descendants of the caterpillar tree.

I loved summer and its veiled sense of freedom that comes with seemingly endless hours of play, when evening's darkness was deferred until fall, but I was antsy for September and the start of school. On the first day of school, I noticed that the tree's leaves were turning. Some had fallen on the grass, encircling the tree like a giant yellow *O*. Steve, Tom, and I raced through breakfast, too excited to sit still or polish off our cereal despite Mom's insistence. We had finally gotten new uniforms; our Immaculate Conception threads were given over to the Goodwill. The boys wore salt and pepper cords and white colored shirts, and I wore a plaid wool skirt and a white blouse. Shoulders back, we wore them proudly, aching to get going. It was Tom's first day at school, and after attending three schools last year, Steve and I embarked on what was to be an unbroken school year. Dad's store manager position would surely keep him here for at least two years.

"Don't slam the door!" Mom yelled, but we were already halfway down the block.

I wasn't thinking of Hunter—not yet—as I rushed down the hall looking for Tom's classroom. The school's layout was somewhat fuzzy, but

I remembered that the classrooms were arranged in order: first grade at one end, eighth grade at the other, by the gym. Steve had taken off and was already in his classroom across the hall from mine. I dropped Tom inside the first-grade door and raced to my room. The number three was etched on the door, and *Sister Mary Lenora* was spelled out on the blackboard. I knew this was my teacher's name. I'd seen four comparable versions before: my first-grade and three second-grade teachers' names all began with *Sister*. I recognized the second word of my teacher's name from holy cards of the Virgin Mary. The last word had me stumped, but I was pleased with myself nonetheless: I'd read the first two words.

I was ready for third grade.

"Take your seats, please," a tall nun said. Her hands were hidden within ample robes, and her silhouette was darker than my blackest crayons except for her white wimple.

Name cards were taped in alphabetical order on the left corner of each desk. I was pleased to find mine right in the middle: the middle seat of the middle row. I whipped open my desktop, eager to see what was inside. They were all there: books about reading and spelling and more, not just math. All summer long, I'd practiced reading, building sentences, and memorizing words deciphered from pictures. I was all set to read just like everybody else.

"Sister . . . Mary . . . Lenora," she said, tapping each letter of her name with a pointer. "You may call me Sister Lenora."

Her skin was pale, nearly as white as her wimple. She stood erectly, like a statue, and she spoke slowly, sternly but not unfriendly, as she outlined class rules of behavior. There were a lot of them. She drew our attention to the stacks of brown paper sheets that were crowding the first desk of each row. They were book covers.

"Keep three and pass on the rest."

An outbreak of crackling paper and chatter ensued.

"Talking is not required for this task," she scolded. Her voice was no louder, just harder.

Trying hard to avoid the crackling noise, I carefully folded and creased the paper, but some crackling escaped. Thankfully, I wasn't the only one struggling to shape the unruly paper. Finishing up, I liked the way my books matched, except for their sizes. I wrote my name on the front right corner of each book, as instructed. Squishing out ornery wrinkles, I looked up at Sister who was announcing the next exercise.

"Open your reading books to chapter one. Let's see what you remember from last year."

I was relieved to see pictures but alarmed by the number of words. There were far more than in the books I'd practiced with over the summer. My tummy fluttered. A gurgle escaped. I was terrified of getting stuck.

The first girl in row one began. Following along, I pressed my finger under each word. She was a fast reader, faster than my finger. The boy behind her stood and read the next two sentences; his were short, so Sister gave him two. Down the row and up the next, each student read. Some readers were slow, some were fast, and some needed help or stopped to sound out a word. I'd never sounded out a word before. My finger tapped nervously, craving my turn but fearing its arrival. There were lots of words I didn't know, and we were moving too fast for my brain to collect and store them. I was up in two turns. My sentence was long, with too many words—one I didn't know.

I was still staring at it when Sister called my name.

"Yes, Ma'am . . . I mean, Sister," I said, startled.

Giggles ruptured around me and across the room; nobody says *ma'am* here. Sister glowered, and silence returned, the sounds sucked from the air. If my stomach rumbled, everyone would hear it.

"Go ahead." Sister nodded encouragingly.

I began slowly. My tongue felt unruly, swelling with each word. I'd never read aloud before, and I didn't realize the words would fight to get out of my mouth. I made it to the middle and stopped, stuck. Five letters mocked me. A gray blur overtook what had been a word a second before. I looked at the picture, took a wild guess, spat it out, and raced on.

"Let's go back a bit. Sound it out," Sister said.

I stood, my knees quavering while my finger pointed at the word. Nothing came. It was hard to see the page. The harder I looked, the blurrier it became. It was hot. I had to go to the bathroom. Sister asked the class for help. Hands shot up accompanied by a tornado of ruffling shirts. A chorus of, "Me, me, me," ended when a girl one row over pronounced my renegade word. I parroted it back, reread the sentence, and sat down. My finger lost its place, and I could no longer follow along.

A boy sitting in the front of the last row completed his first word as the recess bell rang. A cacophony of books closed, concluding the reading and rescuing those in the last row. *Not fair.*

We lined up and filed out. Once we passed through the school door, screaming and laughter ensued. I walked heavily toward the swings, my head still in the classroom, playing the scene over and over. *If only I'd had a better sentence.*

"Hey, Dumb Dumb!" Hunter Schmit shouted, shoving me. "Yes, Ma'am," he jeered.

He had made it clear last year that *ma'am* was not used in the North— "So hoity toity," he'd claimed—but the habit was hard to break. His buddies laughed, their eyes bouncing from him to me. I pretended not to hear him and continued walking.

He moved on in search of fresh targets. Leaning against the swing set, I watched some kids scatter like mice while others banded together, veering away from him like a spooked herd on the savanna. A group of four roamed with him. I noticed he was just as likely to turn on them. They pretended to play along despite being the butt of his jokes. When my turn came to swing, I pumped as hard as I could, hoping he'd stay on the other side of the playground.

I monitored Hunter Schmit closely in the classroom and during recess, studying his third-grade tactics. Second grade taught me to keep my distance but not how to do so. I was watching him when Sister told us to line up. It was a few weeks after school started. We'd just finished lunch, but we weren't in line for recess. Steve's class joined mine, waiting in the hallway.

Sister Bridgett tended her line like a drill sergeant. Marching toward three offenders, she smacked them on the back of the head. I was glad she wasn't my teacher. Sister Lenora hadn't hit anyone since school started.

"Silence!" Sister Bridgett barked, swatting Steve.

He looked over to see whether I was laughing. I knew better. I looked at the wall.

I passed the time by scrutinizing pictures hung high above us. They were graduates from another time, as if plucked from silent movies. Making up stories, I contemplated which graduates were married and had children and which were doctors or criminals.

"All right, class, move forward. Quietly . . . please." Sister Lenora's voice was half as loud as Sister Bridgett's.

We marched to the gym, obedient cadets keeping close to our side of the hallway, fingers brushing the wall as instructed.

The gym was massive. The ceiling was nearly as high as a church's, and it was an ideal space for a mind that liked to wander. To the right of the entrance was an empty stage. It beckoned ghost-like, for habitation. I envisioned Peter Pan swinging on theater ropes. Wendy entered, soaring higher than Peter: a Wendy with red hair and lots of freckles. I was Peter, of course, not Wendy (despite the freckles). My sword ready for battle, I charged Captain Hook—

"Move it," the girl behind me whispered.

Captain Hook vanished, and I stepped forward.

Roused and now fully present, I took stock of my surroundings. The gym was devoid of furnishings except for a table monitored by a nurse. She was draped in white: a white cap, a white uniform, white stockings, and white shoes. We lined up in two rows behind the tail end of the first and second graders who had come before us. Measuring a second grader standing on a hospital scale, the nurse tallied pounds and inches, her officious voice blending with the shuffling of shoes and chattering of kids.

"Next!" she shouted without looking up, her head bent down over a large book where her pencil scribblings lodged.

The other row was monitored by a black robe, a nun I hadn't seen before. A large chart with big and small letters was pinned on the wall behind her. She was checking eyes.

I'd never been to the doctor or had a nurse measure me. Dad marked our heights on the wall using a tape measure, not an official instrument. My eyes were focused on the hospital scale; it was more complicated than our bathroom scale. Fascinated by all the gadgets—the sliding black stones, the floating pointer, the measuring stick—I waited greedily for my turn.

Twenty minutes later, the kid in front was taking his sweet time getting off the scales. I wanted to shove him so I could get on, but I knew better.

"Next!" the nurse shouted.

Fired up and overly excited, I jumped on the scale. The entire contraption shifted, producing a loud clang.

"Eager beaver," she said, pushing the scale back into place with me on it.

She turned me around and laid the measuring stick on my head. I looked up, stealing a peek, but she pushed my head back down.

"Fifty-one inches."

My eyes followed her pencil to a list of names in her book. There were columns for height and weight and spots for each year's measurements. I was delighted when she wrote *fifty-one* in the empty space by my name. The nurse set down her pencil and walked behind the scale. She stood in front of the steel bar with metal weights. I turned to face her so I could watch. She didn't object; she just tapped the black weight until it reached the number fifty. The pointer didn't move. She tapped it to sixty. It didn't move. She tapped it to seventy. Nothing happened. She tapped it to seventy-five, and the pointer dropped as far as it could go, making a slight thumping sound. She moved it back gently until the pointer was floating.

"Seventy-four pounds."

She recorded the number in my column and called out, "Next!"

Mega happy my slots were filled, I hopped off the scale and joined the line for my eye exam.

"Seventy-four pounds! We got a porker," Hunter hissed.

He made a pig face twice as ugly as Steve's and held it until Sister Lenora grabbed his hand and pushed it down to his side. My own hands sought my sweater, pulling it tight around me. I failed the eye exam. My eyes were heavy with tears, making the letters one undecipherable blur.

I buttoned my sweater up all the way and kept it fastened the rest of the day. My eyes searched the room, examining every girl body. Looking around, I saw that I certainly wasn't the smallest girl. Dad said our family wasn't built to be tall and lean; we had strong, athletic bodies built to run bases, jump hurdles, and tackle much larger opponents on the football field. I thought I was strong, but now I wondered, *Am I a porker?*

"Porker, you weigh more than me!" Steve shouted, running past me on our way home. "Oink, oink."

My pace slowed. I didn't want to go home. Looking down and counting the cracks in the sidewalk, I contemplated the note in my pocket. No one in my class or my family wore glasses. Only Grandpa did, and he was old. *Four-eyes—another nickname.* I hoped it was a mistake. I prayed I'd pass the eye doctor's exam.

Reaching my house, I stared at the contours of our door, biding my time before opening it. I turned the knob and stepped inside. Mom was sitting on the sofa folding clothes. Barry James was in the playpen, and Mary was on the couch fiddling with a doll, opening and closing its eyes.

I handed Sister's note to Mom and told her about Hunter Schmit.

"He's a bully. Every class has one. Ignore him. He'll get bored and find someone else to pick on."

I'd heard this before, but I needed her to say something about the number. *I was seventy-four pounds.*

"But I weigh more than Steve."

"Girls take longer to lose their baby fat."

My eyes skipped to Barry James and his baby fat. He didn't have single thighs: he had multiple rolls of flesh meshed from knee to diaper, and he had two chins, great for kissing and imparting raspberries. *Great for him.*

I turned to Mom, waiting for her to say more. She finished folding a diaper and laid it on her lap. She gave me her full attention, her eyes probing, checking me over.

"Less cookies and sweets," she said.

I looked away.

Infant gurgles and angry wails petitioned her. Joey was awake. "Watch Barry James and Mary, and while you're at it, how about folding some of these clothes? I'll be back in a minute."

Dad called me "Mommy's little helper." Mom did too, and I cherished the moniker; it set me apart from the others. But at that moment, I didn't want to be anybody's helper. I wanted her to say that Steve and Hunter Spit—my private take on *Schmit*—were not worth listening to. Mom's response, "Less cookies and sweets," churned round in my head. Massaging my temples, I tried to erase my thoughts, but it was no use.

She agreed with Steve and Hunter.

I folded baby clothes, diapers, and dish towels, then stacked them in piles on the floor. I wasn't sure what to believe of Mom's theory. There were lots of girls in my class without baby fat; some were tall and skinny.

When she returned, I went into the bathroom and locked the door. I stared at the scale, not wanting to step on it, but then I relinquished, taking off my school sweater and shoes. I drew in a breath, blew it all out, and gingerly placed one foot on the scale, then the other. The scale showed seventy-two pounds. *The fancy scale must be wrong! Maybe it was my shoes.*

I stood before the mirror. I'd never bothered with mirrors before, except for carnival mirrors that warp your body to make it seem tall and toothpick-thin or squat and Doughboy-fat. I pulled up my shirt and

examined my belly. It pooched out like Barry James's tummy. I didn't have a double chin, but my cheeks were pinchable. Lifting my skirt, I examined my thighs. They didn't have rolls, but my thighs seemed to grow the more I looked at them, my eyes warping my frame like a carnival mirror. The longer I stared, the rounder I got. All pretense of my body being strong crumbled. Mom agreed with Steve and Hunter. *I must be a porker.*

Years later, when looking at my grade school pictures, the childhood reflection looked wrong, as if tampered with. The pictures revealed a plump child, not a fat one. I remembered feeling fat, seeing fat, hating fat, and hating the me in that bathroom mirror.

Dinner took on a life of its own. It was staring at me, chiding me, while steam escaped from the potatoes and silky butter oozed over their sides. Mom declined the potatoes, choosing cottage cheese instead. She was on a diet. She was always on a diet, and she had zero baby fat. I wanted the potatoes, could already taste them, but scooped cottage cheese onto my plate instead.

"Ouch!"

Steve kicked me under the table.

Making a hideous face, he shoved a huge portion of mashed potatoes into his mouth. My plate, being full of cold and lumpy cottage cheese, was equally offensive. I had just turned eight and didn't want to join the diet brigade. Mom's plates were boring—no potatoes, cookies, cakes, ice cream, bread or butter—but I didn't want to be a *porker*.

A week of cottage cheese muddled my dreams and filled them with chocolate cake, chocolate pie, and gooey maple bars, a favorite Northwest treat that I missed while living in Augusta. But I would have happily eaten my last maple bar and given up my precious box of soaps and favorite toys in exchange for a transfer back to Augusta, where scales didn't matter and I only rejected foods unpalatable to my tongue.

During another night of lying awake, my stomach grumbling, I heard Joey fussing: gurgles mixing with monkey-like cries. He was nursing and not getting enough milk. He mostly took a bottle now; Mom must have been too tired to prepare it. His complaints sounded oddly like Tarzan's sidekick, Cheeta, when he didn't get his way. A vision of the chimp jumping on my bed, his face furious, protesting the attention Joey was getting, momentarily eased the gurgling in my own stomach. A table set for two materialized. Tarzan arrived, his arms laden with the fruits of the jungle: mango, papaya, bananas, and honey.

"Good," Tarzan said, rubbing his belly. "You eat."

I was so hungry I could taste the honey and feel it on my tongue. I dreamed of bananas soaked in honey, and my hands and cheeks sticky with nectar.

The following morning, I woke up famished. For breakfast, I ate a dry piece of toast washed down with half a glass of milk. My stomach gurgled all the way to school. On the walk home, I could think of nothing but sweets, especially chocolate. Entering the kitchen, I listened for Mom and my siblings. Hearing only our dog, Sam, whacking its tail against the table, I attacked the cupboards, rummaging for anything sugary. I found a forgotten Valentine's Day box of chocolates, grabbed a round milk chocolate piece, and bit off the bottom, savoring it while scooping out the strawberry cream filling—I only liked caramel or nougat—in its shell. I left only two pieces in the box. I hid the wrappers and discarded the fillings deep in the garbage bin under food scraps and empty cans.

Chapter Five

Corner to Corner

The school bell rang at three. I took the lakeside path. No traffic lights slowed me down, and I didn't have to get off my bike to cross the road. Crouched over, my butt off the seat, I pumped faster and faster. The bike wiggled from side to side then straightened out as I zoomed down a hill and trudged up another. Last year I didn't need to rush, I always got home before the matinee started. I was now nine and in the fourth grade. We were on our third house. The first one was too small, the second one was nice but pricey, and the third one had a sizable finished basement with ample room for beds and play. It was a good deal according to Dad. The other two houses were on the church's side of the lake. Now we lived on the other side, across the street from a park.

Out of breath and gulping air, I dropped the bike in the driveway. Recalling Dad's threat that any bike not put away would disappear, I resisted the urge to leave it where it fell and picked it up, leaned it against the garage door, dashed inside, tossed my books on the table, and grabbed the TV guide. Flipping the pages, I searched for the day's matinee: *Tarzan the Ape Man.*

"A classic," I said, mimicking Dad's term for his favorite old movies. In this one, my favorite animal saves the day. An army of elephants rescues Tarzan and Jane, by trampling poachers intent on pilfering a sacred burial ground. In my version, Jane does not exist. Tarzan and I save the burial grounds with the aid of our elephant army.

A lot of actors have played Tarzan, but for me there was only one worth mentioning: Johnny Weissmuller. His hair was long, not quite as long as Samson's, but it was notably longer than the buzz cuts my brothers wore, courtesy of Dad, a bowl, and electric clippers. Tarzan's arms were long, cuddle-up strong, and flying-through-the-jungle-on-a-vine safe. In my fantasy world—now more escape than play—neither Steve nor Hunter could come between Tarzan and me. Both perished whenever they tried.

It was three twenty-two p.m. The Tarzan movie started at three thirty p.m. I had to move quickly. Every day, every single day, as regular as Saturday morning cartoons, a chore list waited for me on the kitchen counter. On it, I'd find a collection of tasks considered *girl's* jobs. The boys got away with mowing the lawn and putting out the garbage. There were five of them, including Dad, but fewer chores. Dad refused to lift a finger for *woman's work*. He wouldn't even pick up his dirty socks. If Mom didn't collect them every morning, they'd pile up so high you wouldn't be able to open the door, sock upon sock smashing up against the window, making the glass bulge outward.

Dad's aversion to woman's work irritated me, but it didn't seem to bother my mother. She gave him a get-out-of-jail-free card when it came to household chores, justifying his attitude because his mother was bossy. According to her, Grandma wore the pants in Dad's house, and he hated it. No woman was going to boss him around. Dad often said I was like Grandma, strong and independent. It was a compliment that came with a warning: *be careful, strong women intimidate men.* I looked up *intimidate*, a word Mom used when referring to Grandma. The definition (to make timid) confused me; it didn't fit my perception of Grandma and Grandpa. Grandma was strict and super serious but not mean. When I stayed with them, I never heard her tell Grandpa what to do. He was my favorite grandparent: tall and strong, smiling most of the time. He'd twirl me in the air, and he'd always save a seat for me on his lap. I wanted to be a boy who could be unfettered by women's work and live with Grandpa on the farm in Tacoma.

I hankered for a spot on my dad's lap—we all did—but he wasn't home much during the week or on Saturdays. When he was home, he liked to have his chair to himself to relax. A Sunday afternoon wrestling match with all us kids piled on top of him was our time together. I savored the intimate huddles, squeezes, and tickles, always coming back for more.

A dogpile was not on my mind that day, though Steve and Tarzan were. Tom was outside playing with his new best friend. The little kids were with Mom; I didn't have to babysit. Steve was home or was on his way. My plan was to hide behind the only lockable door in the house until Mom got home. Picking up her list, I prayed for laundry, a task I could do while watching Tarzan on TV in her bedroom with the door latched.

A laundry day! Perfect. Expecting several baskets of clothes, I found two clean baskets of clothes, three dirty clothes piles on the floor, and a batch of clothes in both the dryer and the washer. Roadrunner-speedy, I shifted clothes from the dryer to a basket and from the washer to the dryer, filled the washing machine with a load of diapers, added soap, grabbed a basket of clean clothes, and ran as fast as I could up the stairs to Mom and Dad's bedroom.

I reconsidered the setup. It would be better to have all the fold-ready clothes in the bedroom, then Tarzan and I wouldn't be interrupted. Racing down then back up the stairs as if chased by lions, I flew into the bedroom with another basket. I was out of breath but ready to go. Tarzan would've saved me from the lions, but he'd be of little help folding clothes. He'd had zero practice. As far as I could tell, he owned only one loincloth. His method to clean it didn't require taking it off; he simply jumped in a river with the crocodiles. But he could carry the baskets for me.

I loved this room. The quiet cuddled my ears. I wasn't supposed to be in their bedroom—it was off-limits—but I was ready with an excuse if I was caught: "I was folding clothes," or "I'm dusting," or "I just finished vacuuming."

Thanks
Tarzan

I locked the door and turned on the TV. The movie hadn't started. Mom and Dad's bed was massive and soft. Not a wrinkle disturbed its milky white surface, which enticed me to lie down, though that was a definite no-no. Sliding my fingers through the tiny balls dotting the bedspread, I felt the fluffy bumps press against me. They were deliciously inviting, like it would be to float in marshmallow soup. Mom called the fabric chenille.

It was tidy in their bedroom. There were no toys in the room, no dirty clothes lying on the floor, and no abandoned magazines or newspapers on the dresser. There were no trophies, school art projects, or knickknacks—nothing, save for a family picture. The light gold walls were bare except for a window, a panel of galloping horses above the bed, a mirror over the dresser, and a crucifix to the right of the closet. There were no night tables, only a bed, a matching dresser, and a TV. A clothes hamper hiding in the back of the closet was a necessary embarrassment. Mom's shoes, assorted in pairs, lodged on one side of the closet; Dad's were on the other side.

I was mystified every time I snuck in here, and I wondered how she kept it so neat. The room smelled of lemons, Lemon Pledge. Completely absent of our existence, their room was Mom's sanctuary, but she never spent any time here except to sleep and dress.

Boring commercials monopolized the TV screen. Waiting for Tarzan, I got up and ran my fingers along Mom's dresser and paused at the photo in a gold frame. The picture was old; there were only two kids in it instead of six. A peculiar custom prevailed in my family. Dad was transferred every two to three years, and Mom produced babies in kind. In Tacoma she had Steve and me; in Yakima, Tom and Mary; and in Augusta, Barry James and Joey. She was expecting another one this summer. She had one more to go to complete this town's twosome.

I hoped and prayed we were done with the two-babies-per-town custom. I hoped Mom would deem having seven kids enough so we could leave when Dad fulfilled his two-year stint. In my mind, his job and past transfers were the best indicator of our future moves. I was counting on that. Just one more year and I'd be out of here, begone to another town and another school where there'd be no Hunter Spit.

Steve and I were babies in the photograph. Ten and nine now, we were the only siblings born less than two years apart. He was born October 19.

I came along almost a year later, on October 12. Every year on my birthday, I relished chanting "I'm the same age as you are" to taunt him. But I was careful to croon only in the presence of Mom or Dad to avoid the automatic and repeated recoil of his fists.

Mom had trouble remembering when the picture was taken. "I think you were about six months old, maybe seven, so that would make Steve around seventeen months. It would have been in Tacoma, at the *Bon* or maybe *Penny's*. . . . I'm not sure."

I hated and loved this picture. Mom was beautiful, her skin pink and flawless. Silky hair nuzzled her shoulders. She was composed, almost serene. Dad looked so handsome in his tailored gray suit. He had an athlete's shoulders and a confident bearing. Steve's cheeks were little-boy ruddy, and his hair was a mirror of Dad's short-on-the-sides but curly-on-the-top cut. Steve wore blue dungarees and a red striped shirt and held a block, the letter *W* painted blue. He looked like the perfect firstborn.

The baby—me—was gross, a porker. I had tiny eyes and a tiny mouth, no chin or neck, and fat cheeks that rolled into more fat. I was all tucked into a dainty pink dress that was unsuitable for *this* chunky baby. My wrists were missing, sucked into the rolls of my arms. Luckily the dress covered my legs, hiding my squishy thighs. A conspicuous pair of yellow booties completed my outfit. Mom was meticulous about her clothes and accessories, so this perplexed me. *Why yellow?* It was all wrong.

Scowling at this offensive little piggy, I imagined older versions of her. They were all grotesque. To me, this picture was proof that Hunter and Steve were right. I was a porker. I believed this picture despite how I looked in the recent pictures in Mom's photo albums. I studied these recent pictures with a detective's eye, comparing my body parts with others', especially Mom's slender legs and my pudgy ones. She grew nearly twice her size every pregnancy, but her diet always brought her back to model size. Even when I managed to eat exactly what she ate, the scales were no friendlier. This year, the nurse at school announced that I was eighty pounds as I stood on the scale, staring at my shoes. I waited for Hunter's assault. Weeks later, he was still squawking the revolting number.

I resisted smashing the picture flat on the dresser so I didn't have to look at it.

Music announced the movie's start. I turned the sound up and dove back onto the bed. Grabbing a towel, I placed it under me to prevent round welts forming on the back of my legs. Sitting on the chenille bedspread for even five minutes could create depressions lasting an hour or more. It would be a dumb way to get caught: a sign I'd been watching TV and not doing chores.

Tarzan flew across the screen, his meager costume stiff against his body. I watched closely—a game I played—when he wrestled lions, leopards, and crocs, hoping to see just a little bit more under his loincloth, but it never moved. I figured it had to be glued on. I was also skeptical about Tarzan's appetite for swimming. I knew for a fact that people in Africa didn't swim in fresh water because of the crocodiles. But it didn't matter; I liked to watch him swim and sail over the surface like a speed boat.

Closing my eyes, I let my body relax and settle into Mom's chenille bedspread. The day had been difficult. Hunter had been especially malicious. I needed an hour, a half hour, or even just fifteen minutes before worrying about Steve. Thinking of him, I got up and checked the lock. Satisfied the lock was secure, I lay back and closed my eyes. The clothes could wait for a little while longer since Mom wouldn't be home until five thirty. I floated down a chenille river into an island of jungle foliage, a passage to Tarzan on the other side of the world. Peering through the vines, I spotted a tree house lodged in a regal Baobab tree. The leaves caressed my hair, and the sharp trail of lemon cleaner warmed to an aroma of sweet honeysuckle.

Tarzan waited, poised on the tree house landing. He reached into the foliage, grabbed a vine, and swung toward me. Side by side, we flew through the jungle. A leopard seeking its dinner leaped high above the ground, but we were too quick. Screeching, the cat's enraged complaint pierced my ears—

I jumped, practically falling off the bed. The phone was ringing. Mom checking in, almost as if she knew I was in here. Apparently, she'd be back early. I grabbed a diaper and folded, moving quickly but carefully because Mom liked everything just so. Even the diapers had to be folded exactly corner to corner, and there was another load of clothes to fold, plus more in the dryer.

Three baskets of clothes were a lot to fold, but I had enough time, and I didn't mind. It was perfect, just Tarzan, me, and folding. There were no bullies, lists, or parents in the jungle, only crocodiles, snakes, and big cats. I folded clothes while my mind's eye pivoted from tree to tree, far above the lions, leopards, poisonous snakes, and treacherous white hunters. None of them were a match for Tarzan and me.

Cheeta screeched on the TV alongside me and Tarzan. The chimp was frantic, swinging his free arm while the other clutched a vine. Something was up. Poachers—

A loud woman selling soap powder intruded. *Darn it, another commercial.*

I looked forward to my adventures with Tarzan. I loved living them and loved concocting them, but I also liked the serene moments like cooking in the tree house, traveling through the jungle, and swimming in non-crocodile-infested water. With Tarzan, I was pretty. He stroked my long hair, smoothing the unruly curls. He lifted me as if I weighed no more than a fluffy cotton puff.

I ignored the earnest lady on the TV. Tarzan and I had better things to do. We meandered through the forest on the back of an elephant. He picked a hibiscus flower and slipped it behind my ear. Parrots chattered above us, and the occasional monkey shrieked, but, mostly, it was quiet—

Someone banged on the door.

"I know you're in there, fatso!"

Steve hit the door, slamming his fists again and again. If it broke or cracked, Dad would go nuts, and the belt would fly.

Steve couldn't get in. The door was locked. He yelled louder, using his whole body to smash against the door. I didn't answer or move.

He can't get in.

He wasn't after the TV; he owned the one downstairs. No one would dare change the channel or sit in his chair except Dad. No, Steve just didn't want me in here having a break. Or maybe he was just bored.

"I know you're in there."

If only Tarzan could escape the TV for real, fly out on a magic vine, and take me with him. I focused on the TV, concentrating on Tarzan. He was running through the tall grass, a lion on his trail.

"You're going to get it when Mom gets home!" Steve yelled. His voice was loud enough to be heard across the street. "You got to come out sometime, *pig!*"

Please, God, make him go away.

Steve banged again. The door shook.

He can't get in.

I continued folding. Holding a diaper corner between my fingers, I carefully aligned it to the opposite corner, creating a triangle. I folded the triangle in half and gently laid it on the diaper pile.

Steve pounded the door as if he were trying to break through it.

There were more clothes to fold, but they were in the dryer . . . down in the basement.

Steve's banging grew louder and then stopped.

I stared at the door, frozen, then stood behind it, hiding out well after the banging stopped. Assuming that I'd outwaited him, I opened the door and peeked out, looking left and right. Venturing out, I failed to see him coming. Steve's fist landed on my arm like a power drill intent on breaking concrete.

"Ow!" I howled.

"Gotcha!" He laughed and ran down the hall.

My left arm was red and pulsing. A purple bruise was forming where his middle knuckle had jabbed deeply: a knuckle sandwich. I rubbed my arm and held back tears that ached to fall. I would not give him the satisfaction of seeing my red eyes or knowing how much his jab burned.

Chapter Six

Hunter

My arm smarted from the previous day's events. I was eating breakfast in the kitchen, stalling.

"You're going to be late," Mom warned. She was standing in front of the sink washing dishes. When she spoke, she didn't look my way or interrupt the rhythm of her scraping.

"No, I won't."

I pushed Cocoa Puffs around my bowl. The milk had turned gray instead of cocoa brown. It was eight thirty. The school bell rang at nine. I still had time.

Mom was wearing pants. Lime-green and shaped straight, the pants ended at her ankles. The pants looked comfy like my play clothes. My itchy school sweater inflamed my knuckle-sandwich bruise, and I couldn't stop rubbing it. My skirt was itchier than the wool sweater. When I walked, the skirt felt like sandpaper scraping my legs. I shifted the pleats and sat bare legged. The chair felt cool, but my legs stuck to the plastic cushion and made a squishy sound when I moved.

I was playing for time, attempting to keep as much distance between me and Steve as possible. I tried to avoid him by leaving first, but Mom wanted me to feed Joey. He was covered in jam and was trying to scoop Cocoa Puffs onto his baby spoon. A tiny red glob of jam balanced on one of his eyelashes. I'd been watching it go up and down as he blinked.

"It's time to go. *Now.*"

"In a minute," I said, thinking there was no point in telling her about Steve.

I knew she wouldn't do anything except maybe scold me for being a tattletale. There was the possibility she would threaten Steve with the wait-till-your-father-comes-home speech. If she did tell Dad, his belt would find Steve's behind. The likely outcome of any such punishment was predictable: Steve would hit harder next time. I would not snitch on Steve, but I did want advice on Hunter.

"I'm ignoring Hunter Schmit like you said, but he's still being mean."

"Is that what this is about?" She did a half-turn, wearing her I-don't-have-time-for-this face. "Has he hit you?"

"No."

"Well, then . . . it's only words."

"I know, sticks and stones, but it does hurt."

"There are a lot of mean people, and he won't be the first to try and get your goat."

"Goat?"

"Just a saying," she said, frowning. "Ignore him. He'll eventually get tired of it and move on."

No, he won't.

I knew he wouldn't stop as plainly as I knew the earth orbited the sun. Clearly, neither she nor the nuns nor anybody else on the planet was going to make him stop. I was on my own.

"Go, or you'll be late." She resumed scraping, her elbow jabbing faster and faster.

Steve was probably far enough ahead by now. It was safe to go, and I didn't want to get in trouble for being late. Having waited too long to walk, I'd have to ride my bike. If my calculations were correct, the playground would be empty, and I could simply park the bike and rush into class without running into Steve or Hunter.

Crossing the street, I raced along the path bordering the lake, took a left across the bridge, climbed off my bike, crossed the main road, and pedaled to the playground past the church. But it wasn't as late as I thought. The school bell hadn't rung, and the yard was full of kids.

"Hey, *cow*."

I flinched and turned toward the incoming fire.

Why do I always look? I fall for it every time.

"See, she knows she's a cow!" Hunter shouted. Laughing loudly for all to hear, he sneered, "Or she wouldn't have turned around." Relishing the effect on his buddies, he started mooing. Frozen, I straddled my bike, stunned to have fallen for his trap once again. Jeff, the boy I had a crush on, stood with his hands in his pockets and chuckled feebly, which was not his happy laugh. John yelled, "Touché!" but avoided my eyes. He was looking at the ground as if he were counting the pebbles circling his shoes. Paul mimicked Hunter. From the corner of my left eye, I saw Carol turn briskly and head toward the school entrance. There were others, but I followed Carol and looked through Hunter as if he weren't there. I'd mastered this look; it was a mask I could slip on and off.

Once I was in the classroom, I couldn't pay attention. Mrs. Hickman's words passed right through me. She was the only lay teacher at St. Rose: that is, she wasn't a nun. She reminded me of the grandma in "Little Red Riding Hood." Her gray hair was pulled into a bun, and she wore wire-rimmed glasses with a skinny frame. She was oblivious to predators and didn't seem to notice Hunter's antics. He'd gotten bolder under her tutelage.

I liked her anyway. She didn't lecture me about "sticks and stones" and how "words can't hurt you" as the nuns did. She didn't teach religion since the Sisters wouldn't allow it, and she never implored me to pray for Hunter's soul. Sister Brendan did that for her by repeatedly pulling me aside on the playground, grabbing me by the shoulders, locking her eyes on mine, and saying, "Pray for him. Every time he says a mean thing, his soul turns a little blacker," as if she were telling me a message straight from God. I always nodded respectfully, but I wondered why my prayers hadn't turned him into a saint; I prayed every day and every night, lit candles, and fasted like the saints, but my efforts made no difference.

I stared at the clock, my eyes marching along with the second hand. I woke up afraid of Steve but managed to escape him, only to face Hunter, who was intent on scoring. His next opportunity to do so would be at recess, twenty-five minutes from now.

The bell rang. We marched out in single file. I feared each coming moment. He must have been storing up the insults because they spewed from his mouth like an open faucet. I jumped rope—or tried to—and ignored him like Mom said, like I did every day, but putting all my effort into making him invisible tripped up my feet. I managed not to fall, but I kept stepping on the rope, each fumble inciting more of his howls.

"Ha, ha, come on, piggy," he taunted, with a succession of grunts. Words weren't enough; he pretended to jump but rose no more than an inch off the ground, sneering, "Give it up, *stupid*, hippos can't jump."

He was on a roll; lunch was going to be even worse.

Collecting my lunch bag as if nothing was up, I peeked inside and pulled out a sandwich, hoping for chicken but finding peanut butter and jelly. *Crap, not again.* But Mom did pack Fig Newtons . . . *yum.* I glanced up. He was walking toward me, then he passed me. I heard him plop heavily on the seat behind me.

"Watch, look how she's chewing. Like a camel!" he whisper-sneered. He made chomping noises loud enough for everyone close to hear but stayed under Mrs. Hickman's radar. He always used animal names: hippo, elephant, whale, cow, giraffe (which alluded to my copious freckles). He never, not once, called me by my name.

Cranking up his delivery, he jeered, "I've got the last cookie from the store." Everyone knew he was talking about his parents' grocery store. I avoided the place and only went in there with Mom when I had to.

Stiffly, I stared at the table, picked at my sandwich and resisted eye contact with everyone, but I could envision what his face looked like: scrunched and puckered with glee, a protruding smile baring a mouthful of teeth as he prepared his next blow.

I longed to slip through the floorboards or melt into the chair. My eyes shifted to the rear wall. A prayer poster hung near a picture of St. Rose, but it was too far to read. I focused on the flowers around the poster's border. Centering my thoughts, I imagined picking one and dropping it in a hollow gourd, then placing the flower next to a generous bouquet of daisies from Tarzan. Next to him, meat sizzled on a spit. I could almost smell it. We sipped mango juice and watched a gang of monkeys sparring on the jungle floor—

"Everyone! Quick, guard your food," Hunter mocked. A chorus of sheepish giggles surged.

I stared at the wall, but I could no longer see St. Rose or my bouquet of daisies. My eyes betrayed me, filling with tears. I concentrated, pressing my eyes tightly together to try and suck the tears back. *I won't cry.* I couldn't let him know his stings blistered like a bad sunburn. Staring at the table, I felt heat rise on my face and neck. No amount of willpower could keep my face from turning bright red or my ears, purple. My friends at the table said nothing. Two giggled nervously.

"Hunter," Mrs. Hickman said, placing her hand on his shoulder. "Eat your lunch." Why didn't she smack him on the head like Sister Brendan had?

Laughter ceased, but the looks I felt burrowing into the back of my neck did not. I desperately wanted to run, vanish, but I couldn't move until the lunch bell rang. I had a plan to avoid the playground: hide in the girls' bathroom. He couldn't go in there.

Please, please, please, ring.

Finally, it rang. The clang was grating but welcome. I snatched my lunch bag and the empty milk carton and turned toward the exit.

Don't run.

Tossing the garbage, I headed to the bathroom, counting each step to keep from running. I pushed the door open and dashed to a stall.

I made it.

The bathroom was not the most pleasant hideout, but it was private and reliable. I crouched on the seat, carefully holding my skirt to keep it from dipping in pee-water. Like every other stall, this one was marked with scribbled notes. I knew them all by heart, but I read them anyway. It was like reciting multiplication tables: a mindless, repetitive act that was comforting. I often contemplated etching a response and writing something ugly about Hunter, but I didn't. Getting caught would be an embarrassing affair, one involving my parents and Father McDonough.

I hid from the girls in the bathroom, too, not because they were mean, but because I didn't want them to tell Hunter. I would never let on how desperate I was to hide.

Gingerly balancing over the toilet, I imagined it shifting and morphing. I imagined the hole filling so that the base was now a ridge overlooking the savanna. A herd of wildebeest, thousands of them—

It wasn't working. The sting of Hunter's words roared louder than a hundred thousand wildebeest. "Piggy! Hippo! Cow!"

When the coast was clear, I headed straight for my classroom.

"Where have you been?" Mrs. Hickman asked.

"In the bathroom."

"All that time?" She frowned but didn't scold me. She simply directed me to my seat.

I resumed watching the clock, preparing for the next bell and for Hunter's next move. When the bell rang at three, I'd have two options to evade him: hide in the bathroom or the church. The school was connected to the church through a narrow corridor, but only priests and nuns were allowed to use it. Students entered from the playground—exposed, vulnerable to anyone with nefarious motives. Church visits were only permitted before or after school, which quashed recess escapes. When Hunter was in prime form, like today, I made a mad dash for the church. I preferred the church to the bathroom. It was quiet. And empty.

"Catherine, you're up. Log today's assignments, please."

My spirits lifted; I jumped up and briskly walked to the blackboard. Writing on the blackboard was my favorite school task. Mrs. Hickman only called on kids who wrote clearly. Some kids printed well, but they had no sense of space. The resulting mess swam across the board as if the writer were printing on an ocean wave. I kept the letters proportional and the lines straight. Forgetting about Hunter, I held the chalk steady and pressed carefully, spelling *m a t h*. Then came *c*, for *chapter*. I was finishing the letter *h* when a hiss from behind rattled me. My hand careened down jaggedly, ruining the word.

It was Hunter.

Wiping off the offending error, I peered through the blackboard, envisioning a jungle dripping with vines. I grabbed one, held tight, and disappeared.

Chapter Seven
Mother Mary

Mrs. Hickman made Hunter clean the erasers, so I was able to beat him to the exit, but it was a close call. I sprinted for the church, barreling right into its massive doors. Out of breath and panting, I placed my forehead on the cool surface and collected myself. The leaden sentries swept high above me, their weight a shield against unwanted visitors. Straining, I managed to open the doors wide enough to slide my foot between them to prevent an abrupt slam. I squeezed through and held my breath, carefully gauging if anyone was inside.

Empty.

The doors, accustomed to autonomy, pushed against me, as if clamoring to shut. I hung onto them, using the weight of my body to slow them down. Their bulk pulled me forward, but I stopped them from banging. They closed with a hollowed thump. I didn't dare move; someone in the rectory might have heard. Holding my breath, I could hear my own heartbeat. I listened, searching for the flutter of robes and heavy footsteps, but there was only nothingness. Exhaling, I allowed my body to relax, letting go for the first time since breakfast.

"Capacious," I whispered. A soft echo answered, "—cious."

Capacious was my new word for the day. Mrs. Hickman had introduced it this morning: "Another word for huge." But the church didn't make me feel small. The solitude seemed to strengthen my muscles. Stretching, I felt taller—was taller. I inhaled deeply, welcoming a bouquet of incense, wood, and flowers. It was a little chilly inside, but it wasn't cold. Crossing myself, I genuflected before the altar, walked over to my favorite pew (the one in front of the statue of the Virgin Mary), and lay down; not a move I'd make if anyone was inside. The sleek surface, polished by thousands of parishioners over the years, welcomed my arms and legs. Looking up, I followed the soaring walls up to the cavernous arched ceiling speckled with fading paint. Cracks in the plaster caught my attention; they mirrored the naked branches of winter trees.

I followed the finespun fractures from one end of the ceiling to the other. All at once, a delicate green shoot crept forth, followed by a burst of canopy that crawled out of crevices and unfurled high above my head. Runners became vines and trees, entangling themselves with the chandeliers, the walls, and the floor. The scene was beautiful, like the Hanging Gardens of Babylon, and awash with greenery and peppered with flowers: hibiscus, orchids, and moon flowers.

The domed surface twitched and pulsed, churned by thousands of bats jockeying for a spot to roost. Screeching howler monkeys surged from within the vines, ripping and throwing branches, as if denouncing my intrusion. The monkeys were moving as one body toward a towering Gabon tree that engulfed the altar wall. Tarzan stood at the base of the tree, beckoning me to run. I ran and jumped into his arms.

"Must climb, only way out," he said, lifting me onto his shoulder and giving me a push. High above, I could see light poking through the foliage. I climbed for it, moving as fast as I could. Tarzan followed close behind, shadowing me to prevent a nasty fall. The monkeys were gaining on us. Vines ensnared my ankles and coiled about my arms, but I kept going. We climbed up and up until a tortured face emerged from within the bramble, blood dripping from a crown on his forehead.

His eyes were sad.

The crucifix towered over the altar. The statue nailed to the cross was larger than human size. Upon seeing it, my musings vanished. My eyes drifted from his downcast eyes to the space between his stomach and ribcage, where his skin stretched over bulging ribs then dropped cavernously to an emaciated belly. When I prayed, I prayed to this spot, which was more disturbing to me than the blood dripping from the wounds on his chest, forehead, feet, and hands. His sunken belly affirmed to me that Jesus had given up—the apostles, his followers, and even God had abandoned Jesus. I could imagine him crying out, "My God, my God, why have *You* forsaken me?" Those few words struck me more than any other passage the nuns had read to us and more than any sermon Father had preached during mass.

Staring up at Jesus's belly, I didn't make the connection that I, too, felt abandoned. Instead, guilt tinged my thoughts. It was blasphemy to question God, everyone said so—the nuns, the priest, my parents—and it was wrong to daydream in church, but my musings tagged along anyway, especially on bad days. Looking at the statue, I found it odd that both Jesus and Tarzan wore the same kind of loincloth. Appalled that I'd once again thought of Tarzan, I bowed my head in prayer, apologized, and recited the verse I always said upon entering the church.

"Dear Lord, thank you for your suffering. Bless my family. And sorry my mind wandered again. I promise to do better." A mere whisper escaped my lips, yet the words echoed loudly.

I shuddered and looked about the church, fearing that someone might have entered while my mind was adrift. Sister Brendan would be furious if she knew I was daydreaming, especially about Tarzan. Father McDonough would question the "condition" of my soul. *Depraved* was his favorite term for bad behavior, and I was convinced the description fit.

Ashamed my mind had wandered so soon after entering the church (even before my first prayer), I begged for Jesus's forgiveness and promised to say the rosary. The rosary was a big commitment, but it was justified. In my mind, bats and howler monkeys in church were scarily irreverent.

I prayed to Jesus, not God. I didn't understand God and didn't trust him. God didn't help his own son; why would God help me? I believed that he was all powerful and that he could have rescued Jesus—freed him from the cross and transported him to anywhere on earth—but God didn't. He wasn't a good father. I didn't see the parallel with my own father; I didn't see that he had failed to rescue me from Hunter and Steve's antics. Dad could do no wrong in my eyes. I trusted he'd be there for me in a *real* life-and-death situation, unlike God.

I knew not to confess these thoughts in confession. I knew Father McDonough would go ballistic, and I apologized to Jesus when I had them, but I didn't pray to God. I prayed to Jesus, Mary, and the saints.

The nuns taught us how to pray and how to be respectful when we addressed Jesus—and I was—but my prayers to Mary were different. We conversed in everyday language. I didn't ask whether it was okay to do so. I believed Mary would give me a sign if I was behaving improperly. Sister Brendan told us that Mary had Jesus's ear, since she was his mother, and that praying to her was a sort of shortcut if we had a pressing need. Well, I had one and hoped she'd relay my prayers or answer them herself. She could do miracles, too.

Thank you, Mary, for the eraser trick. It worked. Hunter's probably still pounding away.

I chuckled, thinking of Hunter in a cloud of chalk. *Serves you right.* Closing my eyes, I imagined Mary and me sitting in a garden with loads of flowers. I could smell the roses and feel the soft petals in my hands as we chatted.

Dear Mary, can't you whisper something in their ears? Or switch up their brains and magically make them stop? I know I'm not supposed to ask for miracles, but this would only be a tiny one.

The roses morphed into vines that were crawling up the pew. I opened my eyes, then closed them, hoping to shut out these guests not welcome in the church.

I refocused.

Dear Mary, maybe Steve is just mad. Not mad as in crazy but crazy mad. You could wipe it away, put a happy beam inside of him.

I'd thought a great deal about Steve, about why he was mean, and how the Virgin Mary might fix him. Grandma Lu once confided in me, quiet-like so Mom and Dad couldn't hear, about lickings; they were reprimanding Steve at the time. She told me, "The eldest child is a guinea pig, the one parents learn on, the practice baby." Her comment stuck with me, and I felt sorry for Steve in that moment. Whenever he received a walloping, I felt both glee and pity. Torn between the two sentiments, I'd remember "practice baby" and a rush of guilt would cause my ears to burn. I also questioned Mom and Dad's *practicing* with the belt and wooden spoon. Such *practicing* didn't work. It just made Steve hit harder. He'd get madder and madder and meaner and meaner.

I sat up. The skin around my waist burned. I rubbed it, scratched it, and groaned. I couldn't stand it another second. Two weeks ago, I found a rope in our garage. It was an end piece and was the perfect size to wrap around my waist—not too long, not too wide, and no one would know it was under my clothes: the perfect penance.

Dear Mary, I'm sorry, but I have to take it off.

Yanking up my blouse, I reached under and removed the coarse rope. My skin was red and chapped raw. Applying turbo speed, I scratched my belly hard, but I couldn't reach my back. Working the pew like a bear against a tree, I rubbed vigorously, moving back and forth and up and down. The hard surface helped, but the rough bark of a Gabon tree—

Stop it! No more daydreaming.

The rope was supposed to make me saintlier and worthy of God's ear. We studied the saints in school, and every week we learned about a different one. They all had some penitence program. Sister had said it made them closer to God. I figured that if I got closer, Mary or maybe Jesus would hear me and help. Devout, steadfast, and unwavering, I had tried multiple kinds of penitence, but none of them worked.

Moaning, I threw the rope on the floor. My waist was burning as if feasted on by a scourge of mosquitos, but I promised Mary I'd try fasting again. I hated eating in front of Steve and Hunter, and I was increasingly wary of eating in front of people in general. I figured fasting would be easy. Abstaining from breakfast and lunch was simple, but skipping dinner was tough. *Just one bite,* I'd tell myself. But I was so hungry, my plate would end up clean.

I gingerly tucked in my blouse, used my knuckles to scratch at my waist, left the pew, and knelt in front of Mary's statue.

Mother Mary, why doesn't Hunter give up? I pray for him every day. Maybe you could really make him disappear or make his family move to another town . . . or make Dad get transferred.

Hoping to up the ante on my appeals, I lit a candle and stared into her eyes, concentrating on and praying fervently for them to open like they did for Bernadette. But the Lady of Lourdes did not appear. Mary remained stiff. Silent. Salty tears didn't leak from her eyes or stain her cheeks. Defeated, I thanked Mary for her time and walked over to the kneeler in front of the altar. My eyes roamed from the altar to the crucifix to the paint chipping on the ceiling. *I could fix that, Jesus, with a tall ladder.* Closing my eyes, I cleared my thoughts and focused intently on my prayer.

Please, please, make them stop.

Head bowed and hands in praying mode, I recited every prayer I could remember.

Over time, my zealous nature would abate, but I'd forever be drawn to places like this: cathedrals, mosques, temples (even shopping malls)—cavernous spaces where I could hear my own voice and where there was no one to put me down.

Reluctantly, I said goodbye and headed for home. It was cloudy; rain was coming. I pedaled hard and didn't care when the tears came flooding down my face and slipped under my collar. Hunter had ruined my favorite part of the day, the one thing I looked forward to: my mini triumph at the blackboard.

On Easter Sunday, I was back in church, but I was not in my favorite pew. Hunter's family had claimed my row. I stood on the left side of the church by the statue of St. Joseph. Dad was always late, forever and ever late, except when showing up for a business meeting. It wasn't a problem for regular Sundays, but Christmas and Easter were awash with worshippers. Baptized but not practicing Catholics came for their twice-yearly blessing or, I suspected, to beg forgiveness for not attending every Sunday. I can't remember ever sitting down during Christmas or Easter Mass. Mom was lucky; she was always toting a baby or toddler, so she could count on a gentleman to offer her a seat.

I could see the back of her Easter dress. She held Joey's hand while he wiggled, trying to get away. The pews were packed elbow-to-elbow, and she looked cramped, but she wasn't standing. Barry James and Mary sat on the kneeler in front of St. Joseph. Steve, Tom, and I stood next to Dad in the aisle. I couldn't see anything when the congregation stood; my view was blocked by a wall of Easter dresses and dark suits. But when people sat or kneeled, I had a good view of Hunter and his family. I watched them stand, kneel, sit, and go to Communion, but I took special note of how they paraded back to their seats. I doubted they were really praying, except maybe for the dad. Hunter's mom folded her hands in prayer, but she took an exceedingly long time to get back to her seat. Hunter followed, hands at his heart, until he saw me. Scrunching up his face, he strutted to his seat, making it clear that he had one and I didn't.

Clearing dishes during one of Mom's sorority meetings, I once overheard her discussing Hunter's dad: "He's a clever businessman and Hollywood handsome." He was good-looking in a Tony Perkins kind of way: tall and skinny. Hunter's brother looked like his dad but dreamier, and Hunter's little sister was blonde, pretty, and spoiled: a Shirley Temple with a bad attitude. His mom, as wide as she was tall, didn't strut; she wobbled on top of tiny Cinderella slippers and wore her hair styled like Marilyn Monroe. His mom's Easter dress was a poodle skirt, which only amplified the illusion of a giant golf ball balancing on top of a tiny tee.

I could tell that she must have been delicate at one time—pretty, too. I often wondered whether she gave my mother as much grief as Hunter gave me. Mom's face was different when Hunter's mom was close by. My mom usually smiled freely, acting girlish at church and in town, but never around Hunter's mom.

I observed Hunter's family as closely as I studied animals at the zoo, and I watched for signs that might explain his sadistic behavior. His family were big shots in our town, wealthy owners of the only supermarket. The Bon Marché that Dad managed carried upscale goods, but Hunter's family never shopped there. They bought their clothes, furniture, and expensive items in Portland. Longview shops were too down-market for them. I suspect we were, too.

Hunter was short like his mom, but he wasn't fat. Maybe a fear of fat made him mean. I was short and round. Would I grow up to resemble his mother or mine?

My mom was beautiful, and I wasn't the only one who thought so. "Your mother is as pretty as a movie star," my teacher commented, looking past me and across the room to where Mom stood. "She's a looker," whispered a dad at the pancake breakfast. "Your mom's so pretty," giggled a friend at a slumber party. I wanted to look like her, knew I never would, and was jealous of that fact. Mary was bound to become her look-alike. Grandma Lu said Mom was a princess. I agreed, believing she looked like Grace Kelly, the Princess of Monaco. Later, I would unravel Grandma's comment—she wasn't referring to a *royal* princess.

Mom also had a nice figure. "Lovely," people said. She wasn't skinny but had soft curves, except when she was pregnant, which was a lot of the time. She had platinum blonde hair styled like Marilyn Monroe (like so many women of the day, but Mom pulled it off), and though the color wasn't natural anymore, it was authentic—she had been blonde as a child. I knew so from an old photograph. The picture had yellowed, but her curls were nearly white. Mom took pride in her appearance. Her clothes were fashionable even though we couldn't afford high priced stores. Everyone seemed to like her. They marveled, "How does she do it?" They meant, "How can she look so good and have so many kids?"

After mass, everyone milled about in the front of the church, partaking in the post-church greeting dance. Mom was bubbly and chatted with the ladies as they passed, offering sweet observations about someone's child, outfit, or baked goods they'd brought to a fundraiser. She was in her element—until Hunter's mom walked up.

"Ruthie, you look lovely," she chirped, examining Mom as if she were a piece of produce at the supermarket. "Did you buy it in town?" she asked, not needing an answer.

Mom bristled. Her name was Ruth. Only her closest friends and family called her Ruthie. Dad didn't even call her Ruthie.

I thought Mom looked stunning. Her dress matched the light pink tulips coming up in the church's garden. Only four months along, her baby bump barely showed, and her dress flowed elegantly around her. I noticed the dads chatting with her, all smiling and wide-eyed; they approved. She always looked good, even playing baseball at the church picnic. And she wouldn't have been caught dead in those silly slippers.

Looking satisfied, Hunter's mom turned and walked away, bouncing on her toes. My eyes shifted to Mom. Her face had hardened. That after-church greeting pulled the pretty right out of her. Hunter followed his mom, but not before he flashed me a knowing sneer.

Chapter Eight

Queen of Christmas

"Squish it. Come on, squish it . . . squish." I was on babysitting duty. Joey sat on the counter with cookie dough up to his elbows. Barry James stood on a chair, eating more than he was squishing. "Mash it good, there's still some chips and lots of flour on the bottom." We were making chocolate chip cookies with oatmeal: everyone's favorite to eat right out of the bowl or warm and gooey from the oven. A doubly good babysitting game, making cookies occupied my pint-sized captives and begot yummy snacks. "Don't eat all the dough! There'll be none left for cookies."

Barry James imparted an eye-squinting, teeth-clenching, body-jiggling giggle like only he could. As he wobbled, the chair beneath him thumped the floor, causing an erratic rhythm. His infectious outburst set Joey off and me, too. Our high-pitched giggles and my reprimands riled Mom, who was nursing Greg in the living room. Our newest recruit had arrived a few weeks ago on August first.

"If you make a mess, you clean it up," she said.

Placing a finger to my lips, I shushed the boys. Barry James, a promising mime, wrangled a silent chuckle. We deployed spoons and fingers as we parceled what was left of the dough onto baking sheets and popped them into the oven. Grabbing a dishrag, I reached for their chocolate-chip-speckled hands: "Clean up time!" A race commenced—I was after the renegade chips, while the boys were stuffing them into their mouths. It was game over when I wiped their faces and slipped Joey from the counter to my hip. Swaying from side to side, an acquired reflex, I rocked him and gazed out the kitchen window. Tom and Steve played catch on the lawn. The baseball ping-ponged between them, landing in one mitt then the other. I was nine and wanted to be outside, too—with no dependents.

Each toss was a dig. Envious, I grumbled under my breath. *Mom wasn't babysitting or in the kitchen when she was a kid.*

The kitchen was Grandma Quinn's territory; no one was allowed in except to eat. Mom did have chores, but she wasn't Grandma's *housemaid*. The allure of my previously esteemed role—"Mother's little helper"— had worn off. I wanted to quit; I dreamed of abdicating, but it wasn't an option. Sometimes I fantasized about Mom's childhood; it was positively Old-MacDonald-had-a-farm perfect, or so it seemed to me. She rode horses, played hide-and-seek in a barn, chased chickens, harvested hay, and drove a tractor. Her chores included weeding the garden, collecting eggs, and cleaning the eggs for sale. I imagined the two of us spinning in a time machine, landing flip-flopped, and trading places.

Summoning Grandpa Mel's chicken coop in Tacoma, I remembered the sensation of raw timbers brushing my hair and how warm and quiet the coop was: a dreamy den much like my musings of Tarzan's tree house, snug and safe. Nuzzling my chin on Joey's soft blond curls evoked the feel of feathers on my skin. In my mind's eye, I was fluffing downy plumes with one hand and collecting eggs with the other while my eyes sized up a row of incensed hens. "Don't be afraid. It's just me," I whispered.

"Down. Down," Joey responded, believing I was addressing him.

Not wanting to chase after him—Joey was a runner—I shifted him to my other hip and bounced vigorously, mimicking a pony ride, but my thoughts were still in the henhouse, where I wiped muck off eggs and shined them until they were as pearly as fancy figurines.

"I smell something burning," Mom yelled.

Startled, I checked the cookies. "It's just the stuff on the bottom of the oven."

"Scrub it down when you're done."

"All right," I said, making a face she couldn't see. I hated cleaning the oven. *I bet Grandma Quinn never made her do it.*

Mom was born when Grandma was supposed to be past her childbearing years. Grandma already had four children—Eileen, Naomi, Marian, and Bill—who were grown and married with kids of their own. Mom's nieces and nephews became her almost-siblings, especially Aunt Eileen's boys, Jim and Howard, who lived nearby on their own farm. Consequently, Mom had her own room, the house to herself, and her parents to herself.

I sat Barry James and Joey at the table with a glass of milk and a warm cookie. All was quiet in the living room. I poked my head around the corner and found Mom and Greg snoozing. Her forehead was pale and smooth, her frown lines gone. One side of Greg's face was flat against her shoulder. Mom's mouth was open, just a little, but she wasn't making any noise, not even breathing sounds. She was as still as a mummy. While watching her, my own face melted; my indignation turning to guilt. I resented being her maid and go-to babysitter, but I acknowledged my sin—my thoughtlessness—in confession, though I still struggled to change. I said a short prayer, promising to quit bellyaching.

Mom's childhood stories were enchanting, but I knew they weren't the full story. She shrunk into herself when her family visited, wallowed in their approval, and was crestfallen when they were displeased. She was an *other* to them.

Grousing about her peachy childhood was satisfying as long as I ignored the tumultuous change she endured around her thirteenth birthday, when her family became Jehovah's Witnesses. Holidays were forbidden: no more birthdays and no more Christmas mornings. And there was no more participating in school functions or consorting with *others*.

No more Christmas? No more birthdays? It was hard to fathom and was impossible to ignore during the holidays when Mom made up for all those lost celebrations. Month by month, our house morphed, and by year's end, it had embraced every color of the rainbow: laced red hearts danced across our windows in February; leprechauns made from green paper and tender shamrocks growing in pots clustered on our windowsills and table tops during March; Easter bunnies romped in our living room once the leprechauns were put away in April, while pink, violet, blue, and yellow eggs brightened our kitchen; Fourth of July flags and streamers flaunted our love of red, white, and blue; September gourds and bright orange pumpkins became jack-o'-lanterns come October, joining the Halloween decorations of bats, skeletons, and witches' brooms; and pilgrims dressed in black, copper turkeys, crimson leaves, speckled corn, and over-stuffed cornucopias announced Thanksgiving. But Mom's tour de force was Christmas. Santas and snowmen festooned every room, every nook, and every corner. Mom strung cards across windows painted with fake snow; filled mini sleighs with shimmery Christmas balls; covered every surface with Christmas linens, candles, poinsettias, and evergreens; hung wreaths on doors both inside and out; and whipped the nativity scene into a must-see affair.

She was the queen of Christmas to make up for all those years she was robbed of the most important day of the year. Mom over-indulged on the Christmas dinner, the cookies, the candy, and, especially, the presents. The excess turned Christmas morning into a magical nightmare. Gleeful at first, we bounced out of bed and dashed into the living room to find our stockings and Santa's presents—the unwrapped ones strategically located near our stockings. A mountain of brightly wrapped packages waited under the tree. Playing patiently, but not always quietly, we waited until Mom and Dad got up. All our friends opened their presents in a frenzied burst, but not us. Our method took hours, a one-at-a-time slog, with one eye on Dad who was adding up the cost of each item in his head. Each new unveiling hardened his features and quashed our exuberance.

Year after year, an identical scene played out: Dad adopted his angry-calm voice, demanding to know how much Mom had spent. Mom tried to appease him, denied she'd overspent, and swore she'd bought every item on sale. But it never worked, and the quieter Dad got, the louder her voice climbed. They'd argue until Mom retreated into the kitchen to cook Christmas dinner, her face shiny with tears. We pretended everything was fine—it was Christmas, the happiest day of the year—but our giddiness disappeared long before the last package was unwrapped.

When I was seven, I asked Santa for a Chatty Cathy doll. She was the first item I saw under the tree: a doll standing erect in white shoes, her arms extended straight ahead as if asking to be picked up. When Mom and Dad started arguing, I brushed Chatty Cathy's blonde curls. When Mom's voice broke, I confided in Chatty Cathy, whispering, "I'm never going to beg or get stuck doing women's work. Never, ever." I didn't want to be like Mom. In my mind, she had no voice. Like Chatty Cathy, someone else was pulling the strings, and the one who was doing the pulling had zero respect for *women's work*.

Mom's retreats disturbed me more than Dad's interrogations. I didn't know what I wanted her to do. I wasn't on the receiving end of Dad's cross-examinations, but I always felt humiliated and shaken, terrified of following in her footsteps.

Chapter Nine

King of Tarps

I WANTED TO BE LIKE DAD. HE WAS AN ADVENTURER. GRANDPA
Mel liked to say, "Your Dad's always got a scheme up his sleeve." When
Dad was a teenager, he collected beat-up cars, repaired them, and sold
them for a profit. They drove as if new, or so Dad claimed. Mom said his
earnings were pool money: not from the swimming pool but from the
pool hall. Grandpa Quinn was not impressed. He thought Dad was a
shady character, maybe because Dad met Grandpa Quinn's daughter on
one dubious escapade.

Dad crashed weddings, dined on the free food and drink, and chatted up the girls. One afternoon, while playing pool, he overheard talk of
a wedding taking place close by. Mom happened to be in the wedding
party. That was that . . . but not right away. They were both sixteen, and
her father didn't approve. Plus, Mom had her eyes on a different boy. Dad
was persistent and won her over, but not so with Grandpa Quinn. Mom
was Grandpa's little princess, and he had big plans for her—go to New
York to study Jehovah, become a missionary, marry a Jehovah's Witness,
and settle down close to home—but Mom and Dad were determined to
be together. She studied Catholicism, converted, and, against her parents'
wishes, married three days after her eighteenth birthday when she came
of legal age. Her father disowned her, ordering all family members to
shun her, and they did. After Grandpa Quinn died of cancer shortly after
I was born, Mom's family warmed to her, but she was still and would
always be an *other*.

Dad loved to tell stories. He heightened tales of their romance with
pool-table indecision, that one-in-a-million corner pocket shot. "I'm on a
roll," he'd say, "Should I go, or should I stay and play?" He'd tell the stories
of his dreamy-eyed longing for the cute girl with long, bouncy hair and of

his cagey maneuvers to get her number. He never talked about the shunning, and when Grandpa Quinn's name came up and Mom's face darkened, Dad always had a good word for him.

Romance wasn't Dad's only theme. He always had an adventure on the tip of his tongue, and he recounted his own as well as those of family, friends, and strangers. A favorite of mine recounted his escapades driving cross-country looking for work when he was only thirteen. Along with a friend, he borrowed a car and drove east across the Cascade Mountains to the fertile valleys of Eastern Washington. They were hoping to work in the fields, but they were too late; the harvest was already on trucks headed to market. Undeterred, they drove south, chasing another crop, and another, and another, all the way to Mexico. When they left Tacoma, he didn't know how to drive. He learned on the road. He and his buddy took turns at the wheel, one steering, the other lying on the floor working the pedals. In my mind's eye, I could see him on the floor pumping those pedals all the way to Mexico.

Dad was a mishmash of Daniel Boone, Colonel Hogan from Hogan's Heroes, and, after he grew a beard, Santa Claus. Astute and clever, diplomatic and sociable, he was both larger than life and reserved. He was determined to be successful—he was going to be a millionaire and had no time for fools who got in his way. Someday we would live like the Beverly Hillbillies, swimming in our very own pool every day. He hadn't made his millions yet, but there was time. "Colonel Sanders made his first million when he was sixty," Dad liked to say. He said it often.

Our special time with Dad was on vacation. We never took fancy trips or ate in restaurants: that'd be too costly for a family our size. Mostly, we went camping. Our first camping trip was all things "Dad," and it had all the makings of a family legend. With each passing summer came another telling, Mom and Dad imparting different versions. My rendition amalgamated both interpretations along with my own memories—memories so ingrained and a legend so tantalizing that a tent sighting would forever remind me of my dad, "the Tarp King." His camping strategy was chutzpa with a dash of lunacy.

He didn't believe in wasting money on camping equipment. "Lewis and Clark didn't have showy gear. Why should we?" Ignoring tents, sleeping bags, and camping stoves at the hardware store, he purchased rope, tarp, and, only after Mom's insistence, a cooler. She stripped the bedding from our beds, packed dry and canned foods into boxes, and refrigerated items into the cooler. Rolls of tarp, rope, pots and pans, extra clothing, bedding, and food were tied onto the top of the car.

Mary was a baby, so I must have been four on one particularly memorable vacation. Steve was five, and Tom, two. After an hour's drive, Dad pulled off onto a narrow logging road. Giant cedars breached the edges of the road, their needles flicking the sides of the car. Eventually, we came across picnic tables. Each table was located next to a cleared open space, designated for a tent or trailer.

"Eyes open for the best campsite," Dad said.

He stopped often to check a space for its suitability. They all looked the same to me. He spotted a potential perfect spot and dropped Steve off to save it. Carrying on, he found a better one, and Mom got out to save it. We stayed in the car while Dad retrieved Steve. Once back, Dad cleared a space between two trees on either side of the campsite. "Pick up all the rocks and branches, even the little ones," he told us. "You won't want to sleep on them." We pitched in until it was nearly smooth as sand. He tied a rope around one of the trees, stretched it tight, looped it around the opposite tree, and secured the rope with a wad of knots. Steve and I helped him unfold the tarp. Dad threw it over the rope, and the three of us tugged and pulled until the sides were even.

"Wow! A doozy of a tent," Dad said, hands on hips. "Everybody, grab a rock or log—gotta hold down the sides."

Rocks were hard to find. My first collection, an assortment of pebbles, was rejected. My second attempt, a large branch, was accepted. Eventually, thanks to Dad's batch of logs and basketball-sized rocks, the sides were secured. A second tarp became the tent floor. Dad used another tarp to construct a canopy over the table, tying the canopy's ends to four trees. Ropes crisscrossed our camp like electric wires in the city.

Dad gave the thumbs-up signal. Our tent was ready for occupation. Steve and I scrambled for our bedding, claimed a spot, and made our territory our own. After smoothing out the wrinkles on my blanket, I helped Mom lay out Tom's blanket and pillow. Before long, the tent had five neatly arranged beds. Mary didn't need one—she'd cuddle up with Mom.

Mom warmed up beans in a pot placed over the campfire. We cooked hot dogs on sticks. I didn't like hot dogs, but these tasted better than the ones cooked regularly. We used the same sticks to roast marshmallows. Darkness descended early: pitch-black-can't-see darkness. But we weren't ready to sleep. I could still taste marshmallow goo and hear the fire crackling. The trees above were making creepy noises. In Mom's version, we resorted to kicking, pinching, tickling, giggling, and bellyaching until we heard a crash outside the tent. Then we all froze. I don't remember what I was doing, but I do remember abruptly stopping . . . and listening.

Twigs crackled, not from the wind, but from being under something's feet. We heard heavy breathing and snorting; someone or some*thing* was out there. A box flew off the table, hitting the ground with a thud. Another box turned over, and cans hit the ground, bounced, and rolled. Smashing and tearing and chewing, whatever was out there was eating our food.

"Quiet, everyone," Dad whispered. "They'll get what they want and move on."

"Bears," Steve said, peeking out of the tent. "Two of them."

"Shush!" Dad put his finger to his mouth.

Mom's face was scary-movie petrified. She clutched Mary, fusing the baby to her breasts. As if fearing we were next, Mom's eyes flashed between the openings on either side of Dad's homemade hut. There was no barrier between us and the bears. What if they wanted more, wanted us?

No one moved.

Moments passed.

The bears stopped, sniffed the air, then hightailed it as if interrupted by something or someone.

Hearing nothing peculiar or scary, our tense expressions dissolved. Steve and I smiled. We were ready to celebrate. *There'd been bears in our camp!* A deafening boom sapped our bluster. Lightning flashed. The sky opened with Augusta-like torrential rain. The tarp over the picnic table filled with water and collapsed, drenching what I imagined was left of our food. A river of water gushed through the tent, carrying away anything not weighed down.

Mom swears Mary floated down a river running through the tent. Afraid we'd all drown, Mom yelled, "Out, out! Get in the car." We ran for the car, leaving all our possessions to float away. Damp and chilled, no pillow or blanket, excitement flowed through my veins. Steve, Tom, and Mary nodded off before I did. Mom sat in the front seat, awake and watching.

Come morning, we were eager for the pancakes Dad had promised, but the bears had dispensed of our food—in their bellies or scattered over the campsite. Bits of wrecked cereal boxes, beat-up cans, and trash were everywhere.

"We won't forget this one!" Dad laughed. "Let's clean up."

Mom insists she helped clean up. Dad said she waited in the car with Mary and Tom. I don't recall, but I bet she helped.

I loved this story. I don't know if Mary floated down a river running through our tent, but I do remember a lot of water. I never saw the bears, but I heard them. And I wasn't scared. I was fly-me-to-the-moon excited. Just like Dad.

Chapter Ten
Thunder

SEPTEMBER AND FIFTH GRADE ARRIVED. I WAS FILLED WITH foreboding about another year with Hunter. We should have been in another town. I should have been in a new uniform at a new school—maybe even in a new state—that was miles away from Hunter. Dad had completed his two-year stint, but we were still here. I couldn't sleep. The thought of another year of Hunter gave me hives, not on the outside, but under my skin. I felt the air in my bedroom thicken. I couldn't breathe. There's a legitimate name for an episode like this: an anxiety attack. My word for it was *fear*, and it was physical, like the flu.

Mary's presence wasn't helping. She snored louder than Dad, and he could wake the dead.

Dear Jesus, make her stop! Make it stop!

Mary also sucked her tongue like a newly weaned baby even though she was six. I was ten, and, since we were the only girls, we shared a bedroom and a bed. But it never felt like we were alone, not with all the racket coming out of her nose and mouth. Sleeping with her was like lying alongside a pig trough all night long. I gulped a lung full of air, wrapped a pillow over my head, pulled the covers on top, and stuck my fingers in my ears, but the slurping and snorting permeated, assaulting my eardrums. The battle for sleep was a nightly affair, but it was especially merciless on the eve of the worst day of the year: the school weigh-in.

I was glad to see the end of fourth grade. I could remember only one day when Hunter left me alone: the day President John F. Kennedy died. On that day, every kid in school watched the adults—the nuns, our priest, our parents—roaming the halls and our classrooms, their movements heavy and in slow motion, like a legion of tormented ghosts. I was mesmerized by their tears, especially the held-back ones, and their tortured expressions. I knew who John Kennedy was, but I bore no feelings for him until that day when I absorbed the sadness around me. I didn't feel sad but rather had an odd sense of relief; time as good as stopped along with everything else. It was also the day I felt at one with my classmates. But it was only one day.

Now, only a few weeks into fifth grade, I was counting the days till summer. My head throbbed, burdened with flashbacks of last year's weigh-in. I remembered waiting in line, terrified of what was coming: standing on the scale, straining to be lighter, lifting my body up from my toes, and hearing *the number*, the nurse's voice ricocheting louder and louder, Hunter spitting insults, the whispers, the giggles . . . and the laughter.

We'd both honed our craft over the past two-plus years. His attacks were more frequent and incisive. I evaded him more efficiently by covertly slipping into the girls' bathroom, strategically shadowing Sister when I sensed an attack was coming, and staunchly ignoring him when he pummeled me with vile put-downs. I tried shaking off those past weigh-in nightmares. On most nights, I relied on inventive musings to fall asleep; their plots were either lifted from afternoon matinees or ones that I wrote myself, involving Tarzan, nefarious poachers, and elephants. But tonight, such musings weren't working. Afraid of the fifth grade and afraid that it would mirror last year and the year before, I dreaded tomorrow and every ensuing day.

Nightly prayers betrayed my tongue. I attempted a respectful start, relying on an appropriate verse, but I was angry with God, Jesus, Holy Mother, and every saint—all of them useless. Every morning, every night, during the day, and all the time, I prayed for blackened souls—for help— but no one answered; no one did anything. Seething under the covers, I called them out, venting my doubts and accusations.

I stewed and groused, each slurp out of Mary's sleeping mouth making me angrier. I imagined God and his companions partying, dancing on clouds, and occasionally looking down on earth for entertainment. I needed their attention; I was desperate for it. Night after night, my dutiful prayers were left unanswered. Nerves frayed, fingers pulling and twisting the covers, I was desperate. Picturing the nurse's co-conspirator pencil, I cried out for action.

Do something for a change! I'm not asking. Do something!

I spit demands and accusations into my pillow until fear struck: I'd called on the wrath of God. Horrified, I stopped short. What had I done? Tested God? He had every right to punish me, strike me down, or forge a more ruthless Hunter. Chastened and soaking with sweat, I apologized.

I'm so sorry, dear Lord. I didn't mean it. I know you're busy, and I'm only me. I'm really sorry. Please forgive me. Just let me sleep, and I won't ask for anything else. I'll pray extra hard for Hunter and Steve, and I promise to light a candle in front of the Baby Jesus, Holy Mother . . . and St. Rose.

Praying only escalated my anxiety, sharpened my temper, and riled my displeasure with the divine. It was hot under the covers. I couldn't breathe. Coming up for air, I growled, "Shut up!" to wake Mary, hoping to stop the slurping if only for a moment.

It didn't work.

"Why don't they use the nurse's office?" I barked. I shook Mary, punishing her for not having an answer. "*Why* the gym, in front of everybody? *Why* did the nurse have to say the number so darn loud?" I hissed, pushing her to the edge of the bed. She let out a loud whine and commenced snoring.

I smashed the pillow back over my head and pressed my fingers deep inside my ears until they hurt. The slurp-snorting seeped through. Throwing the pillow aside, I rolled over and pinched her nose, holding it until she woke. She shoved my hand aside, swung a sleeping hand at my face, knuckles whacking my forehead (*probably God's doing*), and turned over.

I pictured God on his throne and lashed out. *I can be mean, too. You're making me mean.* But I didn't want to be disrespectful or mean like Hunter and Steve. I wanted silence, nothingness, in the room and in my head. I couldn't stop thinking about the scales. I'd tried Mom's earlier; it tipped at ninety-eight pounds. I knew the nurses' scales would be higher—they always were—and Hunter would be beside himself, googly-eyed hungry for ammunition. If the scale tipped a hundred, he'd be set for the year.

Exhausted and wrapped in dread, I accused the Virgin Mary of not being holy and berated her for betraying me; she had God's ear but hadn't spoken for me. I thought of Augusta and blamed Holy Mary for Dad's transfer. Longing for Lennit Loop, where Hunter didn't exist and Steve hadn't gone mean yet, I pictured our red brick house, the kitchen where cockroaches roamed at night, and the garage Dad had remodeled into a TV room. I remembered the street in front of our house, the swamp behind it, and the look on Kenny Ray's face when we said goodbye, but I couldn't recall his other faces: the happy one or the miffed one. Pressing my eyes tight, I tried to bring him back, but only bits and pieces surfaced: a game of hide-and-seek and a blurred smile when he was caught.

I dug deeper into my memories, hoping to lose myself. I remembered Kenny Ray, drenched and galloping like a pony. He was running along-side me. It was summer. I was six, maybe seven, and shouting at the top of my lungs. My hair was wet. Strands stuck to my face. Steve, Tom, Kenny Ray, and I fought to out-scream each other. Warm water flowed from my forehead to my cheeks and into my mouth, prickling my body like a bath-shower set on high. I was running through a wall of rain so thick I had to push through it. Black clouds rumbled above us. Thunder boomed louder than a Fourth of July cannon. "God's bowling!" I remember shouting.

Suddenly, the wall of water vanished. It was dusk: frogging time. Steve held a whopper bigger than Dad's Sunday pancakes. A horde of baby frogs no bigger than my fingernails scampered across my hands; their tiny feet tickled my palms. It was like an army of tickles, both creepy and nice. We dropped them into a jar and closed it tight. Steve punched holes in the lid. The next day, they were gone. I recalled staring at that empty jar with the lid still on and wondering how they'd escaped.

The jar melted into water lapping at my knees. I was at the beach. Mom's baby-oiled skin was shimmering. She was lying on her belly, sun-bathing in a powder blue bathing suit. Dad, Tom, Steve, and I held hands, waiting for the perfect wave—a mighty one—then jumped. Salt burned my eyes. The returning wave buried my toes in sand. "Jump!" Dad yelled as another wave approached.

Recalling the joyful expression on Dad's face forced a smile on mine. I felt better until the pristine ocean turned soapy and dingy. Dirty dishes sat on the counter. I was washing; Steve was drying. My back, arms, chest, legs—everywhere—burned and smarted like a zillion bee stings: sunburn. Blisters bubbled over my arms, shoulders, back, and nose. They hurt to touch, but they felt so strange I did so anyway. Steve twirled his towel, grinned, and swatted the counter. I jumped and screamed, "Stop it!"

He wound the towel and struck again, hitting the wall. "Don't be such a baby," he goaded. I ran into the living room. "Cry baby! Gonna cry to Mommy." He whipped the towel over his head three times and struck the table, pushing it toward the sofa and smacking the table again and again. I raced into the bedroom. Fortifying his missile, he whipped the air. He was gaining on me. The towel struck me. My lungs exploded, releasing a cry so anguished it was foreign to my own mouth. "Shut up! Everyone will hear!" Steve yelled, terror in his eyes.

As the pain climbed and my cries muffled with gasps of air, Mom and Dad rushed in. The door slammed. "I didn't mean to; I didn't mean to! It was an accident," Steve said, backing away from Dad.

Mom was at my side: "Hush, stop screaming. You want someone to call the police?" Blister-water oozed down my arms and back. My screams converged in gargled sobs. Steve howled. Dad's belt swung high, whipped down, smacked Steve's bottom, swung back up—

Startled, I opened my eyes and sat up, my body shaking. *Why that memory? Why had it surfaced?* Bewildered and drained, I didn't want to think anymore, but my mind was spinning like a bicycle wheel at warp speed. *I'm gonna get burned tomorrow.* Another lashing, though of a different sort, was coming, but it wouldn't land in a private hotel room; a hundred eyes would be watching, and the lashing would sting deeper. I brushed my arms, stroking them gently as if the blister-bubbles were there, ready to pop.

Throwing the covers off, I grabbed my pillow and held it over Mary's face.

"Shut up!"

Envisioning Hunter under the pillow, I tried to silence him and Mary. She pushed me off, kicked wildly, and scored a hit to my gut—probably God's doing. Minutes later, she was back to sleep.

I rolled over and waited for morning.

Chapter Eleven

Levitating

I STOMPED ON EVERY CRACK. I WANTED TO BREAK EVERYONE'S back, the entire world's back. Mom rejected my pleas to stay home. Last year I'd tried skipping, lamenting a bellyache, but I didn't have a fever and wasn't throwing up, so she made me go. This morning I told her the real reason.

"The nurse is coming today. Her voice is loud. Everyone will hear how much I weigh."

"Don't be ridiculous. Nobody cares but you."

"Hunter will be listening."

The baby fussed, his head bouncing on her shoulder. She turned away. She didn't have time for this. "Ignore him."

I refused breakfast—not to reproach her as she assumed, but to keep my stomach empty. I didn't drink either, afraid of adding even an ounce to the scales.

The tortuous walk to school was both days-long and three-seconds short. Intent on missing the weigh-in, I dawdled yet still arrived in record time. I sat in my seat unable to concentrate, waiting for Sister's command to line up. This Sister and all the other nuns bore no distinction to me anymore: all black-robed-monologues-in-Christ. No matter what she or her comrades said, did, or didn't do, it amounted to "you're unworthy. Pray, pray, pray."

"Line up. . . . Quietly."

I'd put on my lightest tennis shoes despite the rain and ever-present puddles. I took off my sweater and left it on my chair. Compared to last year, the line seemed longer; Hunter, nastier; and the waiting children, antsier. The same loud-mouthed nurse stood by the scale. The line was shrinking fast. Each step I took forward seemed a Herculean task. My shoes stuck to the floor's surface, their rubber bottoms melting into it. I twitched and squirmed as if I needed to pee, but there was no pee to release—I'd already gone to the bathroom. My whole body chafed, demanding release and threatening to burst. I imagined disintegrating into a glittery dust, tiny glitter stars floating up and out through the cracks in the ceiling.

"Next!"

I was in no hurry. Facing the scale, I stepped up softly, hoping to leave some weight on the floor. Holding my breath, daring not to breathe lest I'd somehow add weight, I levitated the bulk of me upward. Focused on the arrow, I implored it to stop before one hundred.

"One hundred and one," the nurse broadcast for all to hear. Even her pencil shouted, scratching the page as she scribbled the number next to last year's abomination. I wanted to grab her pencil, break it in half, take the jagged edge, gouge out my number, then stab her with the tip; maybe I'd induce lead poisoning or slash an artery so her blood effaced my results, leaving a red puddle in their place. Instead, I dropped my gaze to my shoes, silently cursing them for not being lighter.

A high-pitched whistle pierced the muffled chatter of fourth and fifth graders waiting to take their turn or head back to class.

"Whoo-hoo," Hunter whispered.

"Silence," Sister barked.

Hunter clammed up until she walked away.

"How many pounds in a ton? Hey, I'm talking to you, two-ton Tessie!"

Gulping for air, I stepped off the scales, my heart racing. My feet leaden and dragging, I joined the eye exam line, but most of me was no longer in the gym. A numbness crawled over my skin. Suddenly weight-less—too late to do me any good on the scale—I floated away, still in the gym but not really there.

With no Peter Pan, elephants, or accommodating vines, this departure was different, not like my usual flights wherein I disappeared into my fantasy world. A stillness overtook me. I could hear the dull thump of my heart beating and funny dinky sounds like tennis shoes squeaking on the gym floor. It was like being in a car on a long drive, seeing and hearing people on the outside—close but far-removed—behind a locked door and rolled-up window. I saw myself walking back to class in line between Debbie and Carol, and I felt my feet touch the floor, felt my skirt brush my legs, and heard muffled crowd noises and individual conversations. I was present but not there.

I had friends—Debbie, Carol, my best friend, Kathy, and others—but I didn't let them get close. None of them backed me up, stood up to Hunter, or told him to leave me alone.

Once in class, my eyes wandered as if I were in a dream; they looked over the blackboard, at Sister, at pictures on the wall, and at the dirty light fixtures. I noticed the tiniest of things: paint chipping, a fly flitting between ceiling lights, another fly winging its way across the blackboard, the number of tacks on the bulletin board, and a faint colored prism on the windowpane. A hollowness enfolded in me like I was encased in glass, but I could still hear Sister. And Hunter. Calmed like never before, I drifted as if floating on water.

Hunter spat a series of animal names.

I carried on drifting.

Being present but not there was comfortable. I didn't understand it, but I knew it was a place I didn't want to give up. I spent the rest of the day there while answering Sister's questions, writing on the board, playing hopscotch, and jumping rope.

I took my time walking home from school, for there was much to think about. Something important had happened. Sister gave me the vocabulary word for it yesterday—*epiphany*: a religious prediction, prophecy, or breakthrough. I knew mine was the latter. Isaac Newton discovered gravity when an apple fell on his head. My apple dropped on weigh-in day: *ignoring* Hunter wasn't the answer. I had to *disappear* him; I had to act as if he wasn't even there: no more turning around when he screamed an animal name from across the playground; no more making stray chalk lines at the blackboard when he sneered at me; no more tangling my feet while jumping rope during his cruel soliloquies. It was so clear. How had I failed to see it before? Me giving any reaction to him whatsoever was as bad as crying; my reactions were proof that his acerbic drivel had hit their mark; proof that he was the king of mean and I, the gutless mouse.

I knew what I needed to do: look through him—not past him—and see only my classmates, my teachers, and even strangers while not blinking, tearing up, or changing my expression. No more stone-faced looks, never again. I'd keep the muscles of my face loose, as if I were listening to sweet music instead of his drivel.

And no more praying for his blackened soul.

"Practice makes perfect," Sister liked to say. I would practice him away. The me others saw had to be better than him: stronger, smarter, cleverer. When called on in class, I had to be right, unruffled by his barrages and soaring with each insult as if every hiss were a cheer.

I knew the slurs would always burn, but I was euphoric nonetheless, silly to a fault. Nothing I'd tried before had worked, but floating above the classroom and consorting with a fly made for the best day I'd had in a long, long time.

No one can touch me up here.

At first, the transition from ignoring him to acting as if he wasn't there was a minor blip actualized only in my head, but it didn't remain so. In time, the new approach took on a life of its own, altering my world in totality. I studied harder, anticipated Sister's questions, and practiced jumping rope, marbles, and hopscotch until I could do them blindfolded while never showing any sign of weakness to him, to my friends, or to anyone: I was proving that he could not reach me. It took me a long time to realize that no one else would be able to either.

Chapter Twelve

No Cool Whip

Tarzan Finds a Son occupied Barry and Joey while I practiced Chinese jump rope, having tied the ropes between two chairs. The movie wasn't my favorite, but the boys loved it. In my version, Tarzan found a baby girl in that crashed airplane. After dinner, I tied one end of a jump rope to a tree, cajoled Tom to swing the other end, and practiced until I could jump with my eyes closed. After everyone was asleep, I turned on the light and studied chapters far ahead of Sister's lessons, preparing for those surprise questions she periodically asked. The following day, I volunteered for extra credit assignments and turned in double the homework due.

My growing obsession with over-the-top measures didn't stop when the bell rang. I had no conscious plan to become Julia Child or a *Good Housekeeping* home economics whiz, but I was bored with everyday chores, Hamburger Helper, and making cookies. At the grocery store, while Mom shopped, I devoured *Good Housekeeping* and similar magazines, fixating on extravagant meals, desserts, and home decorations. I was ten years old. My favorite books were Nancy Drew mysteries and Mom's cookbooks.

Thanksgiving was the beginning of my domestic fever. I wanted to make it spectacular, befitting a magazine spread.

Helping Mom put away Halloween decorations, I blurted out, "Mom, I want to do Thanksgiving dinner this year."

"Really? What brought this on?"

"I don't know . . . just want to make it special."

"Special?" She frowned. I shouldn't have said special. She worked hard to make holiday meals an event, but she didn't like cooking, so she used shortcuts.

"I want to make everything homemade, from scratch like Grandma Quinn."

Her mother made the best pies. There were always fresh baked goodies on the counter. Same with Dad's mom, only she made lots of canned goods: pickles and jams. Both kitchens smelled delicious, as if something scrumptious were ready to pop out of the oven even when it was empty.

"I'll make a menu and grocery list and everything. You don't have to do anything."

On *do anything*, she started laughing. "That'll be the day."

"I mean it, really," I said.

"Okay. Get me your list, sooner rather than later."

Rummaging through her magazines and cookbooks, I searched for unusual dishes that were suitable for Thanksgiving. Anything labeled *gourmet delight* was circled for consideration. Mom always made sweet potatoes in a casserole dish, melting marshmallows on top. Her casserole was delicious, but I found something better: orange sweet potatoes. They looked heavenly in the magazine and appeared easy to make: cut the oranges in half, keep the juice, cook the sweet potatoes, mash with juice, fill the halves with the sweet potato mixture, top with marshmallows, and brown. Voilà: individual orange sweet potato cups—a gourmet delight and decoration for the table.

My stuffing would include sausage, apples, and cranberries, and I'd make a seven-layer salad and a fancy Jell-O mold. Mom made her Jell-O in a bowl; mine would be layered with fresh fruit, not canned, and set in a copper mold. I'd christen one of the polished molds that were still hanging above the sink, new as the day they were bought. My pie crusts would be made from scratch. And I'd whip real cream for the desserts—no Cool Whip. I added homemade rolls, glazed carrots, mashed potatoes, gravy, two pumpkin pies, a chocolate cream pie, and a yellow chiffon cake—the fluffy cake that cools upside-down on a glass—to my list and made a note to buy extra flour, butter, and cream.

"Where'd you get all this from?" Mom asked, reading my menu.

"Your magazines and cookbooks," I said. "Are Grandma and Grandpa coming?"

Dad's parents always came for Thanksgiving, Christmas, and Easter, but I wanted to make sure. I needed to know my audience, so I could impress each one of them with something special: orange sweet potatoes for Mom, pies for Grandma, homemade rolls for Grandpa—

"As usual," Mom said, grimacing. "Are you sure about this? It's a good idea to have made a recipe before you serve it for company."

"It'll be great."

Three days before Thanksgiving, I launched nonstop into the cooking. Mom accused me of being like Dad and "using every pot, pan, dish, bowl, and utensil in the kitchen." She was sort of right and followed me around, grabbing pots and bowls and washing and drying like a mad woman. Before she could put them away, I had dirtied them again.

Dad said the Thanksgiving prayer and thanked the Lord and the cooks. I was proud to be included, but I mumbled to myself, "You mean *cook*." The spread looked like a magazine shot; it was perfect. I was especially proud of my orange cup sweet potatoes, the Jell-O mold (Mom thought it would come out in pieces, but it was faultless: not a nick, not too loose and not too hard), and my pies. Grandma Lu picked at the pie crust but approved overall. My pies disappeared, and the boys begged for another chocolate cream version.

The day was brilliant, better than I'd envisioned. My over-the-top efforts had been worthwhile.

As I was cleaning up, putting the last dish away, I offered to cook Christmas dinner. Mom's face went blank; she hadn't recovered from the past three-day cooking extravaganza.

"Why don't you do dessert?"

Mom wasn't up for a feast—my kind of feast—because too much was going on during Christmas. She'd take care of dinner. "It'll be special, everyone's favorites, but not so time consuming."

But that didn't mean I couldn't be extravagant dessert-wise. Guests and friends typically stopped by over the holidays. I prepared for a visiting army. Mom had a cookie book. I baked huge batches of six different types of cookies and stored them in tins. I made enough sugar cookies for the kids to decorate and for me to make special. Copying Mom's Christmas edition magazine, I stuffed frosting into a plastic bag and forced the sweet cream into a corner, cut the end, and squeezed intricate designs over pre-iced cookies. Mom brought a dozen to her sorority holiday fundraiser along with a selection of my other cookies. She sold the lot.

I also helped Mom make crafts to sell at the church fundraiser. We made table runners bedecked with Santa, his reindeer, the sleigh, and tiny packages escaping from his overstuffed bag. The project required a lot of cutting and gluing. I had ideas for other designs and made those, too. Mom sold them along with the runners.

St. Patrick's Day arrived. I devised Easter dinner while making a batch of shamrock sugar cookies. Mom declined my gracious offer to make dinner. She requested one cake and one pie, but she never mentioned any limits on Easter eggs. We dyed them every year, all of us, even Mom and Dad. He colored his carefully, holding half in one dye cup, letting it dry, then holding the other end in a different color. Dad made the best two-toned Easter eggs. I helped the little ones. This year, I decided to go big and do a second batch: hand-painted ones, like those available in gift stores.

Using the acrylic paints Mom got me for Christmas and a tiny brush, I painted flowers, leaves, vines, and Easter crosses. I boiled another dozen and decorated them with geometric patterns, diamonds, dots, and swirly lines. Neither batch turned out like the eggs from the gift store, but they were pretty nice. I boiled a third batch, punched holes in the ends, blew out the middle, painted them—better than the first ones—glued on ribbons, and tied them to a branch I found in the yard. The centerpiece turned out better than the bowl of hand-painted eggs. I heard one of Mom's friends say, "You've got your own in-house decorator; send her my way anytime."

I didn't stop with holidays. I set my sights on birthdays, too, and baked huge cakes carved into favorite characters—Winnie the Pooh, Snoopy, Charlie Brown, Bozo the Clown—trains, and sport spectacles. For the adults, I made multilayered cakes of their choosing and whipped lots of fresh cream. Mom and Dad hosted and attended private parties and countless fundraising events for their charities, which all required food. I obliged and made appetizers, sweets, and relish trays decorated with carved vegetable flowers.

Regular was expunged from my vocabulary—there was no such thing as *it'll do*—and it was working. Each *ooh* and *aha* reaction to a cooking feat or craft work boosted my confidence, and my grades were better than ever. Before, I dreaded report card day, but not anymore.

Steve, Tom, Mary, and I sat on the couch, our bodies stiff with anticipation. Dad governed report-card review. In his chair, he sat leaning back with a favorite drink on the side table. Dad began with Steve, and it wasn't pretty.

"You're smarter than this!" Dad growled, methodically appraising each grade. The inquisition made the air feel cold. I relished the berating despite my pangs of guilt, but Steve didn't say a word, flinch, or show that he cared. That was a massive achievement, I thought, but Dad was not impressed.

My turn followed Steve's. The report cards were piled on Dad's lap. He slipped Steve's to the bottom and picked up mine. I was all smiles before he even opened it; I knew his face would light up when he saw my marks. Last year and the year before, he was passive—"Good try"—but today would be different; I was sure of it.

"What is this? . . . All As and Bs?" Dad stared at the card, then looked at me. I wanted to say, "Yes, it's mine," but I remained quiet.

"Well, well. This is worth celebrating. This calls for a dinner out." The prize for an all-As-and-Bs report card was a dinner at a restaurant, but no one had ever achieved it.

"Steve, you could be more like Catherine."

I knew I'd get hit for that comment, but I was euphoric nonetheless, floating on the edge of my seat.

"That goes for you two as well," he said to Tom and Mary. Too busy soaking up Dad's praise, I didn't notice their scowls. This was my day.

It wasn't easy drawing attention in a house of nine. Steve and Tom had sports victories, trophies, and ribbons to crow over. They'd inherited

Mom and Dad's athletic abilities. In high school, Mom played tennis and softball and was a cheerleader. I suspected Mary would follow her lead. Dad played football, baseball, and basketball. I couldn't catch a ball if it was dropped into my hands. But now, I'd found my trophy: my report card.

I inhaled Dad's sweet words; they would keep me going when I tired of extra projects, or when I heard myself mumbling, "It's good enough."

I never considered the effect that being Dad's favorite—at least during report-card review—would have on my siblings: Steve became ever more persistent, and my buddy Tom became resentful. But I didn't care. The approving look on Dad's face was just too irresistible. And without knowing it, I embraced the role of the perfect daughter.

Chapter Thirteen

Game On

"Next," Sister said, pointing her pencil at me.

We were stuck in a mindless review, Sister hammering fifth-grade math back into our vacant summer heads. I was ready for sixth-grade material, but she wasn't—not yet. Stepping up to the blackboard, I grabbed a long piece of chalk, turned around, and faced her. She paused before announcing my challenge, and I could tell she was thinking up a hard one.

"Five hundred and forty-six times forty-two."

I wrote the problem on the board and drew a line under it.

"Hey, Porky," Hunter hissed, for my ears only. "You'll never get it."

Pressing on, I worked the problem in my head: *Two times six is twelve, carry the one.* I wrote two under the six and put a notch above the four, letting Sister see before I moved on. I stayed put while she moved to the back of the room. Hunter watched her decamp, too.

"Give it up, Retard." His voice was still a whisper, but it was louder; everyone up front must have heard the offensive word: his favorite term for me.

Two times four is eight, plus one is nine.

"Piggy, I can't see the blackboard. Your fat ass is in the way."

It was time to liberate a dependable fantasy, one I could inhabit while doing math. I focused on the numbers and the jungle beyond the blackboard. Blades of grass suddenly slashed my arms and legs, but I kept running, hurtling through the bush, and resisting the impulse to look back. The barrage behind me was deafening. The ground shook, tripping me up, but I forged on.

Two times five is ten. Four times six is twenty-six, no twenty-four. Carry the two. Place the four under the two. No. Dammit. Four under the four.

"Give it up, Retard!"

He was gaining on me. I could smell him. A sharp object wedged deep in the ball of my foot, but I ignored the pain. Each pounding on the ground forced the offense deeper, but I didn't let it slow me down. My eyes were locked forward; there was no looking back and falling was not an option.

Four times four is sixteen. Carry the one. Oops, sixteen plus two is eighteen. Four times five is twenty, plus one is twenty-one.

"Hurry up, stupid. I'm tired of looking at your fat ass."

Something was moving in the bush just ahead. A hiss pricked my ears. Standing perfectly still, I eyed the cobra. Its tongue slithered in and out of its mouth, as if preparing to strike—

"Can anybody see around that ass?"

Trapped between a crazed rhino and a deadly cobra, sure to be poisoned or crushed if I stayed put, I pivoted right. The cobra lurched, fangs inches from my face.

The adder's head launched into the air, thanks to Tarzan's blade. The snake's headless body writhed as if trying to escape, only to be trampled by the enraged rhino. It happened so fast, I didn't feel Tarzan swing me up into the trees. Grinning, he wiped the machete on a leaf, leaving behind a gooey red smudge.

Bring down the two. Four plus nine is thirteen. Carry the one. Eight plus one is nine. One plus one is two—

"Twenty-two thousand, nine hundred and thirty-two!"

"That is correct. Thank you, Catherine. You may sit down." Sister nodded in approval.

Smiling back, I turned toward my side of the classroom. Looking through Hunter, I focused on the kids sitting behind him and to the left and right. My expression was poker-faced cool, but I was shaking. Reaching my desk, I felt a great sense of relief; but I couldn't stop fixating on Hunter's ugly words, knowing half the class probably heard every single one.

"That was brave," Lori whispered, barely audible.

Instinctively, I decoded the comment as sarcasm and resisted turning toward its owner. I could spot an insult; I was a pro, having learned my lesson back in the third grade: innocent terms, even compliments, were digs if they came from Hunter, his circle, or even onlookers. I shut out the whispered remark.

I spent most of lunch in the girls' bathroom. Back in class and doodling snakes in the margins of my notebook, I became preoccupied with Lori's words. Had I jumped to conclusions? *Brave* was an odd thing to say. I was always afraid; petrified of the next onslaught. How could *brave* refer to me? *Brave* necessitated a physical response: a kick, slap, punch, or shove-the-bastard-onto-the-floor response, or even a verbal comeback so cutting and clever his tongue would stop working and his eyes would recede, leaving nothing but empty sockets.

It was a puzzle, a puzzle compounded by timing. When she whispered, I was focused on Hunter's words and disappearing him. I failed to notice the lack of malice in Lori's voice or to recognize that she'd whispered to avoid Hunter's detection, not Sister's rancor. I found out years later I'd misjudged her intent; she wasn't referring to the difficult math problem (that I got right), she was citing my gutsy refusal to acknowledge Hunter's visceral attacks—not a flinch, a cringe, or a blink from me.

Waiting for the last bell to ring, I scratched heavy *X*s over the cobras covering the margins of my notebook, obliterating them and clearing my mind of *brave*. It had been a long day. Disappearing Hunter Spit was exhausting.

The bell rang three times. Half the class was out the door by the third ring. I lingered, slowly putting my pencil away, not wanting to stay but not wanting to go either. I hated school, but I hated going home to chores and Steve, who could not be disappeared. His fists made sure of that.

Hunter never hit or pushed me. For years, I checked my lunch and desk for gifts—worms or creepy stuff—and my seat for tacks or glue, but he never touched my things.

Maybe he didn't want to leave any evidence.

My bike stood alone on the rack. The playground was empty. I pedaled fast, my legs juiced, until I reached the lake path. I left the path and walked my bike to the entrance of an old hideout. From the outside, it appeared to be covered by dense shrubbery, too dense to breach, but the hideout was hollow inside: a cave perfect for daydreaming, with creepers for a roof and walls. Steve and I discovered it years ago while fishing—when we used to fish together. It was hard to believe we'd ever played together. But we had. Five years had passed since we'd caught catfish and tormented geese.

I didn't visit the hideout often, but when I did, I imagined being in the jungle, hiding from poachers, nesting with gorillas, or stalking wild animals. The fort had a bird's-eye view of the water. Under my gaze, fowl mutated into an array of creatures all mired in daunting situations requiring my unique rescuing skills. Recalling prior afternoons of make-believe made me smile. Some were pretty silly, but they were nice. I realized it had been a long time since I'd played—really played—and it would be heavenly to do so again.

I thought of my best friend, Kathy. We didn't see each other much, not with chores and babysitting. We played at school, as I did with other girls, but it never felt as free as those pre-Hunter days when Steve and I peeked through the bramble walls of our fort. Twice I went to Kathy's house after school. She had only one sibling, an older brother who wasn't mean. He ignored her: a factor of their age difference. He was in high school. Kathy's mother was plain looking with mousy hair. She didn't say much. Kathy didn't either. Her house was as quiet as the two of them: church-like. Kathy wasn't comfortable at my house. I think she was overwhelmed with Mom yelling, kids yelling, a baby howling, and siblings pounding on my bedroom door or barging in. On her second visit, she fell on our driveway and broke her tooth. She never came over again. I don't think her mother thought our house was safe. Now I never let my guard down, around Kathy or anyone else. She never backed me up; none of the kids did. They were mute around Hunter. Sometimes they even joined in, with forced smiles or giggles, every sheepish grin confirming the error of getting close to the outcast.

Tears, normally withheld until night when under the covers, cascaded down my chin and neck. I didn't want to be second-mom anymore. I ached for a different school and to be free to jump rope, run, somersault, scream, and laugh without the ever-present fear spoiling everything. I called out for Tarzan.

I was so tired. Too tired to think. Too tired to ask another why-Hunter question. Too tired to differentiate a malicious comment from a kind one. Sitting alone while imagining bleaker days to come, I couldn't fathom why Hunter's efforts were intensifying.

I was the only one who failed to see why Hunter would not give up. My method of coping, pretending he didn't exist, endangered his rank on the playground and denied him the validation he sought. Him being invisible was anathema. Hunter could no more stop his assault than I could give in to him. We were forever entwined.

It was time to go home, before I got into trouble. Standing up, I exhaled loudly. *Another eight months to go before I'll be done with sixth grade.* Then comes summer—something to look forward to.

No school!

There'd still be chores and Steve, but no Hunter—except for Sundays, and the church picnic, and the Fourth of July celebrations.

While wiping tears from my face and neck, a twig caught my eye. It was slimy and tinted green from mold and bits of moss. Picturing Hunter's face, I stepped on it, smashing it into pieces.

Chapter Fourteen
Pretty Boy

SUMMER!

No school.

No recess.

No uniforms.

No Hunter.

But there was YMCA Day Camp, a summer gift better than a pillowcase of Halloween candy. Camp occupied only a few weeks of summer, but every day was a glorious diversion. Steve and Tom filled their camp days with sports and nature activities. I spent mine in the craft room with Miss Jo, a teacher I adored. Miss Jo was a big lady. I hated the word *fat*, but she was circus-lady fat. Kids laughed at her and made fun of her in their whisper voices, voices that pierced the air like a submarine ping traveling through water: "She must make her clothes from sheets, or tents. She can't sit down, no chair on planet Earth is strong enough. Bet when she eats, she swallows an entire cake or pie, or cow." They knew she heard. I knew how she felt.

Adults were no different; their disgust beamed equally loudly even when they were silent. Pursed lips, frozen eyes, or severed repartee conveyed more than the kids' insults. Miss Jo knew. I could see it in the apology between her shoulder blades; it was a "sorry" for taking up space. I didn't care what they thought. Miss Jo was lovely. She had kind eyes and a quiet face, and I liked how she rested her hand ever so gently on my shoulder while she looked over my work. It wasn't a hug, but it felt like one to me, and I couldn't wait for another one.

The YMCA was a twenty-minute walk from our house. Steve traipsed far ahead, far enough to suggest we weren't together. Tom and I ambled side by side, lost in our own thoughts. I was thinking about Miss Jo, how excited I was to see her, and wondering whether she would be happy to see me, too.

I didn't know what was on Tom's mind. His eyes pointed straight ahead, but I knew he wasn't looking at anything in particular. I guessed he was playing baseball in his head, imagining himself squatting between second and third base and minding the game's most demanding field position: shortstop. Tom was lightning fast, as fast as I was slow, and he was Mom's favorite. When he spoke to her, she gazed at his face as if it was enchantment itself. When he was up to bat, she cheered him on, screaming over the other parents and the referee: "Okay, Tom! Here we go, here we go. . . . Outta the park!" Her cheerleading skills were resurrected for him.

Tom and I always got along, but we didn't play like we used to. He loved baseball, football, and basketball, but I was a hopeless ballplayer. I tried my best, but it never worked out, like the time he smashed a would-be homer, and I caught it with my teeth. My lips swelled up like a purple balloon on its last leg. For the better part of a month, I ate through a straw, sucking down milkshakes and soup. The dentist said I was lucky: "You could have lost all your new, permanent front teeth." They grew back in. My new smile didn't line up like before. One tooth was pushed back and slightly discolored, and another turned somewhat inward, though not grossly so. After Tom's thwarted home run by virtue of my mouth, I insisted on the outfield—way out.

I liked our walks to the Y; hanging back with Tom was peaceful, and the route was comely. Across the road, tall oaks shaded noisy ducks and noisier geese competing for grass and worms on the lake bank. We passed the hospital where Greg was born. Ritzy houses and a public grade school—the classrooms and parking lot now empty—lined the other side of the street. The Y was catty-corner from the hospital. We were nearly there and had lost sight of Steve. He was probably checking in, which was a quick procedure since the staff knew us by our first names. On weekends, when Dad wasn't busy, all nine of us attended Family Swim and hijacked the pool. All but Greg and Joe took swim lessons, and Steve, Tom, and I were on the swim team (not by choice) because Mom said there were too many of us to keep track of. We had to be strong swimmers to save ourselves and each other. Practically speaking, the countless hours in the pool honed our underwater wrestling and water-torture skills. The foolery required a safety code: three taps, to prevent accidental drowning at each other's hands.

I spotted the Y through the trees. Eager to see Miss Jo, I sped up.

We checked in at the front desk. Tom went to the gym. I raced to the craft room and flew inside. She was across the room sorting art materials into piles. Her bangs were shorter than they were last year. Miss Jo's hair was short, straight, and shiny black. Her eyes and mouth looked tiny, though only because her face was so very big and round. She wore a dress with a flowery pattern. Miss Jo always wore dresses and was meticulous about her appearance: her dresses were wrinkle free; her shoes, polished like new; and she carried a matching purse; but no one noticed. She had pretty chocolate-brown eyes and a gentle, soft voice, but no one noticed. She never diverted her eyes when conversing with her students, and she waited patiently for their responses, leaving each student with a comment worth remembering.

"Miss Jo!" I said, dashing over.

"Well, Miss Catherine, so good to see you." She smiled and stopped what she was doing, giving me her full attention. Behind her eyes, I could see happiness; she was happy to see me. "How was your school year?"

"Eh," I said, shrugging my shoulders. "Summer's better."

"Indeed." She laughed, but her body didn't jiggle like the other kids claimed. "I've got big plans for this summer. Are you ready to work?"

"Yes!"

"Find yourself a seat. It's still early."

Only two other kids were in the room, and they'd grabbed a table together. I snapped up one by the window. We waited until all ten campers arrived. When everyone settled, Miss Jo called us to the big table where she demonstrated projects and displayed samples. On one side of the table were various tiled plates—some platter-sized, others as small as ashtrays—and at the other end were stacks of leather goods, purses, wallets, and wall hangings. The tile works were all colorful: some were without a realistic pattern, just mixes of colors, but others embodied images of flowers, scenery, buildings, and Fourth of July–inspired flags. The leather pieces were likewise impressive. Some were sparsely decorated, with just initials in a corner or edges adorned with modest motifs, but others were spectacular, with nature scenes or lavish flowers carved into the surface. The leather was soft and had a strong smell: outdoorsy, like sun-bleached dirt. The craft room basked in the scent, that and the smell of glue. I had an urge to touch each of the samples; the knobby surfaces were enticing, like pricey off-limits knickknacks. Rolling my fingers over the patterns, I imagined Mom doing the same.

"You'll be doing one tile and one leather project. Take a look at the samples to get some ideas." There was a rush as everyone grabbed for the leather items. "Hold on, hold on. There's no hurry on leather. We're starting with tile." She pointed us to the other end of the table. We responded with groans and mock pouts, which she ignored. "Pick your pleasures, and let's go."

I knew what I wanted to do: make Christmas presents for Mom and Dad, an ashtray for him and a wallet for her. I planned to do a rainbow design on the ashtray, with the design starting in the center and going out. But I wanted to use colors just off the main rainbow bands—that fuzzy mix between solid colors that are less vibrant but more interesting. For Mom's wallet, I was going all out. I was going to use the most complex of Miss Jo's flower patterns.

The tiles were in multiple boxes. Ten kids with twenty hands created a momentary free-for-all.

"Only two people per box," Miss Jo said, gently escorting our eager hands, thereby turning chaos into an organized treasure hunt.

She didn't have all the colors I'd hoped for, but Dad would like it . . . if it turned out as I planned. My first handmade project was not well received. I was six and made what I thought was the perfect gift for Steve: a hand-printed copy of a paragraph from the encyclopedia. I couldn't read and had no idea what the paragraph said, but Steve was sounding out words and making sentences, so what better present than a page of words from an important book of science? It took me hours to copy the paragraph. Mistakes and ugly eraser marks had me restarting multiple times, but the finished piece was clean. On Christmas morning, I was so excited that I begged Steve to open my present first. My eyes shifted from his hands to his face and back again as he opened it, expecting his expression to unfold with delight, but he stared at the sheet of paper. "What is this?" he'd asked, then handed it to Mom. Surprised and utterly perplexed, I retrieved the book and explained, pointing out the passage. He burst out laughing. Mom passed my gift to Dad. They all laughed. The following Christmas and thereafter, I chose my gifts more carefully.

Determined to create a present Dad would appreciate, not because one of his kids had made it, but because it dazzled, I worked diligently, gluing the fingernail-sized tiles to my plate. Excited chatter forged a soft roar in the room, like distant drums. The buzz was spirited and freeing. Some kids fooled around more than they worked, but everyone made progress. I loved it when Miss Jo came around my table, and I resented sharing her with all the other kids. She complimented my choice of colors, my technique, the straightness of my lines, and the arrangement of my workspace. Each time she walked past, I swooned like a maiden in an old movie. When Miss Jo called to clean up, I wanted to burrow under the table and make it my home for the summer.

A week later, sparkly white grout set off my rainbow design. Cleaned and polished, the ashtray was perfect. I stored it and started on the wallet. Miss Jo was worried at first—the design was so complicated I might not finish, and the other kids were just doing initials or borders—but she relented. I was determined to make the wallet look professional, like leather goods I'd seen at the store. Mom was particular. The wallet could not look amateurish. I used a set of three metal tools and a hammer. One tool pounded in the outline of the design, and the others were used for shading and creating delicate highlights. Once the design was complete, I'd have to sew on the inner lining, replete with pockets for money, coins, and credit cards. The final step involved softening the leather by massaging wax into the surface and polishing it with a soft cloth, a process not so different from shining shoes.

Three days of pounding later, Miss Jo said, "I was wrong. You are going to finish, and it'll be beautiful."

"Thanks," I said, looking up. Consumed with pounding, I hadn't noticed she was watching.

I stopped and reviewed my work. It was good. My gifts would stand out this Christmas; I was certain of it. Under Miss Jo's tutelage, I discovered that art was an arena I could shine in. Catching and throwing a ball reigned in my house, but with Miss Jo, my eye for color, my dexterity in wielding a brush or craft tool, and my imagination ruled.

"You deserve a treat for working so hard. How about lunch, at my house? I live nearby. Would you like to come?" she asked me one day.

"Yes! Absolutely. When?"

"I'll need your parents' permission. I'll write a note, and you can bring it back signed tomorrow."

I could hardly wait. I didn't think there'd be a problem, and there wasn't. I brought in the signed copy, and after class we walked to her place for a late lunch. Miss Jo lived two blocks from the Y. She walked slower than Mom, but we were not in a hurry. Miss Jo was finished for the day, and Mom didn't expect me until four thirtyish—I could vacuum and dust when I got home. It was hot, but a light breeze tempered the heat and fluffed my hair. Too short to do much moving, Miss Jo's bangs stayed put. Nervous with excitement, I didn't know where to look and found myself studying her feet. I hadn't noticed how little they were and caught myself wondering how they supported her huge frame. Straightaway, I chastised myself for the mean thought.

We stopped in front of a white single-story duplex. "Here we are."

Miss Jo lived on the left side. She unlocked the door, stepped inside, and laid a hand on my shoulder, nudging me in.

"Hello, Pretty Boy. I brought a guest," Miss Jo said, her voice high and singsongy.

"Hello Jo. Hello Jo." The return cry was growly and strange.

She has a parrot.

I searched the room but didn't see a cage. Her living room was tiny. I passed a small sofa and one chair on the way to the kitchen. It was tiny, too. Butted alongside the one free wall was a two-chair table, and in the corner stood a birdcage, its door eye level with Miss Jo. A blue and green parakeet shimmied side to side on a swing.

"Hello Jo. Hello Jo. Pretty Boy here. Pretty Boy here," he squawked, repeating every line twice. Overexcited, he started flying about in his cage, bouncing off the floor and sides.

"Sweet Pretty Boy . . . calm down. We have a guest."

Miss Jo opened the cage and brought Pretty Boy out on her finger. She petted him, cooing as if the bird were a real baby. "Hush now. Why the fuss?" Once he calmed down, she gestured for me to pet him.

"Pretty Boy, this is Catherine. She's a friend."

"Pretty Boy friend. Pretty Boy friend," he said, pecking Miss Jo's sleeve.

He had an impressive vocabulary and was softer than Kai, my Siamese cat. Petting him, I was afraid he might break; I could feel the bones beneath his feathers. Miss Jo put him on her shoulder and made us sandwiches. She trimmed the edges and cut them into triangles and squares, arranging them on a fine china plate. She set out an assortment of cookies, two glasses of milk, and sliced apples.

A kettle whistled, and Pretty Boy called, "Tea Time. Tea Time."

"Thank you, Pretty Boy."

"Welcome, Jo. Welcome, Jo."

A lace tablecloth, china plates, teacups and saucers, frilly napkins, delicate sandwiches, Miss Jo, and Pretty Boy—I'd never had such a delightful meal. It was like lunching with Alice in Wonderland: positively magical.

We had one more lunch before the Fourth of July break. I dreamed about our lunches, complete with the pretty spreads and the tasty treats. The food I ate at home no longer tasted good. Some days I barely ate; other days I gorged, ransacking the kitchen. I loved Miss Jo but was afraid of becoming her. Steve habitually warned me that I would. I pictured myself as her size but with frizzy red hair and glasses. The image soured even chocolate chip cookies, and it roused pangs of guilt. How could I love her but not want to be like her? I wished everyone would shut up about her size, including the voice in my head.

On the last day before break, Miss Jo tidied my space while I stitched on the inner pockets. Mom's gift was nearly finished; it only needed softening. The wallet looked magnificent. Giant roses, balmy leaves, and delicate vines covered the front and back of the wallet, but it was as stiff as a board. Folding it took a surprising amount of effort. I pressed my full body weight on it and held it down while Miss Jo put a stack of books over it. There it would stay till I returned.

I was afraid to leave it. *What if a burglar stole my wallet?* Miss Jo assured me that it would still be there and confirmed a well-known fact: in all the Y's history, only the locker rooms were broken into by thieves looking for money. I knew this wasn't true—people took towels, toilet paper, and even soap—but I relaxed when I heard the craft room would be closed and locked over the holiday.

"Happy Fourth! See you next week," I said to Miss Jo.

She wasn't going to the fireworks—couldn't leave Pretty Boy—because birds pulled out their feathers when stressed. I imagined Pretty Boy as bald. I didn't think it would make much difference whether Miss Jo was home or not. Pretty Boy was going to freak out. *Poor Pretty Boy.*

The Fourth of July festivities were held on the bank of the lake. I took the kids to the peewee games, but now they were with Mom, and it was my turn. Dad was cooking burgers in the Lions Club food truck. Steve and Tom were roaming around, but they weren't together. I was by myself.

My feet, parted for balance, were planted in the grass. The egg was warm and firm and had no cracks, not even the beginning signs: veiny threads beneath the shell's surface. I was waiting for the man in charge of the egg toss to give the signal. The toss began with a long line of kids partnered and separated by about four feet, which was close enough to hand-deliver the eggs. Only five teams remained, and the distance between me and my partner was crazy far. I didn't know her. We had been assigned. She was younger than me and equally reluctant to join forces with a stranger, but we were a good team. I'd never made it this far, not with this many egg-toss challengers.

"Ready . . . and toss!"

A cavern stood between us. I had to throw the egg with enough force to reach her, but gently, so it didn't break in her hands. I swung my right arm back, aimed for her waist, and threw the egg underhand slightly harder than the last toss. It rose up higher than I intended, then came down fast. With her arms swinging behind her and her body angled outward as if anticipating an egg bath, she caught it, and the egg held firm.

"Yay!" I yelled, jumping into the air.

"Nooooo," a boy cried, shaking yolk off his hands and laughing as the crowd moaned in support.

We were down to four partners.

"Move one step back," the games-leader instructed.

Two feet were added to the distance between us. Prizes were on my mind, despite my doubting that we'd survive the next toss; my catching the previous tosses was an outright miracle.

"On the ready. . . . Toss!"

Giving my partner a target to aim for, I held my hands cupped in front of me. Watching her hands, I followed the egg as it rose in the air and came down like a fly ball. I caught it! *Thank you, Jesus.*

The girl next to me did not. *Three left . . . we can win!*

"Take one step back."

Stepping back, I spotted Hunter. He was prowling; his buddies were following. I'd been keeping an eye out for him—I always did—but I hadn't seen him all day. It was hot and humid, but the heat rising in my body and the dampness climbing along my spine had nothing to do with the temperature. He was going to ruin everything, I knew it. A perfect day was about to unravel.

Hunter pointed at me then spread his arms outward, wider and wider, signifying how much space I was taking up. Laughing, his buddies joined in. I focused on my partner. They were behind her. She, too, was focused and hadn't sensed their presence. I homed in on her.

"Ready . . . toss!"

This time I threw it lower but further, and she caught it easily.

I'm getting the hang of it!

Everyone else was, too: three teams stood strong and in place, because there was no room to take another step back.

Hunter puffed up his face and widened his arms. He moved closer to my partner. His arms were waving, and he was blowing wisps of her hair; but still she didn't notice, thanks to the crowd screaming and cheering us on, anticipating the next egg bath.

He whispered in her ear. She giggled.

What did he say? He's gonna ruin it.

"Okay. Ready? . . . Toss!"

She threw hastily, seemingly without calculating how the egg would reach my hands. I caught it, but she'd thrown too hard, and the egg collapsed. The shell crumbled as if it'd been smashed on the floor. Egg yolk and white slime oozed between my fingers and onto my shorts. I heard laughing—his laugh, her laugh, their laughs—but I didn't look up. I didn't look at her. I didn't look at them.

I scrubbed my shorts in the girls' bathroom, but the yolk stain wouldn't come out. Later that night, watching the fireworks, I lay on a blanket squished between Steve and Hunter. They weren't physically there; they didn't need to be. Their taunts had become my thoughts, my inner reality.

I could have won.

Fat . . . circus lady in training. I pulled my sleeves down over my knuckles to hide my freckles. *Stupid giraffe arms. Ugly, ugly, ugly, ugly. I need a veil, like Arab women wear, so I can cover my face, too. Why did I think I could win a prize? For God's sake, how stupid. What a fool.*

I groused on, barely noticing the fireworks. They were a hit, and everyone oohed and aahed, but I couldn't forget the humiliating egg toss: Hunter laughing, the girl laughing, the town laughing. Imaginary slime burned between my fingers. I wiped them on the blanket, hoping the wool would cleanse them. It didn't.

❖   ❖   ❖   ❖   ❖

On the last day of camp, I smothered the wallet with a waxy balm and massaged till my muscles ached. I sat alone, disappointed, because Miss Jo wasn't there. I needed to see her, hear her voice, and look into her welcoming eyes. It wasn't like her not to show, especially on our last day. I was at a loss; it made no sense. Miss Jo loved our class. She'd want to see my wallet, want to help me make it perfect, and want to say goodbye. I grilled the substitute teacher, but she was useless—more like a babysitter than a teacher—and didn't know anything about Miss Jo, or why she was gone, or if she'd come down with a cold or flu bug. I stared out the window, fabricating my own reasons: Pretty Boy was sick, and she had to take him to the veterinarian; Miss Jo was sick and didn't want to pass the bug on to us; there was a flood in Miss Jo's house she needed to attend to; Miss Jo was transferred. I latched onto the transfer idea and imagined Miss Jo in another town, living in a yellow cottage with Pretty Boy, and having tea with me on her patio.

When I got home, I hid Mom and Dad's gifts. Mom asked about class—a first—but didn't inquire about my projects. She didn't notice I came home empty-handed after three weeks in craft class. . . . *How odd.*

Later that night, after everyone was in bed, I overheard Mom and Dad talking. I was in bed, too, and I'd been asleep until I heard their voices coming from the living room. They spoke softly, but their words carried like a strong scent. "It was bound to happen. Her heart couldn't take that kinda weight. I heard she was only in her thirties. In a way, it was her own fault."

In a daze, I sat up, sensing they were talking about Miss Jo.

"Heard it was a massive heart attack. . . . Nothing anyone could do."

I wanted to run in and tell them they were wrong. I wanted to scream, "You're stupid! You know nothing!"

My parents weren't alone in their assessment. No one seemed sorry Miss Jo died, and they were all quick to blame her. Since she couldn't hear them, demeaning comments were spoken openly. "If only she'd taken care of herself. What was she, three, four hundred pounds? Surprised she lasted this long." Kids were more direct: "She croaked on the hospital steps. They couldn't get her on the gurney. She was too humongous to fit inside a normal casket. Bet a Mack truck had to tow the hearse."

Her presence lingered when I went to the YMCA. I missed her and longed to see her, to sit with her, in her tiny house. Colorful birds—blue jays especially—reminded me of Pretty Boy. I never stopped wondering what happened to Pretty Boy.

Chapter Fifteen

John Patrick

SEVENTH GRADE: EVERYTHING WAS DIFFERENT YET EXACTLY THE same.

Hunter's attention seemed to have waned. Apart from a welcoming insult on day one, he ignored me. Days turned to weeks, and he'd scowl— a just-you-wait dirty look—but nothing transpired. I hoped, prayed, dreamed we were done, but I was wrong. He simply changed tactics to striking less often but with greater precision and caustic effect. He replaced juvenile animal name-calling with slights about my changing body and my never-to-be paired-up destiny. No more insult bombs lobbed into a crowded playground, but he struck razor-sharp when I was alone or when those nearby were distracted. I was grateful for the breaks . . . the blessed breaks. But I could never relax. I was always looking over my shoulder or anticipating his next move. When the blitz came, I responded as before: zoning him out while internalizing every insult he spat.

Reflected in the mirror one day, my boobs appeared as if by magic. I loved their marshmallow softness and doughy quality, and, though only shooter-marble size, they filled my training bra as amply as Mom fit her thirty-six Cs. All the girls had training bras or pressured their mothers to buy one; the girls begged even if they were flat as a pancake. Jumping rope, hopscotch, or any bouncy activity was curtailed; the up and down was too treacherous on our tender breasts, despite no evidence of us having boobs large enough to jiggle. During recess, groups of girls meandered in circles chatting about boys, bra size, and the current yummy rock star. Boys, obsessing over sports, avoided us, except if they were paired off—were *going* with a girl. The boys gossiped, too—grandstanded—and assigned points to rookies who'd scored. They got more points if tongues were involved or depending on where their fingers had roamed.

Patrols of freshly aligned cliques monopolized the far end of the playground. The guys played basketball, and cheerleaders practiced routines while choreographers, critics, and fans cheered and shouted suggestions. There were times we drifted from our designated area on the playground, wooed by a faded hopscotch rendering or a discarded jump rope, yet no younger kids dared venture beyond the invisible barrier of our territory.

For some, Friday night spelled *p a r t y*. I was not a participant, but I heard about the artless dancing, loud music, parental eruptions, and "Turn it down, *now!*" ultimatums.

I had a crush on Jeff, but I didn't think he noticed me. His reddish hair was cut short, not quite a buzz cut but close, and he was kind. I never heard him say a mean word to anybody or about anyone. He was more of a word guy than a sports guy, and he was very funny and smart. His desk was behind mine and two rows over. I couldn't see him unless he was answering a question posed by Sister and it was okay to turn around, but I could listen to his chatter until he got reprimanded for talking. I watched him during recess, slyly looking just beyond or to the side of him, like a detective on a stakeout. Jeff never sought me out, but he was always nice when our paths crossed. I savored those moments, and they rekindled in my imagination on tough days.

Seventh grade was like last year and every year. I negotiated the classroom and playground in much the same way. At home, Steve operated like Hunter. Maybe it was the hormones, boy-girl distractions, or years of practice that had honed their tactics. Or maybe it was my conditioning. Regardless, their mere presence was enough to make school and home unsafe. Even so, dealing with Steve and Hunter was my norm, and I'd perfected my response.

Nothing had changed at school, but other changes coming had me worried. Mom was pregnant again, and unlike previous times, this one wasn't routine.

Dad made the announcement; his eyes were serious, and his chest was puffed up like an actor's when preparing a monologue. "You kids are gonna need to give Mom extra special help—"

Mad joyous—my feet itched to do a Fred Astaire—I couldn't wait to pack. Two kids equated moving. Our family's story was preordained: we'd always moved after two new kids.

Dad did all the talking. We cheered; I was the loudest, for I was celebrating no more Hunter forever and ever and ever. I looked over at Mom, expecting to see an elated grin, but her face and lips were mismatched. Her smile was clearly bound by dread. Dad pretended her smiling mask was authentic. I registered Mom's dueling expressions and Dad's denial, but caught up in euphoria, I soon forgot all about them.

The elation was intoxicating. In truth, I'd already moved and invented a new town and a school with nuns who wore mid-calf uniforms and wee veils pinned to the back of their heads. They'd have no wimples; I retired them along with Hunter. I waited for the boxes to pile up in our house, for the word *pack* to become the order of the day. We now lived in our fourth house, another ranch-style home with a full basement. This house was only one block down from the house across the street from the park. Quick turnarounds never mattered before, but the all-hands-on-deck call to pack never came. Mom and Dad had sprouted roots like an aspen. Their roots went deep and broad.

We'd been here too long for me but not for Mom and Dad.

Popular and gregarious, Mom was active in numerous clubs: driving fundraising events and holding office as treasurer, secretary, and even president of a Phi-something sorority. What's more, she had a job, one she loved and considered important. She was forever bragging about the character of the doctor she worked for. "He never turns away a patient who can't pay, even when the nurses say he should." Dad was entangled, too, more so even. He was part of the Lions club, Knights of Columbus, and Chamber of Commerce, and he aspired to run for office, maybe for county commissioner or to be in the House of Representatives. They also had loads of friends—more than I ever wanted to have—parties, housewarmings, baby showers, and impromptu get-togethers to attend.

We weren't going anywhere.

Resigning to stay put with the rotten-egg stench and the same old Hunter crap soured my new-baby outlook. I hated the idea of another baby, changing diapers, rinsing out gag-inducing poop, the stink, the puke, and the snot. The baby would just add more laundry for me to fold corner-to-corner and be another kid to babysit.

I detested the little worm. Sulking, I informed my friends at school but drew zero sympathy. Bewitched by new-baby magic, they were ecstatic. The brat-to-be had cast a silly spell on everyone. Mom's friends sprouted crazily. They arrived at our door cooing "Sweet little angel cakes" with rising voices spewing octaves that'd alarm the shrillest of birds. *Angel cakes* wasn't even born yet. Those who galled me the most spoke in hushed pastels or peculiar baby-talk and inflated the role of Mother's helper to royal stature, either warning me, "Your mother is going to need a lot of help," or cheering me on, knowing very well I already had the job.

Mom ballooned overnight. She looked six months pregnant in her fourth month. By her seventh month, she struggled to drive; her belly was so huge she barely fit behind the wheel. She drove ballerina style: foot extended with toes pointed and stretching to reach the pedals. And she stopped dieting. Early on, food tasted rancid. Then she gave up, knowing from seven previous ordeals that dieting began in the tenth month. Watching her inflate had me thinking of Miss Jo and my own round belly.

I became hysterical around food. I'd already tried every diet mentioned on TV or promoted in magazines: fasting every other day, eating nothing but grapefruit, counting calories, sipping broth, boycotting fruit and bread, consuming only protein (lots of eggs and cheese), chewing super slowly, drinking gallons of water, chewing gum, and sucking on cough drops. Determined to stick to my current diet, which was eating exclusively high energy carbs and counting calories, I wrote down every crumb, even my cough drop consumption. I lasted three weeks before sneaking cookies and ice cream.

Exercise wasn't helping either. Swim team practice was brutal, but missing a workout or a swim meet was not an option. Mom wouldn't allow it, and I was afraid of the unburnt calories. Despite the diets, endless lane repetitions up and down the pool, and sprinting crawl stroke, butterfly, breaststroke, and backstroke, my seventh-grade weigh-in was mortifying: one hundred and fifteen pounds. A few girls weighed on or near one hundred pounds, but only one student topped my weight, and he was a boy. "It could have been worse," Mom said, justifying swim team practice. Dad said that if I held my stomach in and pushed my shoulders back, I'd look a size smaller. Neither remark made me feel good, but I did take Dad's advice, sucking my stomach in all day and only letting go at night when I slept.

School dress code policing loosened up—thank God—which was an advantage of being a seventh grader. Girls were now allowed to wear their blouses over their skirts. I wore mine untucked to create a more slimming line. I'd read numerous magazine articles on how to look slimmer in your clothes, and I kept a list in my head when shopping and dressing: dress in one color, cover up with outerwear, wear vertical stripes, avoid pleated skirts and dresses, dress in dark colors, and never accentuate the waist. My uniform broke all the rules, but now I could at least follow the do-not-accentuate-the-waist rule. And I always wore my dark navy sweater, no matter how hot it got in the classroom or outside.

With a month to go, Mom topped one hundred and ninety pounds. Her eighth pregnancy was proving difficult. Her last two babies had come out yellow, the telltale sign of liver damage. Both had spent their hospital stay under lamp lights to clear the bilirubin from their systems. Mom's blood type, RH negative, was incompatible with Joe and Greg's RH positive blood type. Another RH positive baby would not be good. This one could die or be damaged. I knew all this from overhearing, not spying. Adult conversation shifted when my siblings entered the room, but no one shied away when I was present, co-opting my support without asking for it.

If given the opportunity, I would have chosen ignorance.

I was uneasy. What if I did affect the outcome? Unable to sleep, I tossed and turned most nights, fearing my mean thoughts had already damaged the little angel. Determined to expunge all negative thoughts, I imagined the baby as a girl, dressing her in dainty frocks and swaddling her in fuzzy pink blankets. I clung to pink and prayed to Mary and Jesus, "A girl, please, a girl. . . . I promise to be a super Mother's helper."

Mom cried often and for no apparent reason. She was louder, too, when she did speak. When Dad got home, often late, they argued. She wanted him home. He defended his after-hours meetings—work didn't change because she was pregnant—but I thought she had a point.

The bickering elevated at night when we were all in bed. I could hear them, probably everyone else could, too. Curious at first, I listened, trying to make out every word. The specifics were mostly garbled, or I'd heard them before, like boxers throwing the same one-two punch. Bored, I'd drift off, eyes heavy. One night, I woke abruptly. Mom was yelling, "Do you want me to lose this baby?" I cringed and pulled the pillow tight over my ears to try to erase what I'd heard, but her words recoiled in my head, louder and louder. I was afraid her despair might partly be my fault. She was yelling at Dad, but was I doing enough?

Compelled by Mom's distress, I entered the hallway. As I drew nearer, the effect of their mumbled words seemed to press the walls closer and closer. I felt smaller, like I was shrinking or like the walls were swelling. Mom pushed the door ajar; she must have heard me. She waved her hand, beckoning me to come forward.

"Catherine, you talk to him. He'll listen to you."

It wasn't a suggestion. I slipped inside. It was too bright. Light from the ceiling lamp assaulted my eyes, causing my lids to flutter. Adjusting to the light only confirmed my desire for darkness, for anything to obscure what I was witnessing. Dad sat on the bed—he looked unsteady—trying to remove a sock. I'd never seen him this way, and it scared me. He didn't look like Dad.

"Talk to him. He'll listen to you," Mom said, pleading to him and me.

The sock was caught on his big toe. He twisted and pulled at it, his body waving in slow motion. I thought he was going to fall off the bed. I'd never seen anyone drunk before, except on TV. Dad always had a drink after work, but I'd never seen him like this. Appalled and shaken, I couldn't believe it, didn't want to believe it, didn't want to be here.

Dad paid no attention to Mom or me.

Mesmerized by the sock, I stood watching, my stomach coiling in synch with Dad's movements. He managed to discard the left one, dropping it on the floor. Not wanting to look elsewhere, I stared at the abandoned sock.

What does she want me to say?

I wanted to run, but I knew not to move until excused, plus Mom was blocking the doorway.

"Go to bed," Dad mumbled.

I jumped at the offer of escape, flew past Mom, ran to my bedroom, and dove under the covers, hiding like a child afraid of monsters under the bed. I willed sleep to come, ordered and begged it, but my eyes refused to close. I tried to flee into dreamland, but that infernal sock and Mom's pleas intruded. Dad was my hero, a man of adventure with a stockpile of stories. Fragments of them pervaded my thoughts, especially that summer of his thirteenth year when he took off with a school buddy and traveled through Oregon, California, Mexico, Texas, and the Dakotas seeking opportunity and risking peril like the gold diggers and pioneers gone by. He'd only been a year older than me. I wanted to be him, to be as free and risk averse as he was then and still appeared to be; until now. Picturing him bested by a sock and with his invincible status crumbling, I was overtaken by rage. He should have been the target, but he wasn't. Mom had committed the crime by exposing his vulnerability and eviscerating his hero status. I despised her for shrinking him down to human size.

Mom's doctors didn't wait for her to go into labor. The pediatrician decided it was too dangerous to wait. She was induced two weeks before her due date.

"It's a boy!" Dad announced.

I said, "Send him back. We have enough boys."

He laughed.

I meant it.

Dad took Steve and me to the hospital; the under-twelves weren't allowed past the lobby. At thirteen and twelve, we got the royal treatment. We were still kids but had mini-adult privileges. Nurses, doctors, and administrator types embraced us with wide smiles and salutations, raising our big brother and big sister monikers to dizzying heights. Standing erectly to project our best behavior, we waited next to the information desk, which had a partition separating hospital people from outsiders, while Dad checked us in. The place was awash in green: sea green walls, pale green curtains, and jade-flecked floors. Even the staff wore green. Why green? I thought, watching an army of hospital soldiers zip past.

"Down the hall, take the elevator to the second floor," the desk lady said, throwing Steve and me a practiced buddy-buddy wink.

Dad led the way. We followed single file. An unpleasant odor caught my nose: antiseptic mingling with a sickly-sweet flower—hyacinth, honeysuckle, or rose from a recent visitor's bouquet. I marched face forward and let my eyes wander into open doors. Every room was a green clone accessorized with machinery, buzzing, beeping, and flashing. Equally flashy staff darted from room to room, yet they still managed to throw a smile our way . . . my way. The attention cajoled my steps into a chassé.

A rotund nurse, white shoes squeaking against the tile, winked at me. "Gorgeous hair—just like Ann-Margret's," she said. "But hers isn't real."

Blushing, I smiled back, dazzled by the royal treatment. The hospital wasn't scary or intimidating as I expected. It was heavenly. I pictured myself tucked under warm green blankets with a cadre of attentive, smiling nurses at my beck and call, all stroking my hand. Getting sick wasn't so bad. In a misguided moment, I willed it: nothing too painful, just a mystery disease requiring a long stay.

We turned a corner and approached a large glass window: the baby gallery. "There he is, in the incubator," Dad said, tapping his finger on the glass.

Squishy-looking like all the others, he was wrapped in a blue blanket, not the pink I'd requested. He was RH positive, and from Dad's description, I expected corn-cob yellow skin, but he looked honey-orange. Haunted by the babies swaddled in pink, I turned away from him.

Mom's room was the same color as the hallway, but she had her own TV and a view of the lake. A nurse came in with fresh water and a glass of juice. "How are you feeling?" she asked, flashing a happy smile married with a serious frown.

"Fine," Mom said, faking.

She was still swollen, and the worry hadn't left her forehead. John Patrick—Dad named the boys—had a blood transfusion right after delivery, but no one knew whether the procedure worked. We had to wait and see. Dad explained the transfusion. I understood how they got the blood in, by pumping it in through a needle, but how did they get all the old blood out? In any case, Joe and Greg needed only lights to cure them; this one was a vampire baby.

Mom came home empty-handed. No one knew when John Patrick would be released. Leaking from her eyes, nose, breasts, and privates, Mom was a mess. I came home from school one day and found her sobbing, splayed across the stove door with a spatula in her hand. She'd been cleaning to keep busy and try not to dwell on John Patrick, who was still in the hospital with no one to hold him or to love him like only she could. The state of her shocked me. Gawking at the contours of her back, which were significantly smaller than three weeks ago, I reconsidered my sullen attitude despite wanting to hang onto it forever. Guilt rose in my throat; I could taste it. Afraid for Mom, for John Patrick, and for my soul—now speckled black—I started praying, begging.

Dear Lord, Mother Mary, bring him home. I promise to light a candle every day for a week . . . and say the rosary.

I washed the dishes, vacuumed, made a snack for the little ones, settled them in front of the TV, and prepared dinner.

Two weeks and two transfusions later, John Patrick came home: a celebratory moment that lingered. Friends came by bearing gifts and seeking a peek at him or an occasion to cuddle him. I made loads of goodies—cookies, cakes, and brownies—for the drop-ins. Despite not holding a newborn for four years, I soon became an expert; I supported his neck and protected the soft spot on his head. He took a bottle—he couldn't have breast milk; it contained Mom's antibodies—and I'd landed the afternoon feeding when I came home from school and she needed a break or had to go grocery shopping. We rarely used our living room since there was no TV in there, making it a perfect spot for feedings and naps. I sat on the sofa with a pillow tucked under my left arm and his head nestled in the crook of my elbow. John Patrick was a good eater and didn't gulp or choke. I checked his consumption regularly, burping him every five minutes or so, and rested his head on a diaper covering my shoulder to catch the occasional upchuck.

I liked to watch him, especially when he dozed in my arms or slept in his crib. Mom put him on his tummy to prevent choking or perishing from crib death. She also oiled his head against cradle cap, crusty yellow patches that'd defile a baby's scalp. We did a lot of crib-endangerment prevention. Fearing crib endangerment, I'd sneak into the nursery to check on him, willing him to wake so I could take him out. Everything about him was touchable, edible. Stroking his cheek with my nose, I inhaled him. Why did he smell so delicious? I struggled to place the aromas: fresh bread and steamy chocolate milk? His hands always looked like miniature boxing gloves, with his fingers curled into his palms. Every so often, his whole body quaked, and the little gloves swatted air. Fern-spiraled curls covered his head and framed his face. When he was awake, I twirled them around my fingers. Diaper changing wasn't even a burden—including the ripe ones.

It was John Patrick's doing. Seventh grade ended with a bang.

For years, I dreamed of hitting back, kicking Hunter Spit in the balls or smashing his ugly mug. Riled to the point of no return, I finally did. Unfortunately, I decked the wrong guy.

The girls in my class were agog to see the baby. Sister gave us permission to have lunch at my house, considering it was within walking distance. A gaggle of twelve- and thirteen-year-old girls, with me in front emulating the Pied Piper, bolted down the lake path, eager to make the most of every second of lunchtime. I'd never had so many friends come to my house, and I was nervous, but I counted on John Patrick's baby magic to win them over. It did. They ogled over him and grappled to get close to him, to touch him, until Mom put him down for a nap. Then they went through my closet. Being the last week of school, we were allowed to wear street clothes. Debbie pulled out a dress she liked and pressed me to put it on. I liked the dress; it was covered with tiny flowers and flared when I twirled, but it reminded me of one of Mom's maternity dresses: pleats were sewn under the breast, causing the dress to poof out like hers did. I rarely wore it, fearing I looked pregnant in it, but agreed nonetheless.

Back in class, we huddled and shared darling-little-angel baby stories. "How's the baby?" Jeff asked, staring at me. Jumping to conclusions—I thought he was eying my stomach—and without warning to him or me, my fist smashed into his jaw.

"What'd you do that for?" he yelled.

Horrified, I stuttered, "I thought . . . you said something mean. Never mind. . . . Sorry!"

I spun around and bolted to my desk. *What have I done?*

He really did want to know about the baby. He wasn't implying that I looked pregnant, and he wasn't being mean. I just heard it that way. After all those years of holding back, I lost it, saw Hunter's face, and hit Jeff. Heart pumping, my face red as fire, I lifted my desk's top and stuck my head inside, pretending to dig for something. I wanted to cry but couldn't stop laughing.

I smacked the good guy.

I ruined any chance of pairing up with Jeff, but I could not stop laughing.

Three months later, I began my last year at St. Rose. John Patrick was five months old. He'd come home skinny but plumped up lickety-split. Before setting out that first day, I lifted him up, submerged my lips into the soft folds of his neck and planted copious kisses, then I raised him higher and deposited fat raspberries onto his belly. He responded with fits of delight and squealing, practically begging for more. I took his aroma and the softness of his curls with me, both of which lingered on my cheeks well into the day. At school, I watched the clock with an unfamiliar energy. I had a reason to come home—I actually wanted to come home.

I was hooked on the little bugger.

After school, I swooped him up and set about my daily routine. Consulting the chore list, I cheered, "A laundry day, perfect!"

This time, I wasn't alone in my parents' bedroom or in my dreams. I had a sidekick. A real one. I placed John Patrick in a laundry basket. He couldn't sit on his own, so I tucked clothes on either side and behind him. Wired with brand-new zeal, I turned on a Tarzan movie and let my imagination go. The basket soon lost its toothpaste sheen, displaced by hefty forest reeds. John Patrick played with his toes, a recent fascination, while I pulled him up to our tree house. Cheeta, jealous of the jungle's newest orphan, threw a tantrum; he was screeching and pelting us with mangos that I caught and mashed for my charge. Tarzan didn't appear, there was no need: I was John Patrick's protector.

The school year progressed, and so did our time together. He learned to crawl and walk and say my name—*Catrun.*

Some families are huggers; mine was not. We were physical but not affectionate. Babies were coddled and kids were molded. Hounded day after day, by Hunter at school and Steve at home, I was depleted most days. An emptiness bled inside me that only tenderness could ease. John Patrick became my effervescent shadow, a bottomless vessel for untapped affections, and a source of utter joy.

Chapter Sixteen

Too Tight

M<small>OM AND</small> I <small>TRAVELED FROM STORE TO STORE SEARCHING FOR A</small> dress for me to wear at my eighth-grade graduation breakfast. I tried on dozens of dresses, but none of them worked because they made me look fat or dowdy, or they were too short, exposed the freckles on my arms, or were pretty to Mom but ugly to me. Finally, I found the perfect dress: a pale blue one with pastel flowers, a sloped neckline exposing my collar bones, three-quarter length sleeves, a slim A-line cut, and feathery soft fabric. The dress shimmered as if each stitch trapped a star. Looking in the mirror, my only concern was how tightly it clung to my thighs. "It looks fine," Mom said, clearly antsy to be done.

I was antsy to be done, too—with school—and I wasn't the only one. Everyone was ready to dump St. Rose and move on to ninth grade and public school where there'd be no uniforms, no nuns, no catechism, no confession on Friday afternoons, and, for me, no Hunter. I would attend Monticello Junior High, and he'd go across town to Cascade Junior High.

On the eve of my graduation breakfast, I shampooed my hair, slopped on Dippity-do, and rolled my curly mop into giant foam rollers. I harnessed my bangs with tape that I put across my forehead. I carefully inspected my dress, moved other garments a good distance away, set the alarm for seven, and climbed into bed hoping the night would flash by. I slept fitfully. My mind would not rest. I was too excited: tomorrow was the last day of Hunter.

When the alarm rang, I jumped out of bed and raced to the bathroom to check my bangs. Sometimes the tape left dents and I had to repeat the whole process, but no need. They were fine except for a slight flip at the sides. Shedding the rollers, I brushed through the donut-shaped curls and smoothed them into a pageboy falling right below my chin. The front strands stubbornly flipped up instead of falling straight like the models' hair in *Teen* magazine, but the waves were soft and shiny with no frizz. Good enough.

Turning and twirling in front of Mom's full-length mirror, I eyed every angle of me with a smile. I looked good, though I wished the dress were a little looser. Beyond the door, I heard giggles and the muffled sounds of small bodies wrestling. The mood was electric, as if the floorboards were dancing the rumba. The little ones checked my outfit, and laughing, smiling, touching my dress, and oohing and aahing, they signaled their approval. Dad oversaw the cameras; he had one for movies and another for snapshots, and his arms were laden with light bulbs, film, and extension cords. He stationed the camera in the living room in front of the fireplace and repeatedly took my picture—alone, with Mom, with the kids, and with the whole family, using a timer. The movie camera lights were blinding. I struggled to keep my eyes open, but nothing could unseat my smile.

Both Mom and Dad escorted me to the big event. Pulling into the parking lot, I surveyed a sea of cars and bodies. Parents hugged their kids and reluctantly departed, stealing a last look as their children entered the building. Everyone looked sharp. Girls in pretty dresses with their hair fixed attentively, a few even had beauty-parlor updos, tiptoed across the blacktop as if crossing a stage. Boys in suits and ties, their hair slicked back, nervously tapped their shiny black shoes. I modeled a composure of a seasoned adult—mimicking my classmates—despite aching to run and cheer.

Once inside, propriety ebbed as a herd of juvenile graduates dashed to find their places. Clicking heels and thumping leather soles—ones never usually allowed on the gym floor—echoed off the gym walls, suggesting double or triple the number of graduates. Whiffs of bacon and maple syrup intermingled. I approached three long tables elegantly dressed with blue crepe streamers atop white tablecloths. Cards handsomely penned for each student were poised above the plates. I darted to the middle table, assuming the names were grouped alphabetically, but mine was missing. I looked around; everyone was sitting. I was still searching. Then I saw it.

No.

It can't be.

My card was next to Hunter's, and not just his—his cohorts, too.

My skin turned cold, and my body stiffened like a teetering ceramic doll. I stared at the card in disbelief and panic. It couldn't be a coincidence. Why would anyone put us together? Then I saw Hunter casting a malicious smile, expectation filling his face. His sister, one of the seventh-grade servers, walked past carrying a pitcher of orange juice. She was grinning, too.

He switched cards. Or she did.

"Hello there," he chimed, in an overly gentlemanlike voice. "What do you know? Hungry? Have a seat."

I looked through him and sat down, cautiously avoiding his leg draped in front of my chair. The dress was tight and stubbornly creeped up my thighs. I pulled the hem toward my knees and concentrated. I needed a focal point. Staring at the stage, I remembered Peter Pan and swinging on imaginary ropes that first weigh-in day. I wanted to wrap a real one around Hunter's neck. No matter where I looked, my eyes landed on the faces of exuberant classmates, their mouths open and laughing. Bitter memories poisoned the happy laughter, making it menacing. The laughter assaulted my ears. Holding my dress down, wanting to be elsewhere, and longing for the breakfast to end, I castigated Mom. *This dress is not fine!*

The Mom-chefs cooked my favorites, but the smell of maple and bacon churned my stomach, and my fancy china plate became an ashtray of fetid stew. I sipped orange juice and observed the festive table adjacent to me, wishing I were there and not understanding why I wasn't. Hunter and his chums blathered loudly over and across me, their voices squeezing out what was left of my morning's excitement.

Pretending to ignore me, they watched my face, looking for signs their antics were working.

"You want mine, too?" Hunter cooed, pushing his plate toward me. They laughed. I stared beyond my plate, consuming the barbs each giggle inflicted and refusing to give them what they wanted.

That afternoon, I lay buried under my covers, not wanting to get up . . . ever. I felt utterly alone, defeated, and certain nothing was going to change. Hunter would go to a different school, but his entourage, channeling him, would attend mine. *I'll never be rid of him.*

I spent the day in my room, only venturing out to do chores. Days passed, and my routine remained unchanged. Exasperated and aware something was wrong but not knowing what—I wasn't about to share what happened with anyone—Mom and Dad stepped in, insisting I accompany them to a dinner, an American Field Service fundraiser.

I did not put on the fancy dress.

The event was held in a dark hall. It needed a coat of paint and smelled old. A faint sting of bleach in the air camouflaged something nasty. Mom and Dad grabbed three seats while I checked out the food. I was more interested in the meal than the forthcoming slide presentation. As I approached the table, the aromas of fried chicken, chocolate, yeasty breads, green beans, and sugary frosting ripened agreeably. Admiring the chocolate cake—dark, rich, and fudgy—I imagined a morsel gracing my tongue, causing saliva to swirl in my mouth.

Someone made three tapping sounds.

Startled by the wood-on-wood salvo, I turned and spotted a reedy woman, the American Field Service chapter president, banging a gavel, so I dashed to my seat, noticing the head table for the first time. A dozen or so teenagers milled around deciding where to sit; they were exchange students; their national costumes were a giveaway. The chapter president droned on about the American Field Service student exchange program, but I was distracted by the teens to her right and left. Gaping at the foreign students, I created flashy back stories for each of them: an Indian Princess, a Somalian Prince, a Kenyan Warrior, an Australian Trapper, and a Turkish Belly Dancer, and I wondered what American students wore for their national costume.

A girl from Iran stood and headed to the podium. I listened to her—and every student after—talk about their country or what it was like to be an exchange student. Deliveries varied, especially when language was an issue, but one element never deviated: the response from the crowd. The audience was captivated, not by the words spoken, but simply because these kids were foreign: passport celebrities.

To me, the concept of *exchange student* embodied possibility, not the romance of studying abroad or living in a foreign country (though that was clearly enticing), but as a way to escape. My mind was racing; this exchange-student business could be a way out, a way to disappear and restart thousands of miles away from here. I was desperate to run from Hunter, Steve, grown-up burdens, and the me I was becoming. I feared my own soul was turning as black as Hunter's.

At home, I'd become Mary's nemesis just as Steve was mine, and I hated myself for it. We no longer slept in the same bed, yet our nighttime battles continued. A line drawn with tape delineated our territory: a twin bed on either side of the room. Any personal item found on the wrong side disappeared, or worse. Her beloved Mickey Mouse clock bunked deep in my dresser drawer; its incessant ticking was unbearable. Sixty strikes a minute pulsated, becoming a metronome for Mary's snorts and slap-slop sucking. I terminated the clock, but I could not expel Mary. When her hideous chorus began, I got out of bed, crossed the tape, and squeezed her nose, or pushed her into the wall, or yanked her pillow free and pressed it over her head—whatever it took to stop the insufferable racket.

The nightly battles left me ashamed, as did my adoption of Mom's penchant for the wooden spoon. Babysitting had become the devil's chore. Tom, my buddy and ally against Steve (I wasn't Steve's only mark, just his favorite), was safe from me. The little ones, Greg and John Patrick, were safe, as was Mary—we clashed after hours. It was Barry and Joe, now eight and six, who faced the wrath of my spoon. Lately, they'd made mischief on purpose, howling when I deployed the spoon and darting off laughing, as if daring me to chase after them and start another round.

After each episode, I heard Sister's voice warning me, "Your soul just turned a little blacker." I despised myself, yet I still reached for the spoon when I became exasperated and overwhelmed with housework and kids: just like Mom did.

I was thirteen and didn't want to be like her, not this side of her (or Steve). I needed to get out before I murdered someone. Dad said that every kid gets bullied, but that it built character and would make me stronger. But I didn't like *this* character; she scared me. I had to get away from *her* and everyone else.

My head throbbed with what-ifs. I'd barely eaten and didn't notice that the presentation had come to an end and people were getting restless. I couldn't take my eyes off the exchange students. I pictured myself sitting with them and dressed in a national costume of cowgirl finery, an adoring crowd in attendance—

"How's the cake?" Dad asked.

"Delicious! You should get some."

So excited my feet were tapping, I hadn't realized I was eating. I didn't even taste the fudge. There was hope after all. Becoming an exchange student could be my way out. All at once I was hungry, famished, but not for the food or even for the cake.

I waited until the last student finished and the thank-yous were parceled before I sprinted to the podium.

"What do I need to do to become an exchange student?" I blurted, addressing the American Field Service lady.

A long lecture followed.

Back at my table, I scribbled a few notes on a napkin, next steps that I planned to start tomorrow. Under my breath, a new mantra simmered.

I will be an exchange student.

I will.

I will.

Part Two
Fleeing the Jungle

Chapter Seventeen
Red

We moved yet again, but we didn't go far this time. We were on our fifth house since leaving Augusta. This one was in the same neighborhood and a block over from the last one. We moved from the house across from the park because the landlord wanted to sell it and Dad thought the price was too steep. This time we moved because Dad bought a house. It looked a lot like our first house—two stories, a tiny living room, two bedrooms downstairs and two upstairs—except this one had a large unfinished basement. Dad's plan was to finish the basement and spiff up the main floors, then sell the house at a profit to buy a bigger and better one. I wondered how much I should unpack.

Dad painted every room eggshell white and installed orange shag carpet on the floors, except for the kitchen and bathroom floors. He said white walls made the rooms look larger and the bright carpet added pizzazz, but the combination made me think of orange peels. My new school was two miles down and on the other side of the lake. Riding my bike, I could get to St. Rose in fifteen minutes, but it would take me a good half hour to walk to Monticello—girls didn't ride bikes in junior high. Tomorrow was the first day of school. I hadn't been this excited about school since that first day at St. Rose.

My bedroom was on the second floor. I raced up the stairs, dumped the contents of three shopping bags onto my bed, and tossed the empty sacks on Mary's side. Light from the window illuminated only items in its direct path. My new clothes lay in the shadow cast by the sloped ceiling over my bed. I flipped on the overhead light. The piles remained in shadow but loomed a bit brighter. Admiring my new shoes, I made a mental note to bandage my toes and heels before heading out to school. The navy flats, crowned with buckles across the toes, were cute but deadly. They were stiff as wooden clogs and bound to cause blisters. I placed the shoes at the foot of the bed; the buckles were simpatico with the orange carpet.

Every year, Mom bought us new school clothes. Come the latter days of August, old uniforms were inspected and hand-me-downs were assigned and sewn to measure. An account was made of what inner- and outerwear everyone required. Most years I got a new blouse, and every couple of years I got a new skirt and a sweater if the old ones were ragged, but this year I needed a whole wardrobe: no uniforms in junior high. Church dresses hung in my closet, and run-around clothes filled my allotted dresser drawers, but none were right for junior high. In preparation, I gorged on fashion magazines and took Dad's challenge: lose the weight, drop to model size, and get a free wardrobe from store samples. Apparently, clothes worn once on the runway were giveaways. I stuck to my diet all summer but did not get free clothes. But my efforts weren't for nothing; I dropped a full size. Pleased with my reflection in the store mirror, I happily forked over my babysitting money.

I had a fair number of babysitting clients: my second-mom reputation had spread. Babysitting for other households was *supercalifragilisticexpialidocious*, a favorite word I'd picked up from the Disney musical. There were no wooden spoons, no you're-not-the-boss-of-me sibling snark, and no chore lists at these other households. I felt fancy-free and at liberty to be silly: I pretended to be Mary Poppins and sang while my charges and I tidied up. Parents returned to freshly baked goodies, a clean house, and sleeping children. While pretending to search for stray dollar bills, the dads snatched cookies and swiped frosting from my three-layer cakes. I was paid well and saved my earnings to buy school clothes and Christmas and birthday presents. Monetary advantages aside, the main reason for hustling non-family babysitting jobs was because they'd look good on my exchange student application.

I handpicked my own clothes; no adult guidance. Mom and Dad were in the living room, waiting to see the end results. I organized my trove into piles—jeans and cords, two skirts, two blouses, one sweater, and one dress—and perused the lot. Keyed up, my lips vacillating between a quiver and an ear-to-ear grin, I couldn't decide which to model first: the sleek and slimming classic *Mod Squad*–inspired A-line dress with a mauve collar and cuffs and brass buttons down the middle, the plaid skirt and navy sweater, the powder blue skirt and matching blouse, or the cords. I especially liked the plaid skirt's unusual colors: lilac and navy highlighted with lemon yellow threads. Now that I'd dropped a size, I figured I could break some of the dress-to-look-slimmer rules. I tried them all on and scrutinized the front, side, and back of the outfits in the mirror. The dress and both skirts fell one inch above the knee. Even girls at St. Rose wore their skirts shorter, at least three or even four inches above the knee, to emulate Twiggy, an international model and the poster girl for the miniskirt. She wore hers much shorter, four inches down from her bottom. It was 1967, and miniskirts were everywhere, even in church, but they weren't that short. I knew I'd never be a Twiggy, but I thought I could wear a mini dress—I hoped I could—like the other girls. The dress would need hemming, but the skirts could be shortened by folding the waistband.

I changed again and again, diving into my closet for blouses and sweaters that might work with the new skirts and slacks. My room was trashed; I'd heaped discarded clothes on both beds. I chose to model the plaid skirt and sweater; I added navy knee socks and slipped on my new shoes. I rolled the skirt's waistband and inspected my profile, making sure all was smooth. I took one last look in the mirror, set my shoulders back, sucked my stomach in, and put my chin up—I looked good.

It was after eight, and the little ones were asleep. Steve, Tom, and Mary were watching TV in the basement, and Mom and Dad were in the living room. Dad was still in his suit, minus his jacket and tie, and was relaxing in his favorite chair by the fireplace. A toothpick-speared olive floated in his glass. Vodka martinis were his go-to drink. He would have another after this one. Sometimes I watched for any sign of the drink taking control, but none surfaced, not since that late night with the sock. Glancing over the newspaper, he eyed me at the top of the stairs. I paused while he folded the paper and placed it on his lap. When he was settled, I continued down the stairs and struck a pose in front of them. The crinkling paper had roused Mom; she'd been sitting on the sofa reading a magazine. She'd lost the baby weight and then some. I couldn't help wondering why our similar shapes—average height, broad shoulders, and rectangular frame—looked so different or why she was solid despite giving birth to seven kids and I was soft despite swim club and habitual dieting.

I waited, studying their faces and examining every nuance. Mere seconds passed. I couldn't wait any longer. "Well, what do you think?"

"Looks great. The colors suit you, and the dark top and straight skirt . . . very slimming," Dad said. "Let's see the back."

I twirled. Dad nodded, awarding me that look, the one he shares when one of us does something right.

"It's a bit short," Mom said, a crease forming between her eyebrows.

"It's allowed. I measured. It's only four inches above the knee, and six is the limit."

"You bought a miniskirt for school?"

"No, I just rolled the waist. Everyone does it."

Her mouth stiffened, "Why do you want to wear it so short?"

"I think it looks good."

"Let's see the real length."

I rolled it down.

"That looks better—smoother. Falls like it should," she said, eyeballing my legs and middle. I felt naked and ached to run back up the stairs. "And it's slimmer."

Dad said, "You could hem it, but I don't think it needs to be shorter."

I turned around and marched up the stairs, brooding. I thought the length looked good, was pissed Mom disapproved, and wondered, what if I were model size? Would she have reacted differently? *All frou-frou-fabulous like she does with Mary?* Mary was nine and looked more and more like Mom. Mary had long blonde hair that dropped to her waist, and she looked cute in everything: dresses, shorts, even swimsuits. I'd cover up, but she ran free on the beach and at the swimming pool. So did Mom.

I put my clothes away. The fashion show was over.

My right heel smarted. One Band-aid was too little too late. I should've triple-plastered both heels. Entering the school, I was assailed by a chaotic scene; kids were screaming hellos, roughhousing with friends, and slamming lockers, and metal was clanging on metal, tennis shoes were grating and squeaking, and the bell was clanging. It was an assault to my eyes and ears that were accustomed to St. Rose's sterile halls, where no one talked and everyone walked single file. I joined the melee and searched for familiar faces, but I didn't see anyone from St. Rose. Curious stares greeted me, likely suspecting I was one of the Catholic school transfers.

I looked past the students, but I took in every detail and was relieved to see an array of outfits, dresses, skirts, jeans, and slacks. Most people had dressed up; only a few girls were wearing jeans. Skirt length varied, too; some girls pushed the six-inch rule, others had skirts that fell just above the knee like mine, and some skirts were in-between. I considered rolling my waistband and hiking the skirt up a bit, but I decided it wasn't worth it; I'd be self-conscious all day wondering whether my hem looked even. I rounded two corners before finding my locker. Homeroom and first period were a short distance down the hall. I dumped my things, grabbed my English book, and slammed the locker door, adding to the high-pitched clanging and banging around me.

"Hello," a boy said as he passed by. He was walking with two other boys. All three of them were wearing cheesy grins and laughing.

My stomach stiffened. I knew this game: If I smiled, they'd laugh, reveling in my stupidity. Pointing, ogling, and laughing, they'd mock, "What? You think we meant *you?*"

I wasn't about to fall for their tricks, not this time. I dropped my eyes and ducked into the girls' bathroom. A barrage of tears streaked my face. First period hadn't even started, and the incessant crap had already begun. Locked in a stall with fresh graffiti, I pressed my eyes with wads of tissues, but still the tears came.

I recited my AFS mantra—*I will be an exchange student. I will. I will*—while washing my face. Composing myself, I envisioned Cairo, Tokyo, Rome, and new foreign friends.

Looking in the mirror, I tried on different expressions: poised, aloof, casual, impervious. Shaking my hands (and unconsciously trying to expunge the memory of the hallway jerks), it never occurred to me that his hello might have been a friendly gesture, a courtesy to a newcomer.

Like Jeff's innocent question, all commentary was suspect, especially from males.

The warning bell rang. I was late.

Beefing up my courage, I snarled under my breath—"Try it on someone else, jerks. I'm no fool"—but when I entered the classroom, I scurried like an overwrought squirrel recovering from a close call with a hound. The teacher didn't look up from his desk. I couldn't see the contours of his face, but he was bald on top and wore dark-framed glasses that he shifted from his nose to his head. Looking for a seat, my eyes landed on the boy from the hallway.

No! He's here.

He flashed a wide smile. An arc of blue-black hair covered his forehead. His brows were thick, and his eyes were dark, like the color of Christmas fudge. I looked away and found a seat on the opposite side of the room.

Mr. Holbrook introduced himself and called out attendance. Each student responded with a single "Here." He rarely looked up, as if he already knew them. Maybe he was a coach or the band teacher. He called my name, stopped, searched the room for my raised hand, and asked, "Catherine or Cathy?"

"Catherine," I said. Dad disliked nicknames and insisted we use the version typed on our birth certificates.

"So be it . . . Red."

I blushed. Several students looked my way, waiting for a reaction. Familiar with insult-laden nicknames, I didn't know what to make of *Red*. There was no ill will or sarcasm in his voice or expression. I smiled inwardly and kept my eyes forward, looking beyond Mr. Holbrook at a worn smudge on the blackboard.

"Pick a poem from an established author." He was looking down at his desk with his glasses atop his head, which made him look like a noseless, mouthless being. "Try the library. I don't care who you choose, but memorize their poem. Be ready to recite on Monday, without notes, in front of the class."

He spoke with authority, and it was clear he would not repeat himself, today or on any other day. The assignment incited a collective groan, an overly animated one. They liked this teacher; his reputation clearly pre-ceded him. I wondered if he was a hard grader. The AFS lady stressed getting good grades and said they were the number one decision maker—foreign schools were tough, and there'd be a new language to master. I had to ace my classes to prove I could handle school abroad.

When the second period bell rang, I waited for the boy to leave then rushed to history class. He wasn't in that class or in my math class. The day dragged, and the next two classes were blissfully uneventful. I brought money for lunch, which was a new experience since St. Rose didn't have a cafeteria. Standing in line, I searched for a familiar face but didn't see anyone. The menu selection included macaroni and cheese or a ham-burger and fries.

"Hamburger and fries, please." The lunch lady loaded up my tray with fries. "Thanks," I smiled. Other than replying "here" for attendance, I hadn't spoken to anyone else all day. I added a carton of milk to my tray and searched for a spot to sit down. An empty corner table beckoned. I headed for it but was cut off halfway there.

"No way," a girl said. She was short and solid, and her voice was as loud as her purple blouse. "Come on. You're not going to meet anyone that way."

With the chutzpah of Harold Hill from *The Music Man*, she motioned for me to follow. I did. Her table of eight was full except for one spot: mine. They introduced themselves and filled me in on the layout of the room and its occupants; they explained who was who: the popular ensemble of sports stars, cheerleaders, and student council members; the nerds and potheads; those to be avoided; the cool kids; and the rare mortals who were both popular and nice. They pointed to the boy from the hallway, "He's one of the nice ones."

Maybe he wasn't being mean. How could I have been so foolish?

The table of eight adopted me and volunteered themselves to set me straight on the ins and outs of Monticello. I learned about them, too. Plugged into the social hub of the entire school, they were like the fill-ing in a layer cake that held the crumbly tower together. There wasn't a cheerleader in the bunch, but they went to every game and made posters, fliers, and banners; several were in the band, choir, and theater, but they never played lead roles; two served on the school council, though only as secretary and treasurer, not president; one wrote for the newspaper, and another took the photos; they were all prom and homecoming committee members, but no one was likely to be voted Prom Queen. They were the worker bees, buzzing from one event to the other, and were determined to pull me along. I decided to let them.

The sidewalk was dry and warm thanks to a late summer. My toes gripped the pavement, happy to be free: I'd removed my shoes and socks once the school was out of sight. The day hadn't panned out as I expected. I was anxious about the episode with the boy, my flight into the bathroom, and my tear-trashed face ushering me into first period. I couldn't disentangle his motives or my reaction. The table of eight girls said he was nice, but could I trust them? Was I rude, wise, or stupid? Later in the day, while rushing to the next class, I saw a few girls from St. Rose. They said hello or waved in passing. It felt like a new norm, a friendlier place, but was it?

I looked up at the sky. The sun's warmth was soothing, stirring me to rethink. It was a beautiful day, and school hadn't been that bad. I'd met some people, maybe even new friends. I thought of Mr. Holbrook, *he called me Red*. I whispered, "Red," and it rolled over my tongue like soft ice cream.

Smiling but still puzzled, I opened the door and dropped my shoes at the base of the stairs.

"Cafrun!" John Patrick squealed. He was a proficient walker now but wobbled side to side when he ran. Halfway to me, he plopped on his diaper-padded bum. "Up, up."

"What have you been doing, rascal?"

I swooped him up, jiggled him high over my head, then lowered him to my waist, his legs curling around me. I snuggled his neck and kissed a favorite spot below his ear.

"Wanna go to the park? Go on the swing?"

"Me, too! Me, too!" Greg yelled.

Poking around the corner, Greg's red and white striped T-shirt appeared first with his bellybutton exposed. The shirt was ready for hand-me-down storage, though John Patrick was growing so fast he'd be wearing it before the year's end. Greg's hair was as white as the stripes on his T-shirt and was straight and feathery fine. He was five now—Joe's shadow.

"What about me?" Joe hollered, though he didn't need to; he'd followed Greg into the hallway. Soon to be seven, he once was our little runaway. Between the years of two and five, he was slippery, and watching him was a nightmare. Thank God he'd stopped fleeing. I was tired of chasing him.

"I'm coming, too," Barry James said, folding his arms. He flashed a just-try-and-stop-me grin, which revealed new permanent teeth that were too big for his baby-teeth mouth.

"Okay, get your shoes on."

John Patrick wiggled, commencing our routine shoe-wiggle-war, and waved his arms and legs like a riled octopus.

"Mom, I'm taking the boys to the park!" I yelled, not waiting for a response. If she didn't hear me, she'd figure it out. Where else would they be except with me?

The boys barreled out the door. I carried John Patrick on my hip.

"Wait up. Don't cross the street till I get there."

They stopped at the curb with their backs to me, three restless boy bodies clad in jeans and scraggly T-shirts: one striped, one white, and one pale blue.

"Hold hands, everybody," I said, my voice in authority mode.

Barry James crossed his arms and took a step onto the road. "I don't need to. I'm not a baby."

"Me neither." Joe joined Barry, folding his arms and scowling.

"Greg, give me your hand." He obeyed without a fuss. "You two . . . *no* running ahead. If you do, I'm taking you home. You can forget the park."

Crossing the road safely, we entered the park and headed for the swings. The boys were already swinging by the time I arrived with John Patrick. I pushed all four of them, nudging John Patrick's baby swing, vigorously pushing Greg's, and grabbing Barry and Joe's swings by the seat, running beneath them, and pushing as I let go. Sometimes the chains would buckle and swing wild, making Barry James and Joe nearly collide, but still they'd scream, "Higher! Higher!"

Bored with the swings, the three older boys took off for the slides and monkey bars. I lifted John Patrick out of the baby swing, turned him toward me, and sat down on what had been Greg's swing. Pumping my legs, I got a good swing going. John Patrick held tight with his arms around my neck and his legs circling my waist. I straightened my legs and flattened my body into a bed. We flew in the air like a glider. I kissed his ginger curls and whispered, "We're flying, like birds in the sky." Returning a sleepy smile and blinking heavy lids, he was falling asleep. A jet plane soared above us, momentarily catching his interest. "Plane," I pointed.

If I could get high enough I'd stowaway.

Too tired to play along, he didn't repeat the word—just closed his eyes and dozed off.

I watched the plane until it disappeared, leaving only a white trail in the sky.

"I'll be up there one day, flying high, looking down, waving so long," I whispered. John Patrick didn't hear me. I held him and pumped my legs. We swung gently. He slept. I watched for planes and envisioned faraway places until he woke up.

Chapter Eighteen

Steps One through Four and More

GRANDIOSE HOUSE AND SCHOOL PROJECTS EASED AFTER JOHN Patrick was born, but exchange-student mania renewed my compulsions and monopolized my thoughts. I needed a plan. Dad repeatedly drilled all of us on the importance of a five-year plan: "Aim high, visualize where you want to be, and set concrete steps to get there." Dad rose from modest means—his father was a barber; his mother, a housewife; money was tight—but he had a plan and now managed the fanciest store in town. I didn't need a five-year plan; I just needed a two-year road map. I converted my napkin notes into a four-pronged attack:

Step 1: High GPA: Study mad and do extra projects.

Step 2: Diverse interests and team player: Join clubs or find a sport.

Step 3: Volunteer work: YMCA? Church?

Step 4: Demonstrate responsibility and leadership: Get a real job.

Dad also liked to say, "You got to be wholly focused and willing to take on the big challenges no one else will." I was focused; so zeroed in on my goal that I failed to notice much of anything that didn't move it forward.

My approach to school epitomized my singularity. I was going to get A's and would wrestle the cosmos into submission if need be. I dove deep into my schoolwork, beginning with my English poem. It had to be exceptional: long, enticing, and tough to recite. Dad said we were related to the poet Henry Wadsworth Longfellow: apparently, he is on a distant branch of our family tree. Dad suggested Longfellow's famous poem *Song of Hiawatha*, which was based on a real Ojibwe chief, Manabozho. I found the poem in the school library, and to my surprise it wasn't one, two, or three pages long. It was a full-length book. Already committed, I decided to memorize an excerpt: the first twenty pages.

On Monday, while my knees bounced under my desk and my hands fiddled with a pencil, I watched and listened to one recital after another. The poems were short, consuming only minutes. It took me a good fifteen minutes to recite mine. I was having second thoughts. *Should I stop after five minutes? Ten? Do it all?*

"Catherine . . ." I stood up before Mr. Holbrook said my last name. "Eager, are we? Okay . . . go for it, Red."

Heat rose to my face; I was still unraveling the meaning of *Red*.

I took my place in front of the class and looked straight ahead, not daring to look at Mr. Holbrook. I began.

"Should you ask me, whence these stories? . . ."

Most people paid attention through the first minute or so then doodled or stared out the window. Slowly, one by one, they reengaged, likely wondering how much longer I could keep going. I couldn't feel my legs or feet, a tingling sensation hugged the back of my neck, and my lips were numb, but my mouth kept going. I couldn't stop. I recited all twenty pages.

"Why not the whole book?" Mr. Holbrook quipped, motioning me to sit down. He shook his head, but I couldn't tell whether he was exasperated or impressed. There were more than a few chuckles, but none came from the dark-haired boy.

I took my seat and lowered my eyes. Staring at the desk, I berated myself for being so stupid.

I went too far—should have stopped halfway in.

Several poems later, I found the courage to look up. I studied Mr. Holbrook's face for clues, but he'd moved on. Scanning my classmates, I was afraid they thought I was showing off. An instant replay would have captured my timid performance; I was too self-conscious to actually show off, and I was oblivious to the reality of how others saw me. The harder I searched for clues, the less I understood. My classmates didn't know what to make of me. When the bell rang and people rushed out, a few smiled at me, and some shot me a look I couldn't interpret. No one mentioned the poem.

Mr. Holbrook gave me an A+ and never mentioned the length of my reading. Grinning, ogling the A+, and tracing it with my finger, I concluded my efforts had paid off, and I dismissed what people may have thought of me. What mattered was the grade; I'd soon have foreign friends. Step One was off to a great start.

Step Two was a bigger challenge. I detested clubs and sports, but the American Field Service lady made it clear she was looking for well-rounded candidates—no eggheads focused solely on books or sports stars who couldn't do math. I disliked the posture of importance and the giddy commitment to participation that belonging to a club entailed, but I had to pick at least one club. Because it required the least commitment and was the least offensive, I chose the school newspaper.

Picking a sport was easier but equally painful. I'd only recently persuaded Mom to let me quit the YMCA swim team. The thought of stuffing my body into a skimpy Speedo and always coming in last was nauseating—a recurring nightmare—but swim team was my only option. I was an excellent swimmer, but I was slow. Unfortunately, I wasn't excellent or even middling in another sport.

Monticello didn't have a pool or a swim team, which meant that sports could wait until next year. The high school team needed swimmers, and winning wasn't a prerequisite. I only needed to show up, go to practice, and compete, which I knew how to do. Steve, Tom, and Mary accumulated the trophies decorating our basement shelves. A few pearly third-place ribbons belonged to me; I won them when only three swimmers were in the pool: me and two other competitors. I hoped to do the same—score third place wins—for R. A. Long High, next year. My chances of winning first or second place victories were nigh on impossible unless I raced against myself or only one other swimmer.

My Saturday mornings were devoted to Step Three: volunteer work. I signed up for the YMCA Special Children program, a program for children with disabilities. The sessions were designed to improve the social and physical skills of the participants, as well as providing caregivers a much-needed break. Capabilities varied widely: some children had only physical disabilities, some had only mental disabilities, and others had both mental and physical disabilities. The differences between participants made it difficult to plan the day's activities. The kids without mental disabilities hated being aligned with those who did have them and loathed being stuck while their caregivers went off to play. Understandably defiant, these kids targeted new volunteers.

Arriving nervous and very keen on my first day, I was greeted with, "Another Goody-Two-shoes? What are you here for?" The child, swimming in her wheelchair, was tiny; I guessed she was maybe seven or eight. Discounting her opening parting shot and groping for something to say, I complimented her outfit. Her knee-jerk reaction was flush with colorful language, demonstrating an adept knowledge and vocabulary of insults. It turned out that she was not seven or eight, but my age: fourteen.

She pegged my disquiet and do-gooder posturing, reading me like an ABC book. Avoiding her and her coterie when possible, I was equally uncomfortable with the excessively affectionate children who draped themselves on me and demanded hugs or fought to hold my hand. The hour dragged. An appalled voice in my head castigated every blunder. I was glad when the last Hokey Pokey played and I could go home.

Predictably, our leader always patted me on the back. "You did a great job today." She was short of volunteers. Every Saturday was a hairbreadth from chaos. With no time to notice my shortcomings, she'd be a great reference.

I needed three.

Step Four was an easy one. I had already demonstrated responsibility with a long list of items and experiences to include on the application: family responsibilities, babysitting jobs, catering, a Red Cross lifeguard certificate, and being a YMCA lifeguard in training. Once I turned fifteen, I'd be an official YMCA lifeguard and swim instructor. I assumed Step Four was fulfilled, but I was wrong.

A week before Christmas, Dad left his job as manager of the Bon Marche over a grievance between him and corporate. He'd had enough, and they had, too. Dad defended *his store* by resisting changes he felt were inappropriate, but it wasn't *his store*. I suspected corporate tired of his initiative. Christmas was always tumultuous in our house—this one more so. We opened our presents, oohed and aahed, and then put them back in their boxes to be returned. It was especially galling when Dad insisted the color TV had to go back, too. The previous spring, Tom and I had launched a secret plan to buy a color TV for Mom and Dad—we had an old black and white one. I saved all my babysitting money and pushed for more jobs. Tom mowed lawns. Come fall, we raked leaves off the large ritzy lawns facing the lake. But all our efforts and money were for nothing. Dad appropriated the TV-return, telling us it was an investment in the new store.

I stewed while he announced his dream had come true: "We'll be the owners of a new store, the best women's clothing boutique in town. Women with a fashion sense won't have to drive to Portland. Not anymore!"

Everyone would have a role. Before long, a drab building on Main Street was transformed into our new family business. From the street, the shop looked like a storybook cottage. Dad used recycled bricks and faux shingles: he wanted real ones, but they didn't pass fire codes. Inside, the space generated a cozy ambience that sublimely fulfilled Dad's original drawings.

Mom did the books and helmed the front. She was a natural with customers and knew how to start up a conversation and sell without "selling." Steve and Tom worked in the back, unpacking and marking merchandise and doing odd jobs. Dad ran the operation, was the store's business face to the bank, and was the primary merchandise buyer. He also tinkered with the displays, swept the sidewalk, wiped smudges from the mirrors, cleaned the toilet after messy customers, appeased cranky patrons, and turned animosity into sales. I'd never seen him this attentive. Like Mom with a newborn, the store was his baby.

My favorite job was designing and assembling the displays; I'd choose outfits and accessories for the front window and piece together intimate clusters of purses, scarfs, and jewelry to decorate counters and racks. The second-best duties included unpacking, marking merchandise, and steaming clothes, which were all back-of-the-store jobs.

But I was also expected to work out front: another *girls'* job. I got paid more for selling and received a commission—I bought loads of new clothes—but I detested selling. Like Saturday mornings at the YMCA, I was tongue-tied. Dad would offer prompts, and they sounded great coming from his mouth, but when I offered them, they came across forced. My efforts didn't sprout small talk like his greetings, his tit-for-tat bantering that mustered smiles. Customers cottoned on to my spurious attempts and responded in kind: "I'm just looking," "I'll let you know, if I need help," or worse, "Stop stalking me." Silenced, I'd back away and hide behind the cash register.

If it weren't for Step Four, I would have stayed behind that counter, no matter the extra pay, but I was collecting bounty, leadership responsibilities that would look impressive on my application.

I was miserable at selling and thankful there was only one Saturday in the week, but I was making progress. My grades were good, my name was listed as a contributor on the school paper, and I had a volunteer job,

a potential reference, and a job that required a social security number. I was a taxpayer! Every second of the day and late into the night was given over to executing my plan. Even tender moments with John Patrick were filed under family responsibilities. I did not attend Friday night games or go shopping with friends on the weekends. Leisure wasn't in the plan.

Did I do enough?

Chapter Nineteen
Smile

Yearbooks were distributed on the last day of school. We all rushed about to get as many signatures as possible, as squirrels do when collecting nuts in late summer. Forty people signed mine. I read some of them during school hours, and the rest I read alone in bed, resting the book on a pillow. I pored over the signatures, deciphering every word. They were penned neatly, covering bare fields with red, blue, and black ink. I was tickled reading comments on the first page; they were all complimentary. I laughed reading "So crazy Mr. Holbrook kept calling you Red and Carrot Top," and smiled when my poem was mentioned. As I turned the pages, baffling patterns emerged, and the cozy sloped ceiling above me began to close in. I felt like I was being watched. Many of the entries were eerily similar, as if stamped with the same phrases: "You're so sweet. You're really nice. I didn't get to know you, maybe next year." The word *sweet* stuck out like raspberry Kool-Aid on a white shirt.

"Twelve times," I mumbled, counting the banal term.

There it was on the first and last pages and peppered in between. *Nice* showed up nearly as many times as *sweet,* as did the phrase "I didn't get to know you, maybe next year." There was one passage I fixated on. I read it over and over, my stomach tightening after each read: "I think you're nice, but I don't really know for sure because you never talked to me." Thinking back, I couldn't recall one instance when I deliberately refused to talk to someone who was being nice to me.

How had this happened? *Sweet? Nice? Wouldn't talk to me?* These were not the comments I was looking for or expecting. Granted, I'd spent the better part of ninth grade terrified; the school hallways and lunchroom were minefields. Loud laughing sent me running, though I didn't move, having given up escaping into the bathroom. Like a spooked animal—not so much like a noble deer in the headlights, but like a dazed possum—I stood rooted, afraid to even look to see where the laughter originated or whether it was directed at me. Despite the initial paralysis, I thought I'd improved (or at least covered my tracks) by following Dad's advice: "Shoulders back, stomach in, slim and strong."

Guess not.

Studying the headshots of my classmates, I realized not one of them had ever cut me down or mumbled a slur; I just expected them to. Sitting with my table of eight friends, I'd worn my school face, the face I practiced in front of the bathroom mirror—the face that denoted interest, confidence, and cleverness. I didn't trust those eight friends any more than the friend-pretenders at St. Rose, but I thought I fooled them and was baffled by the uniform scribbles and the too-sweet-to-speak innuendos. How had this happened?

I wasn't shy or withdrawn in class. Overly prepared, I debated every topic my teachers posed. Frankly, it was a joy to speak up and partake in a battle of wits after so much time spent in my head. I was careful not to hijack conversations or be a bigmouth. It never occurred to me that my wholehearted focus on my exchange student plan might also have been a factor.

I searched for the text written by the boy with Christmas-fudge eyes. His remarks hadn't implied me being shy or sweet. In the bottom corner on the second to last page, he'd penned, "Those square-offs in Mr. H's class were out of this world." I wanted to destroy the book (except for that page) and erase every mention of *sweet*. *Sweet* was boring, slight, forgettable: not an adjective the AFS lady would ever use. The word burned my eyes as if sand had been thrown into them. Stewing, I lay back on the bed, replaying ninth grade in my head.

"Catherine, set the table!" Mom yelled.

"Coming!" I yelled back. Slamming the yearbook shut, I vowed to do better. *Sweet* could not appear in my high school yearbook anymore—absolutely not.

Determined to talk more and smile more, I began sophomore year with new vigor, starting poolside. Swim team was a downright smile zone. We were undefeated thanks to Debbie Moon, who swam like an Olympian and won every time she graced the pool. Coach Prebish consigned the 500 m freestyle to me, noting my forte was endurance—it certainly wasn't sprinting. The race was ten lengths in an Olympic-sized pool and twenty in the standard twenty-five-meter pools our high school competed in. It was not a popular race, and I didn't smile on the starting block. However, this race had one advantage: more than four swimmers rarely ever competed. When there were three, I garnered smile-worthy third place points for the team.

Debbie was popular but didn't huddle in girl groups, gossip in the halls, chase boys, or turn ditzy when a cute one passed by. She was friendly to everyone and collected her winnings matter-of-factly, without pretense or false humility. There was a quiet repose about her. It was easy to smile around her. When she talked to me, she paid attention and saw through the fortifications I'd built to keep everyone out. I practiced talking to her, mostly in the locker room after swim practice.

One afternoon, we were alone in the locker room, our teammates having already departed. As usual, I didn't know how to start and waited for her to say something. We stood in front of the mirror in awkward silence. My hair was a chlorine-frizzled mess; hers, smooth and shiny.

"I look like Ronald McDonald or that crazed clown, Chucky," I said, grinning, pointing to my unruly mop.

"Don't do that," she said, frowning.

I didn't know what she meant. Was there a better way to comb my hair? She looked at me for a brief moment, as if wondering how to say what was on her mind.

"People can't wait to put you down. Don't help them." Her voice was kind, and she delivered her words without airs or expecting a quid pro quo. "Your hair is beautiful."

Embarrassed, I looked away. Desperate to change the subject, I groped for something to say, but she was long gone before I thought of anything. Her words cut deep. She may have poached them from an inspirational quote, but she spoke as if she meant it—had lived it. I took her words to heart, believing they were for my ears only, and committed to follow them.

I stepped outside. Raindrops mottled my glasses. It was getting dark. I picked up speed, hoping to get home before the oncoming downpour. My head was rushing faster than my feet. I needed to think. Hunter Schmit wasn't ambushing me in the hallways, deriding how I chewed in the lunchroom, or scoffing at my bathing-suit body at swim meets—his presence wasn't required. Like Debbie inferred, I was doing his dirty work for him. *Enough! No more apologies for existing.* I felt an odd sense of relief. Beaming, I broke into an intoxicated jog, my body suddenly light as air.

Debbie became my secret weapon. I thought of her when I was stuck— *What would Debbie do? What would Debbie say? What expression would she don?*—and it worked. Channeling Debbie opened all sorts of avenues. Talking to customers got easier. I used Mom and Dad's prompts, but not their tone of voice: too gregarious for me. Instead, I channeled Debbie. I said less, waited patiently, listened more, and painted her face onto mine—calm, interested, confident—despite feeling the opposite. My sales increased, as did my commissions. I channeled Debbie on Saturday mornings, soothing overly affectionate campers (making them less clingy) and confusing the smart ones, who were uncertain why their attempts to goad me no longer worked. I channeled Debbie at lunch, in the classroom, and in the hallway. At the end of sophomore year when the yearbooks were handed out, I rejoiced: every available spot in my book was taken and not a single comment mentioned *sweet*, accused me of avoiding conversation, or claimed another year was necessary to get to know me.

When spring arrived, I gathered my recommendation letters and completed the exchange student application. Kissing the envelope, I said a prayer before dropping it in the mailbox. I crossed my fingers, elbows, and knees; searched the sky for a sign; and begged for a miracle.

Chapter Twenty

The Envelope, Please

"Open it! Open it!" Barry, Joe, and Greg screamed. Jumping up and down, they were three pogo sticks in danger of colliding.

I'd been checking the mail for weeks, combing through the daily pile left on the kitchen counter. Every Saturday, I waited for the mail carrier, my eyes glued to the mailbox. Spotting the mail truck, I'd race outside, collect our batch, and—finding nothing addressed to me—retreat to my bedroom with my hopes and resolve crushed yet again. Imagining my application in a stack of "Nos" that was perilously leaning toward a trash can next to a vacant desk, I began to panic. My mind was littered with doubts: I should have done more volunteer work; my grades weren't good enough; my essays were lame. . . . *They were awful.*

Staring at the envelope, I was afraid to open it. My hands were stuck to my sides, as rigid as a piece of petrified wood. Mom grabbed the manila envelope and placed it in my hands. I wasn't the only one on mail alert; she and Dad had been watching, too. I'd kept my escape plan to myself. I told no one about my four-step plan, even resisting repeating the steps aloud in the privacy of my own bedroom for fear of jinxing my chances. But Mom and Dad picked up on my crusade, the all-night study sessions, the essays that turned into books, the extra credit projects, my closed-mouthed hysteria upon receiving a C, and my dogged pursuit of one more job—just one more nugget for my application.

There was relief in Mom's eyes when she saw the envelope—its size foretold the results—but I couldn't move and misread the depth of her sympathy. I'd taken my parents' concern for granted, believing it was their duty to prepare us for failure, to ease the disgrace of a missed fly ball, the crucial free throw that bounced on the rim, or the failed audition for that coveted part in the school play. Duty-bound, they'd made every effort to ease my certain belly flop. Mom had pointed out the difficulty of being chosen, the tiny percentage of accepted applicants, and the import of preparing for rejection: "Very few make it. It's a win just to apply. It shows what you're made of." Dad had taken a different tack and lectured me on failure, "An opportunity to learn and get better." He'd used a laundry list of examples: Walt Disney was fired from a newspaper for lacking imagination, Thomas Edison tried ten thousand different versions of the lightbulb before he got it right, and Colonel Sanders was fifty-six when he made his Kentucky Fried Chicken millions, only discovering his special recipe after making one thousand lousy versions of fried chicken.

Mom and Dad's efforts backfired. They didn't believe I could do it. I rejected Dad's pep talk and Mom's implication that I should aim lower. I'd show them. I heightened my efforts and grew even more manic, fearing I wasn't doing enough. I was spinning out of control and had no idea they were on to me and were convinced I'd suffer a breakdown if I were rejected. I'd lain awake at night fretting a *no,* unaware that Mom was awake and pondering the steps to take when her basket-case daughter lost it.

Tired of waiting, Tom shouted, "Open it!"

I ripped the top seal and pulled out the contents, spotting *congratulations* typed in regular black letters. The word pulsed like a blinking red light. The room spun as if I were standing in the center of a Tilt-A-Whirl.

I'm an exchange student. I'm an exchange student . . . exchange student.

Flipping through a sea of documents, I frantically looked for the name of a country, taking care not to drop the mass on the floor.

"What does it say?" Tom asked.

"What's the country?" Mom asked. "Where are you going?"

"I want to look!" Barry yelled over Mom.

"Let me see! Let me see!" a chorus of voices said. John Patrick pulled at my shirt, wanting up. There were too many papers and too many words; it was all a blur.

At last, I spotted it: *host country New Zealand.*

"New Zealand," I said, my voice barely audible.

"New Zealand? Where's that?" Mary asked.

"It's near the North Pole," another voice chipped in.

"No, it's not. You're thinking of Iceland," I said. "New Zealand is at the other end, by Australia."

Someone fetched the globe. Four heads touched, searching for a country no one had heard of. My head throbbed amid the pandemonium, emotions bouncing like a bag of marbles dropped on the floor. I didn't remember seeing New Zealand on the list; maybe I was too focused on Thailand, Brazil, Egypt, Japan, or Italy: exotic places in my fantasies.

New Zealand? It's so tame. They speak English.

"Up! Up!" John pleaded, his voice shifting from whiny to panicky.

"Just a minute," I said, pushing him off. His lip quivered, and tears bubbled in the corner of his eyes. I placed the papers on the table and picked him up. Only three years old, he didn't know what the commotion was about, but he understood I was going away.

"I want to come, too," he mumbled, his head resting on my shoulder.

Holding him tight and swaying back and forth, I soothed him, but I was restless. Words lodged in my throat, doubts rising. I thought about John Patrick and what my leaving might mean for him and us.

The following week, the American Field Service chapter leader came to our house to go over paperwork and explain the next steps. Mom and Dad pored over the parental forms—immunizations, healthcare insurance, passport, visa, flights, school transcripts—while I read about my New Zealand family: three brothers, Mark, Greg, and Ricky, and a little sister, Sarah; they were all under the age of twelve. This was Twilight-Zone freaky; how could this happen? So many brothers—three more brothers—and the sister was a toddler. *Did they want a babysitter?* Where was my teenage sister-buddy? Every exchange student was supposed to have a teen in the house to be their mentor and guide.

"You're the first match ever with a family that doesn't have a teenager," the AFS lady explained, clearly pleased with herself. "The national council wants to know if exchange students really need a go-between at school. If not, we could significantly expand our pool of host families."

"I'm an experiment?"

"No, of course not. We're looking at the host family unit."

Noodle thin, the AFS lady had hair shorter than Tom's and didn't need Dippity-do gel. She sported a satisfied grin. My ire grew as I watched her jabber away with Mom and Dad, explaining the jury's decision process and laughing all buddy-buddy-like as if sharing an inside secret. I overheard her say the deciding yes votes were cast based on a three-second moment during my interview.

I remembered the interview clearly, but I couldn't recall an aha moment. Two months earlier, on a Sunday afternoon, three AFS representatives knocked on our door. They'd arrived five minutes before my scheduled interview. I'd been watching the clock. The noodle-slim one wore a dark blue sweater and matching skirt. She was friendly but formal and sat down in Dad's chair. An average-shaped lady who looked fortyish and was wearing slacks and a blouse—very teacher-like—sat on the sofa alongside a younger gal I no longer remembered except for her platform shoes. I sat on a kitchen chair placed in the middle of the room. I'd chosen my outfit carefully, focusing on items that looked serious and professional, but also plucky with a little style. My slacks were a deep rust color and wide at the bottom but were not full-on bell-bottoms. The coppery hue matched the delicate flowers on my blouse. I wore a single gold chain, and I sat straight with my legs folded at the ankle (like Queen Elizabeth), as I was taught at a Campfire Girls etiquette lesson.

Sitting at the kitchen table, Mom was out of sight but still within earshot. My siblings were in the hallway. I could hear them rustling and Mom's occasional shushes. The threesome was well rehearsed. They never talked over each other or gave away their thoughts as they grilled me about grades, after-school activities, home responsibilities, and my desire to be an exchange student. Twenty minutes in, John Patrick escaped the hallway troops or Mom's lap and entered the living room. Seeing the strangers, he ran to me, crawled onto my lap, and folded his face into my shoulder. I rocked him—a reflex—as much as was possible given the stiff chair. I placed a kiss on his forehead and finished the question I'd begun answering before he appropriated my lap.

". . . I've been on a swim team since I was eight." I kissed John's ear. "You will be, too, in about five years."

I looked back at the panel. They'd gone quiet and were staring at me. I assumed it was my time to ask a question. Dad said I should; he said that it was a good interviewing technique and shows you have "gumption."

I can't remember what I asked them, but the interview ended soon after.

It turned out that John Patrick had won me the scholarship. Ms. Noodle told Mom and Dad they'd expected me to shoo John Patrick away. The fact that I didn't clinched my acceptance. Clearly, I was the perfect candidate for a host family with young children. I could see their point in respect to young children, but I wondered how this moment had demonstrated I'd succeed without a teenage liaison. I was stunned and furious. The other exchange students would get a go-between, so how was I supposed to navigate without one? And what about the past two years? Nauseating clubs, early Saturday mornings at the Y, late nights, and extra-credit papers: had any of it made a difference?

As Mom, Dad, and Ms. Noodle partied in the kitchen, I sat in Dad's chair, where they couldn't see me sulking. John Patrick came in and crawled onto my lap.

"It's your fault, you little stinker. Now I'm an experiment," I whispered, my breath tickling his ear.

He giggled and squirmed, which took the edge off my funk. Holding him tight, I recalled our times together: the mingled laughter as we slid down the slide; the pair of us gliding high in the air, the swing a pretend spaceship; making sandcastles at the beach and jumping waves with his hand in mine; and playing in our make-believe tree house high above the jungle floor. *My little buddy.*

Absentmindedly, I curled his downy hair around my finger. Disquiet flooded my thoughts: *Maybe getting out wasn't the best solution.* The best part of me would still be here.

Chapter Twenty-One
Seatbelts On

Humming a tune from *Man of La Mancha*, I floated down the aisle of a Qantas 707. Mom bought the soundtrack when I was in the eighth grade, and *The Impossible Dream* became my theme song. I played the album constantly, driving Mom and my siblings mad. I could recite the lyrics to every song, but, more often than not, I belted a bastardized version of *The Impossible Dream*, singing of unbeatable foes, of marching into hell for a heavenly cause, and of following that star no matter how hopeless. I sang it aloud in my bedroom, hummed it at school when celebrating a good grade, and chanted "no matter how hopeless, no matter how far" when I'd floundered or had a miserable day.

Finding my seat, I hum-giggled, "to reach the unreachable star." I wanted to belt the words, to throw my hands in the air, to dance a jig. It felt beyond surreal. . . . *I did it, the impossible dream.*

Shimmying past two seats, I picked up the blanket and pillow on mine and sat down. I unpacked the blanket and inhaled its toasty scent, hugged the wee pillow, and looked out my very own window. I knew it was silly, but I reveled in my pocket-sized alcove that was more mine than any place at home. Floating, my bum barely touched the seat as the butterflies in my stomach do-si-doed in merry circles, which was a welcome change from their usual antics. With a liberated grin, I imagined the troupe of butterflies flying me to New Zealand sans the plane.

"Miss. Pardon me, Miss," the steward said, trying to get my attention.

Turning, I spotted a flash of red: his red, gray, and white Qantas tie. A stewardess worked up ahead. The pair were unmissable in tailored tomato-red suits and matching accessories: a pocket hanky for him and a neck scarf for her, both of which mimicked the design of the plane's tail—a white kangaroo over a red backdrop.

He offered me a cloth bag.

"Thank you," I politely replied, my dopey grin excised and replaced with grown-up composure.

The bag contained a collection of Lilliputian flight essentials: a toothbrush, toothpaste, a comb, socks, a sleeping mask, and a Qantas flight badge. I removed my shoes and put on the Qantas socks: the rest I'd keep for souvenirs.

My new tribe—exchange student buddies—sat next to, in front, and behind me. Our gang of twelve represented mostly the western states; another dozen or so students, from eastern locations, would arrive on a different flight. After a short stay in Auckland, we'd fan out across New Zealand's North and South Islands. My town was located in Hawke's Bay on the North Island. Pam, a California girl, was posted to Napier, too, but we were going to different schools. Her teen sister, Mariah—like the song about calling the wind Mariah from *Paint Your Wagon*—was waiting. They'd exchanged countless letters.

I'd already forgotten the awkward goodbyes with my own family and the perplexing flight from Portland to San Francisco. Attempting hugs, my siblings and I bumped into each other. Affection was not our strong suit. Mom and I air-kissed; lips mislaid, we brushed hair instead. Dad was the only exception. He bestowed a lingering bear hug. Afterward he said, "No phone calls—too expensive. Remember, tapes and letters only." He'd bought a tape recorder, and we'd already shipped one tape to my host family to introduce ourselves and demonstrate how Dad planned to keep in touch. Mom said she wouldn't be on the tapes; she'd send letters. She held back tears at first, but then she let them flow. I was surprised; surprised my eyes were tearing up, too.

John Patrick cried, "I want to come, too!" His hands had to be pried from around my neck.

Flying as an unaccompanied minor, the stewardess escorted me to my seat. She noticed my tears. So did the stranger sitting next to me. "I'll watch over her," he'd said, a concerned look on his face.

I couldn't stop the tears or wipe away my angst in John Patrick's curls as I usually did. My exit strategy no longer seemed so wonderful. Would he replace me and entrust his affection to someone else? Mom had cried. Was she really going to miss me? Did I misjudge her—misjudge all of them?

The Good Samaritan pressed his body into mine. He unfolded a Playboy magazine and contorted the pages so I'd get a major-league view, though he closed it when the stewardess walked by. I could feel his heat on my arm and leg, and I leaned as far away from him as possible. Anxious, spooked, and out-of-the-blue lonely, the magnitude of my actions hit hard. I was headed for a country of strangers. This one was creepy and gross. What would the others be like?

I tried to drop all thoughts of Playboy-man and watched the airline-army maneuvering on the tarmac, racing about in mini buggies and pulling trailers filled with luggage or meals. Men in flight suits scurried about, avoiding the fleet of carriages. I turned back to my seatmates, now strapped in but no less lively, who were organizing their spaces and whose voices were rising in anticipation of our layovers in Hawaii and Tahiti. "Do you think we'll be greeted with flower leis?" Jenny asked.

I wept from Portland to San Francisco. Thankfully, a super friendly AFS lady met me at the gate and drove me to a hotel where other AFS students were staying and awaiting the flight to New Zealand.

I met Jenny at the hotel in San Francisco along with other exchange students headed to New Zealand and Australia, plus a few who'd recently returned from Down Under, a colloquialism referring to the two countries. Chaperones drilled us about AFS behavior befitting representatives of the United States, but it was the in-the-know exchange students who captured our attention. Newbies and edgy, we were hungry for firsthand information. The experienced students happily laid out some of the dos and don'ts: never use the word *fanny*; only say *crap* and *bugger* with friends; don't chew gum around adults; do not laugh at Māori rituals, especially the sticking-out-of-tongues during the *haka*; and never flash the victory sign backward (better yet, don't use it at all). We were expected to attend AFS events, give presentations, and perform in talent shows.

Only one student fit the exchange-student model in my head—perfect in every way—and he was a guy. John was a football star, was over six feet tall with a caramel tan and sun-bleached hair, and had a honey-rich voice that dropped deeply at the end of his sentences. His eyebrows were thick, framing eyes accented with spidery lashes. He was dreamy but nice. I'd expected every student to be a boy or girl version of him—and a grandstander—but it wasn't so. I did not stick out, and our backstories didn't matter; we were all exchange students, brand new sheets that were clean, fresh, and without stain or wrinkle. They embraced me, and for the first time ever, I dropped my guard and reciprocated: I giggled, laughed, and told stories, my behavior ebullient, as if in a dream.

"What's so funny?" Jenny asked, staring.

She'd caught me grinning; I was halfway to a dream state and was reflecting on my new demeanor. "Nothing," I laughed, searching for a cover-up comment. "I was thinking of those cheap plastic leis."

"Oh, yeah. They're gross. My mom and dad brought leis back from Hawaii. They were made from orchids."

I imagined soft petals on my neck and the scent of orchids tickling my nose. I inhaled the imaginary blossoms, setting off an attack of the sneezes—airplane dust—followed by an onrush of the giggles. *I did it! Brought that frigging unreachable star to its knees!*

Part Three
Home

Chapter Twenty-Two

Someone Cool,
Someone Fabulous

My inaugural week in New Zealand was head-spinning; it was over and above even what I'd cooked up in my own imagination. I'd fantasized one thrilling happening after another, but the reality was better. We were famous. Our story aired over the radio, beamed on national TV, and circulated in newspapers, with images of American exchange students descending the airplane gangway or posing with the mayor of Auckland. Technically, our being exchange students wasn't what caused all this fuss; we had survived a cyclone. Cyclone Mary had hit us without warning, swallowing our 707 and spitting us far off course. We never made it to Tahiti. We never got any leis. No orchids tickled my nose. We ended up in New Caledonia, an island 1,500 kilometers east of Australia. After refueling, we flew to Sydney. In Sydney, we were unceremoniously ushered to an Air New Zealand flight bound for Auckland. Unescorted, tired, and wired, our teenage troop finally touched down on New Zealand soil one day later than scheduled.

The reality of our almost misfortune was a blur and was at odds with disaster films—films where the captain imparted calm to the passengers, and a ravishing stewardess, often his girlfriend, racked up acts of bravery by rescuing feeble passengers and troublemakers who didn't deserve to be saved—which had been my only insight into drama in the sky until now. Three hours out of Hawaii, halfway to Tahiti, our sturdy 707 jerked as if tossed by Zeus. The intercom buzzed and hissed. The captain came on, yelling, "Put your seatbelts on! Heads down!" The clinking of seatbelts followed, but few heads went down. Alarmed but curious, I, too, looked up as I was hurled to the left and right, my body pitching along with the plane. A storage compartment opened, dumping its contents. A suitcase flew across the aisle, barely missing a passenger's head. The bag joined other dislodged objects tumbling down the aisle. Ear-piercing cries of mechanical torture, as if the plane were splitting apart, battered my ears. The plane cracked, whined, and screamed. I put my head down and jammed my face into my thighs. We churned as if in a blender. Items not tied down rained upon us, yet no one screamed; or maybe they did, but their cries were muffled by their legs or the plane's deafening roar. Ours was not the hysterical screams from the movies, but a scream of silence.

I was not scared. I was curious, my entire body wired. I'd felt a similar sense of awe nine years prior when I watched water rise up around our car in Louisiana during our drive through that flood. I was only seven, an age when ominous endings, like drowning, were beyond me. I wanted to know what was going to happen next. Now sixteen, my body thrashing and pressing against the seatbelt, I was likewise unfazed even though I knew bad endings were a possibility. To me, Hunter and Steve were far scarier. Years of conditioning had warped my fear gene: the cyclone was an adventure; people were scary.

Abruptly, the shaking ceased. All was still—too still. Eerily silent.

We were in the eye of the storm. Minutes later, we flew out, and the rumble and shake returned, but not a cry or word was spoken. The stewardess did not soothe us with a calm voice, nor did the captain. There was no explanation of what was going on. We would learn of our near-death predicament later when we watched the broadcast on TV.

No one spoke when the storm cleared. I don't remember whether the captain or stewardess came on the intercom. We landed in New Caledonia. A case of communal stupor kept us in our seats until the captain announced, "Sorry, folks, air traffic control rerouted us to New Caledonia. All passengers must exit so we can refuel and clean the plane. Thank you for your cooperation." We rose in silence, descended the jetway mute, and lined up for customs. Trauma-zombies, we responded to passport officials with nods and the odd word.

Chaos greeted us in Sydney. People in the know accosted airline officials and rebooked flights. We wandered about the airport, twenty-four teens marooned without a chaperone, until a Qantas official rounded us up, arranged passage to Auckland, and escorted us onto the plane. We were giddy from Sydney to Auckland, loud, unrestrained, frolicking in the aisles, and starving—we hadn't eaten in fifteen hours. I felt sorry for the stewardess, but I joined in the milieu.

We spent our first week in Auckland attending induction lectures on New Zealand and on proper exchange-student behavior. The lectures came with assigned tasks: study the handouts on New Zealand, write to our host families, and create a talent show; a bonding activity and practical exercise central to our spread-the-word duties. Halfway through the year and during a school break, we'd be traveling the country, plugging the AFS program to potential exchange students and host families.

No one wanted to do a talent show, so we created a lineup of comedy skits inspired by *Saturday Night Live.* We also wrote silly lyrics lampooning American caricatures, pairing the ditties to melodies from popular songs. Unable to control the exchange-student enthusiasm pumping through my veins, I volunteered to be in the chorus line. How was it possible that I was in a skit about chewing gum—me, who normally avoided joining in? I loved theater and theatrics, and I created a family Christmas play every year, including making costumes, tickets, and posters, but I was rarely in the plays past the age of ten.

If it had been up to me, I would have ditched my host family and spent the year roaming the country on a bus with the new friends I'd bonded with—no poker face, no looking past or through people, no staring at my shoes, no calculated moves. I was overwhelmed with emotions and unhinged in a good way; I felt eager and alive, raw and fragile—as I did when embracing John Patrick after a bad day and letting his allegiance purge my distress. When it was time to say goodbye, I did so with reluctance. I wanted more time to bask in the warmth I felt with them, my exchange student friends.

Pam, the other exchange student assigned to Napier, and I traveled the last stretch of our journey together. Pam was gregarious, loud, lively, and utterly upbeat—the flip side of me—but we'd bonded nonetheless. More to the point, she'd taken me under her wing.

I spotted Pam's family first. Two teenage girls stood in her group. Four kids, my appointed siblings, fidgeted in front of my New Zealand parents.

Eying them, I questioned my New Zealand parents' intentions—maybe they wanted a babysitter—and approached with caution. The mom, Judy, pushed forward, took my hand, and drew me in for a robust hug.

"Welcome to New Zealand. You must be knackered." Her accent sounded different than other New Zealanders I'd met. She sounded more British, like movie stars I'd heard on TV; my ear was not yet tuned to the difference in New Zealand accents. Hers was merely a highly educated one, honed from boarding school and university—not British. She was a big woman, wider than two of me standing side-by-side. Her eyes were kind and deep brown. She was a vision in browns: mahogany hair, bronzed skin, beige purse and sandals, and amber flowers on her sundress.

"Gidday," the dad, Ralph, said, shaking my hand. His body was lanky and bubbling with energy like a thoroughbred eager to sprint. His Buddy Holly hair and a fixed grin implied that he was friendly. He stepped back, pushing Mark, the eldest, forward. Mark had his mother's prominent nose and his dad's hair. He was twelve and ungainly, not a boy and not yet a teen.

"Hi. Welcome." His face offered little, an expression I recognized. *This one is like me.*

"Gidday!" Greg laughed, as if he'd landed the perfect joke. Nine years old, he reminded me of Alfred E. Neuman from the *MAD* magazine: big ears, freckles, and ginger hair.

Ricky waved a hello. I recognized him from his picture: dark hair and large, swimming-pool eyes. He was the cutest, but little Sarah outshone him on the adorable scale. Four years old, she hid behind her mom's skirts. Her hair was fine and curly, like John Patrick's, but blonde, not ginger. Hues of unripe corn crowned her head, and she had her mother's dark eyes. A year older than my John Patrick, she appeared equally shy.

Cyclone Mary consumed our conversation in the car. Listening to their patter, how they aimed to please, I watched them, looking for clues to who these people were. Mark watched me and said little. Like his dad, I suspected he broke silence when there was something worth saying. Greg hadn't stopped talking, just like the mom. She was a herder and could wrap the unsuspecting in her enthusiasm, which I found captivating and frightening. Before I knew it, I was calling her *Mum*. AFS encouraged students and families to use *Mum* and *Dad* instead of their given names. *Dad*, however, wasn't coming out of my mouth as easily.

Mr. Ralph had me thinking of my own dad, who was outwardly gregarious, the life of the party, yet reserved. I'd heard Dad described as "outgoing, but hard to get to know." I knew people said that about me, too—not the outgoing part, despite wearing Debbie's smile—and I was content with the assessment. It was safe, and it was like Dad, who I still aspired to be like, but after Auckland, I wondered: I was different here, not so guarded, not so invisible. Was it a fluke?

My doubts were uncomfortable: I'd spent a decade cultivating my smart-and-independent-but-don't-get-too-close persona. Proximity to this new dad, for reasons I didn't understand, challenged my perceptions, and I didn't like it. He wasn't the life of the party, but he was present, without a veneer. Scarily so, for me. I kept him at a distance, and it was a good month before I could call him *Dad*.

The drive home took longer than I expected. They—we—lived in the country. Pinched country roads, hairpin curves, and hills dotted with sheep reminded me of Ireland: *The Quiet Man* version with John Wayne and Maureen O'Hara. Ireland was on the AFS list, too, but I hadn't checked it as an option. Not foreign enough.

I fell into my customary car position: staring out the window.

A chenille blanket, with wool tufts.

Greg noticed. "More sheep than people in New Zealand," he said.

"Looks like they're all here," I said.

"Don't be daft. These aren't even serious farms."

"Greg! Manners, please," Mum scolded. Greg scowled.

The dad turned right. We pulled into a gravel road, drove about thirty feet, and stopped in front of a sturdy-looking steel gate.

"What's that for?" I pointed to the metal bars across the road.

"A cattle stop. Aussies call it a krud knocker. Keeps cattle and sheep from crossing. . . . Afraid their hoofs 'ill get stuck," the dad explained.

Mark jumped out and opened the gate. Once we crossed, he got back into the car. We drove up a winding unpaved road, the car dipping and swaying in and out of rain-dredged channels and craters. Twice we stopped for sheep. Unlike deer who scatter after a momentary freeze, these creatures didn't budge. The dad edged the car forward. Chewing, the sheep eyed us, their mouths moving but nothing else.

"We have thirty-six sheep," Mark said.

"Less if they don't get a move on," Mum said, laughing.

We edged closer. They kept chewing, parting only when the car didn't stop. We reached the top of the hill and pulled up to a ranch-style house with three-hundred-and-sixty-degree views of the countryside and thousands of sheep grazing on their not-serious farms.

"Everybody out," the dad said, unloading my bags. "We call this the boot."

"I know that one," I said. We were warned about *boot* in Auckland, one of many hand-me-downs from the King's English. "And *garage* is pronounced *GARE-idge*."

"Good on ya," Greg said, impressed. "How 'bout *dunny*?" he asked, testing me.

"No idea."

"Toilet!"

"Off you go, Greg," Mum said, grabbing one of my bags.

She unlocked the front door, and we entered a foyer facing a hallway. Glancing left, I saw furniture and a piano.

"Kitchen to the left. Bedrooms to the right." Mum shuffled me right, stopping at the first bedroom.

"This is yours."

I stepped inside. It smelled warm. The room was cozy; a large window was its prominent feature. Two single beds, in an L-shape, butted up against the left and front walls; a dresser and closet were on the right.

"For visitors, school friends, and AFS buddies," Mum said, pointing to the two beds.

I doubted the extra bed would get much use, except for discarded clothes.

The window—*my window*—was wide open. Lace curtains flapped against the window frame. I remembered looking out the car window as we drove up and noticing all the windows were open. *Why did they bother locking the doors?*

"Your room is the only one with a heater." An off-white accordion-shaped electric heater stood behind one of the beds. "Doubt you'll need it. Come winter, a hot water bottle will suffice." She smiled. Her eyes conveyed that I needed reassurance. "You're used to central heating, but it's rare here. Doesn't get cold enough."

I nodded, despite not believing her. Average temperatures were similar to Washington's according to the AFS handouts and research I'd done before leaving.

Four children stood motionless in the doorway like toy soldiers. Three were wide-eyed and still, while the fourth, Greg, jiggled and ventured forward. "Away with you. Give the girl some peace," Mum ordered. They scattered. "Plenty of blankets if you need more."

"Thanks."

I could hear the boys giggling as they shuffled down the hall: a familiar sound. Closing the door, I thought of John Patrick and reopened it a crack. The room was all mine, and I breathed it in, detecting scents of fresh linen and grass. I ran my fingers over the bedspread: smooth, no cotton balls. Laying down, I spread my arms out wide and made snow angels on the cover. *All mine.*

Week two was abuzz with welcoming parties and exchange student events. We were warned that the average weight gain for the year was twenty pounds. I was determined to go home slimmer, surprise everyone, but the spreads were so tempting. I ate cream buns, pavlova, sticky toffee pudding, pikelets, trifle, and fairy cakes, my sweet tooth intoxicated.

I was the person of honor, the star attraction. Nobody knew my history, my fears, or my foibles. I was the "American Exchange Student," someone great, someone cool, someone fabulous.

It was exhausting. I prized the attention but grew weary of answering questions, of talking, of people. Mum noticed and suggested a trip to the beach. They had a beach house! Embracing my good fortune—I had two homes!—I envisioned a lavish bedroom with spectacular views of a private bay rimmed by ragged cliffs and crashing waves, a feather bed, the scent of salt, and dozing on seabird chatter.

"Catherine, get a move on!" Mum yelled.

"Coming!"

The drive was long. The last two hours were hair-raising; we had to traverse S curves on an unpaved two-lane road barely wide enough for one car. There was no way of telling whether a vehicle was coming down while we were going up. Several close calls, one requiring a terrifying blind reverse, shattered my composure and provoked Greg's acute case of carsickness. The dad, on the other hand, finessed the wheel and gears as if the ride was an everyday occurrence, which for him, it was.

I was glad to get out of the car.

The beach house was not lavish, but it was comfortable and located in a landscape made for fairy tales. Giant beech trees and mamaku tree ferns hid the house from the road. Washington is famous for its ferns—maidenhairs, ladies, deer ferns, and giant horsetails—but they only carpet the forest floor. New Zealand's tree ferns grew to heights of sixty-five feet, defining the forest canopy. Walking under a mamaku—a feathery kaleidoscope of spring greens—reminded me of Egyptian hieroglyphics like Cleopatra sitting on her throne, with servants on either side cooling her with opulent feathered fans.

"Swim trunks, everyone, while it's still light." Mum dug through a duffle bag searching for Sarah's swimsuit.

"I can't find my togs!" Ricky yelled. "Never mind—got 'em."

I may not have envisioned the house correctly, but I did get the beach right: small, private, and surrounded by cliffs. We had it all to ourselves but had to hike in. The dad and the boys were already in the water by the time I finished walking through the woods. Mum walked with Sarah, adjusting her pace to mine and Sarah's. I was slower.

We strolled down to the water. I put my toe in, expecting icy water this close to Antarctica.

"It's warm!"

"It's summer," Mum said.

"I know, but the ocean's never warm in Washington or Oregon. It's freezing. Turns your feet blue even in summer."

This place is paradise.

I watched the boys wait for a wave, pick one, ride it in, then stand up before hitting the sand. They weren't jumping the waves or swimming.

"They're bodysurfing," Mum offered, reading my mind. "Want to 'ave a go?"

"Maybe."

"Go on. You can swim, right?"

The dad was supervising the boys. I waded out, stood next to him, and studied Greg and Mark. Ricky crashed and burned every time but came up laughing.

Their dad yelled, "Good one!" or "Hold on!" as the waves passed. I watched, trying to figure out what made a wave worth riding. They all looked the same to me.

"If it's flat, pass it up. Avoid pitching waves. Look for meaty swells." He was trying to help, but what on earth was a meaty swell? "Catch one too early, and it'll go over your head." He looked to see if I understood, and clarified, "Wipeout."

"Okay, don't want that."

"Kick off too late . . . there's nought to ride."

He demonstrated, catching a wave and riding it to the beachhead.

"Good one, Dad!" Mark said, cheering.

Greg whistled. Mum cheered from the sidelines. Sarah clapped.

"Come on," Greg goaded, watching me hesitate. "The wipeouts are choice—better than surfing."

"Okay, okay."

I faced the incoming waves.

"Good one!" the chorus cried out, so I went for it. The wave passed me by.

"Faster, you gotta swim faster!" Mark yelled.

Piddly waves approached. I was tempted by their diminutive threat but let them go. Tired of waiting and sensing all eyes on me, I took the next one, riding it a measly three feet, a stunt I could have achieved by simply floating.

"Here comes one!" somebody yelled.

Feeling confident, I went for it. Five seconds later, I was eating sand. Wrapped in the ocean's belly, I churned in a hail of somersaults. Helpless in its grasp and disorientated, I couldn't find the surface. Painfully, I encountered the bottom, scraping my shoulder, my toes, and my knee, before my feet fixed firmly and I stood up. Salt burned my nose and eyes. I coughed and spit.

"Whoa, that was a shocker," Greg said, hands over his mouth, trying to smother his giggles.

"Are you all right, love?" Mum asked.

"Best take a break, aye," the dad said.

I didn't need any encouragement. Fazed and embarrassed, I joined Mum and Sarah sitting on a blanket. Mum handed me a towel. Cocooned in terry cloth, I avoided her, the dad, and their brood.

It was only a wipeout. I would suffer many more before mastering bodysurfing. Greg's giggles had silenced me, dulled my senses, and sent me back to the playground with Hunter on my heels. I spit him out along with the remaining sand in my mouth. Shaken by my overreaction, by Hunter's visit—a stowaway like rats on a ship—I realized "Catherine the Exchange Student" was not invincible or capable of suppressing that other me. Not yet.

Chapter Twenty-Three
First Day of School

I DON'T REMEMBER MY VERY FIRST DAY OF SCHOOL IN GEORGIA, but I do remember day one of ninth grade in Monticello when I fled to the girls' bathroom and hid from Hunter who wasn't even there, an agonizing and unnecessary move. I felt the same urge entering my new high school: the locals called it secondary school, sixth form. Mum marched alongside me, spouting words of encouragement. She never walked. She didn't possess a meander gene. Struggling to keep up while scanning for potential hideouts, I heard her words brush past my ears like a breeze. I didn't catch a word.

Modern and unlike the red brick colonial back home, there were no hallways in my new school. The campus-cum-hamlet embodied identical one-story white cottages that were shrouded with expansive windows and topped with flat roofs. A pixie could fly from one end of the campus to the other by skipping across the rooftops. Trying to curb my nerves and dampen the compulsion to scratch my itchy-everywhere, I imagined running over the rooftops: an ideal getaway, but how would I get up there?

I couldn't stop squirming. Vertigo from the wipeout wasn't the only thing I'd incurred bodysurfing: I now had a scorcher of a sunburn. My back, shoulders, nose, and forehead were peeling like loose wallpaper, tormenting me. I scratched because it itched, and it peeled because I wanted it off. Loose flaky skin repulsed me—it had since I was little—and I couldn't leave it alone. Mum was horrified by the sunburn, "Crikey, how can you burn once the sun's quit?" I told her not to worry and that I'd fried countless times before. However, searing after sunset was a first. Mark explained, "UV levels are higher in New Zealand"; he'd heard it on the news—bad news for redheads. The merciless rays cooked my skin. Mum came to my rescue, stockpiling sunscreen and sunburn remedies. She'd slathered on a mystery paste this morning, but it wasn't working.

"Brighten up; she'll be right," Mum said, noticing my unease. "And try not to scratch." My eyebrows joined ranks, as if trying to scream *not helpful*.

"I'll pick you up after school, and we'll go to the shops. Get something special for tea."

Tea was one of many mystery words I had to decipher every day. I thought tea was a brown liquid; not so, it could be a snack, dinner, or a drink. I couldn't make heads or tails of it.

"Cheers. I'm Mrs. . . . English teacher."

Preoccupied with decoding *tea*, I didn't see her coming or catch her name. Apparently, Mrs. *English* was my go-between in lieu of a teenage sibling. She was tasked to show me around and escort me to my first class, English, which doubled as my form class—somewhat like homeroom in high school—and her territory.

"Cheerio," Mum said.

Prior to coming here, I thought *cheerio* was a dead word only spoken in 1930s English movies, but Mum used it liberally. Her farewell tone conveyed "You got this!" and "It will be great!" but I heard "Adios, I'm out of here," and I longed to race her back to the car.

Mrs. English stepped outside. I followed. She filled the air with questions. I answered Mrs. English in one or two words. I couldn't help thinking of Pam at her school, chatting with her teen sister, Mariah. A fresh wave of animosity toward the AFS lady back home engulfed me. *I'm the one who needs a go-between, not Pam.*

My uniform taunted me. I pulled at it, yanking it down as I'd done during my eighth-grade graduation breakfast. Was it too short or too long? I didn't know. Mum was versed in school rules, had studied them, but knew nothing about the important ones dictated by students, not teachers. Pam would know; Mariah would have told her. They probably dressed together. Pam would be wearing a uniform, too. I wondered what it looked like and where it fell above her knees.

I had both a summer and winter uniform. The winter version was uncannily similar to the one I wore at St. Rose—white blouse, green and blue plaid kilt, navy sweater—plus a striped tie and blazer. I was wearing the summer concoction, a frivolous gingham dress with bloomers, suitable for a three-year-old. The kit also came with a sweater, but it was hot and I didn't need it, except to cover up: the smock was unduly skimpy. White ankle socks and black shoes completed the ensemble. The outfit was perfect for masquerading as a Kewpie doll on a warm Halloween night.

Despite the absurd ensemble, I was pleased by how the frock draped—loose around my waist and hips—thanks to a loss of eight pounds since leaving home. Fifteen hours without food on the flight launched my diet. Picturing the look on Steve's face when

I bet it was designed by male teachers.

I returned skinny as a model had made me newly diligent, despite the lure of gourmet delights, especially the cream cakes. Resting my hand on my flat stomach, I looked straight ahead and focused on Mrs. English's enunciation. Mum spoke more eloquently, or as they say here, *posher.*

After a whirlwind tour of the grounds, Mrs. English opened the door of her—my—English class.

"Catherine, our exchange student from America. Please, make her feel welcome."

I replayed her words in my head, *our exchange student from America,* with a sense of wonder and elation.

The ensuing hospitality was overwhelming. I answered a zillion questions.

"Where do you live?"

"Washington State, not Washington DC," was always a point of confusion.

"When did you arrive?"

"A week ago."

"How'd you get here?"

"Drove to Portland, flew to San Francisco, then to Hawaii, then to New Caledonia, a rerouting thanks to Cyclone Mary, then to Australia, and finally arriving in Auckland two days after departing."

"What's your favorite band?"

I didn't have one, but I said, "The Beatles."

"Were you a cheerleader?"

"No." *Not in a million years.*

"Can you surf?"

"No. The water is too cold, and I don't live by the ocean."

I wasn't a tennis pro, nor did I play an instrument in a band, or sing opera, or play the lead in my school musical, or act in a movie or TV commercial. I didn't fit their model for a female American exchange student: a blonde and tanned athletic cheerleader who surfed on the weekends and spent school breaks on a movie set. But I didn't care: I was *The Exchange Student.*

First period flew by. Annabelle was assigned to walk me to second period, European history. Chipper, she was round but not chunky and wore her hair in a ponytail, though there wasn't much tail. Unlike most of the girls, she didn't wear ribbons but opted for strategically placed bobby pins and clips instead. She walked slower than slow. Short legs. Comparing her height to my own five-foot-three and three-quarter inches, I guessed she was five foot. At her pace, we'd miss period two. She explained the route. I did reconnaissance—on her.

Her friend Faith joined us, tagging alongside me. Thankfully, Annabelle adopted Faith's stride, and our pace increased. It was Faith's turn, and ever so discreetly, I gave her the once-over: pretty, a knockout, but she didn't know it or didn't like the attention. Faith sunk into her shoes, a fruitless attempt to look ordinary. Curly jet-black hair tied in braids highlighted her porcelain skin; flecks of green in her eyes matched the silk ribbons around the ends of her braids; and she possessed the kind of freckles I wished I had: sparse and pinprick-sized. The two were a pair, but by the end of the day, we were a threesome.

Entering history, I eyed a tall boy sitting on the back of his chair. He was animated, professing an earnest opinion—something about Vietnam—and enjoying the attention of every student in the room. I'd hoped for a reprieve from the war rhetoric; it was all-consuming back home.

Guess not.

Vietnam was the topic over the dinner table and after the evening news; Dad didn't allow talking during his programs. Every night was the same. It started loud and ended loud. Steve, Tom, and I were against the war. Dad was pro: "As the leader of the free world, it's our job to stop the spread of communism." Our nightly brawl routinely stopped when Dad shouted, "If you don't like it, move!" He meant to another country. We were teenagers, where were we going to move to? Regardless, questioning the president was tantamount to treason in our house.

The teacher, Mr. Reid, fiddled with a stack of papers on his desk. He was dressed like a nerd who thought he was one of the cool guys. His face was nondescript, and he talked into his chest or at the ceiling. Midway through taking attendance, he called my name.

"Here," I answered, without thinking.

"Sir," he said, glaring at me, making eye contact for the first time with anyone.

"Excuse me?" I said, forgetting *excuse me* was a rude way of saying *get out of the way* in New Zealand.

"It is customary to say *Sir* when addressing a teacher."

"Sorry."

Recalling the yes-ma'am-no-ma'am-yes-sir-no-sir custom in Augusta, I almost smiled.

"Sorry, *sir*," he corrected me.

"Yes . . . sir."

Mr. Reid looked down at his list and called the next name. The student acknowledged with a singular, "Sir." After class, we filed out and merged with a mob of students advancing to the auditorium for our first assembly of the year—the headmaster's welcome. Kids stared, some said hello and some asked versions of the questions I'd already answered in English class. The quiet ones conveyed they knew I was the American by the way they looked at me or stepped aside, letting me pass.

"You're not what I expected." It was the boy from history, the one sitting on top of his desk.

"What did you expect?"

"Someone more gregarious," he baited.

"You mean a California surfer girl?"

"No." '

"Blonde-haired bouncy cheerleader?"

"Maybe."

"Not all American girls are Barbies."

I was astonished by my own mouth. Someone clever and bold had stolen it. We started playing word ping-pong. I countered his lobs, scoring again and again. Nearby, a posse of popular girls giggled. A collective identified by their sameness, they wore tight uniforms cut to identical lengths, their hair long and pulled high in ponytails or braids, and sweaters tied just so around their hips. He noticed the chuckles, too. His ears turned pink, as mine did when I was embarrassed, and he walked away.

Rosemary, one of the giggly girls, sidled up and clarified, "That's Headly. He thinks he knows everything, loves to hear his own voice. . . . You squashed it," she said, finishing with a whistle.

"I did?" I said, flashing a puzzled smile, not knowing what to think of the interchange with him or her.

You squashed it spun in my head. Studying Rosemary's sassy grin, I realized my exchange-student voice was oodles more powerful than my former one. I didn't know whether to trust it, but I salivated in its potency: the smart-ass boy had run away.

"I'm glad you're no Barbie," Rosemary teased. A lime green ribbon laced in her braids singled her out from the pack. "He's off to the safety of his mates."

I followed Rosemary into the hall and took a seat next to her. Headmaster Turner stood at the podium. He was wearing a black robe, as were three teachers sitting on chairs behind him. Moments after everyone was seated and quiet, the entire student body stood up in unison as if pulled by the same string. I missed the stand signal and joined them three seconds late. The timbre from a single piano key reverberated from the stage to the back wall. Everyone broke into song: "God Is My Shepherd." They sang loudly, full-throatedly, like a polished choir performing for a dignitary. The last note sung, students and teachers sat down, creating one thunderous thud. Headmaster Turner bellowed a welcome, introduced the new teachers sitting on the stage, and started announcing a long list of rules and regulations students might have forgotten over the summer break.

Twenty minutes later, he wrapped up. We stood until he walked off the stage, then the mass of flesh and energy filed out in an orderly fashion, like soldiers dismissed from a military exercise. I'd never witnessed anything like it. I was pondering the pageantry when Annabelle popped up to take me to art history. She deposited me outside the door.

My other classes were geography and liberal studies. Social studies kicked off my liberal studies regime, which changed every six weeks. Mum and I confirmed my course schedule with the headmaster three days prior. He decided math and science were no-go subjects for me, explaining, "We do things differently here. We don't carve up math and science into little pieces like in the States." When he said *States*, his mouth curdled as if chewing unripened fruit. It was the first time I'd heard the popular euphemism spoken with distaste.

Perturbed by the tone of his voice, Mum stepped in and explained, "Our children are exposed to calculus and physics in primary school." Since I'd missed out on elementary calculus and chemistry, my chances of passing a secondary-level course were slim. I was torn. My future plans were to be a doctor. I needed math and science, but if I failed to earn credit for classes taken in New Zealand, I would not graduate when I returned. The headmaster and Mum argued. Watching them, I thought of San Francisco and the sage advice from returning exchange students, "Academics are harder, and the exams, brutal. Beware." My high school diploma had to come first. I went along with his ruling, deciding to worry about college later.

It didn't occur to me that there might be an upside to a schedule devoid of science and math. I'd never taken an art class or elective outside of the sciences, despite having a passion for painting, photography, and decorative crafts. Walking into art class, my eyes roamed in wonder. Paint stains were everywhere, on the walls, the floors, even the ceiling. There were tables and chairs instead of desks, and they were covered with paint blotches, too. Giant easels stood against one wall. A sink in the corner was bathed in an array of paint colors, and next to it was a table covered with tubes of paints and piles of brushes. I'd never been in an art room, except for Miss Jo's craft room, but I immediately felt at home. Art history would quickly become my favorite subject; its absorbing curriculum, antiquities to modern art, would stay with me long after the minutiae of my other classes disappeared from memory.

"We will create art and travel through its history," Mr. Campbell (the art teacher) said, sporting an eager smile and attempting eye contact with everyone in the room. His eyes crossed at one point and were so large and invading, I had to look away.

"It'll be crushing, I warn you—daft, even—but we'll get through it." Apparently thrilled by the challenge, he announced that we would cover everything from cave paintings to Picasso. I was thrilled, too, until he announced that a test would be given every week to prepare us for our certificate examinations. We'd be hitting the books more than squeezing paint tubes.

I knew all about certificates—the General Certificate of Education or GCE—from AFS lectures in Auckland. New Zealand's academic system included thirteen years of school, ending in the Seventh Form; however, students were only required to attend through the Sixth Form. Most students left after Sixth Form and accepted jobs or entered technical schools and professional colleges. Those going on to university continued on to Seventh Form, which was on par with the first year in US universities. GCEs were at the end of Sixth Form and were a big deal, influencing employment opportunities and college hopes. I had to pass, or I would not graduate high school when I returned. The scary part was the pass rate. Unlike the American system, where poor performing students received their diplomas as long as they remained in school, here fifty percent of students failed their GCE exams. Mr. Campbell made that fact scarily real.

Staring at the floor, I filed out of art history, my mind occupied with GCE angst, but I didn't fret very long. A deluge of greetings from upper and lower classmates engulfed me. Like feeding bread to a hungry duck, more arrived every time I waved or nodded hello. It was lunch break, an opportunity for them to meet the celebrity exchange student. Rosemary swept through the gaggle of enthusiasts, grabbed me by the hand, and escorted me off the common square to her friends on the periphery who were idling under a tree.

"Where's your lunch?" she asked.

"I left it in first period." Her eyebrows shot up then dropped just as quickly. The term *period* had two meanings here, neither referred to a school subject. "Sorry, I meant *English*." We both broke out laughing.

Annabelle appeared from behind. "We take lunch in E2." I wasn't sure what she meant by *we* or *E2*, but she pulled me away.

"You should be careful about that lot." She chose her words carefully. "They smoke, and not just cigs."

"Rosemary's nice," I said. The nicest person I'd met so far, but I kept that to myself.

"Right you are—and trouble," Annabelle said, nudging me into the classroom where I'd begun this morning. *E* obviously meant English, but the *2* made no sense: it was my first class. I made a mental note to ask her but soon forgot.

Faith sat at her desk waiting for us. Two rows over, Headly was on top of another desk, spewing factoids about Vietnam's history: a country forever at war, who they'd fought, and how they'd suffered. He turned his gaze to me.

"It shouldn't even be called the Vietnam War." Pausing for effect, he added, "It's the American War."

Australia and New Zealand fought alongside Americans in Vietnam. Their presence was small by comparison, but that didn't matter—soldiers died. The war was controversial, especially among young New Zealanders. Anti-war protests were frequent and focused on more independence, independence from the US. A year earlier, Vice President Spiro Agnew had visited New Zealand on a goodwill mission, hoping to ease rising anti-Americanism. He wasn't very successful, and protests turned violent in response. Headly was clearly anti-American or a darned good pretender.

Annabelle and Faith's expression telegraphed a clear aversion to debating with him. I would have taken the bait had the subject been anything but Vietnam, a topic that raised heat but no answers. I ignored him. We ate our lunch in peace, discussing nothing more controversial than high school fashions in the States versus New Zealand.

After lunch, Annabelle walked me to geography. Mr. Taylor loved rocks. Fifty-five minutes of rocks later, I was delighted to see Annabelle. Rushing for the bus, she stopped briefly to point me in the direction of the Māori club, my after-school activity, which was culturally meaningful and nonnegotiable for all AFS students. I learned that Māori, the indigenous people of New Zealand, were Polynesians who arrived in New Zealand by boat in the early 1300s. Europeans who landed in the seventeenth century encountered a significant rival in the Māori, but epidemics, sham treaties, and land confiscations devastated the population, just as the Europeans devastated the Indigenous people of the US. Māori have fared about as well as them, too. Māori have recovered, somewhat, but they have lower incomes and a lower life expectancy than white New Zealanders.

I was one of two *Pākehā* (non-Māori) students in attendance. It was clear why I was present—I had no choice—but the other girl's appearance was a mystery. While waiting for the club to start, I invented backstories for her, settling on two options: she was collecting résumé tokens, or she had to fill in time until her working parents picked her up.

Qiu Rātana was written on the blackboard. I assumed it meant hello but discovered it was the club sponsor and teacher's name, Mrs. Rātana. She silenced the room without saying a word. Standing in place as still as a stone—a magnificent stone—her every muscle conveyed a purpose. Silver strands framed her forehead. The balance of her mane was dark and subdued in an ample bun resting on her neck. Her skin glowed as if washed by the sea and daubed with a breeze. Casting a bewitching gaze, she lured us in.

"*Kia ora koutou katoa*," she said, voice commanding and fierce, but not aggressive. "*Haere mai. Haere mai.*"

A few students responded, "*Kia ora.*"

I recognized *kia ora*—hello. For the most part, the expressions in the room evoked a polite boredom. But I was hooked. I wanted to spend the entire day with this mysterious goddess.

I waited for Mum's car to pull up. A small coterie of students approached and said hello or stayed back and stared. I wore my exchange-student smile and chatted amicably while my eyes searched the road. It'd been a long day, and I was tired of being in the spotlight. I longed for my bedroom and its emptiness: no questions, no obligation to engage.

"Gotta go," I said, spotting Mum's car.

"*Kia ora*," Mum said, poking her head out of the car window.

Climbing inside, I averted her eager expression imploring me to talk. I was done with talking, had filled my quota for the day.

"Come on, give us a clue. How'd it go?"

"Exhausting, but good," I said, looking out the window, brushing her off.

"Your teachers? Anyone stand out?"

"The Māori teacher; she's striking."

Just drive. For heaven's sake, drive!

She continued, poking and prodding. The more she dug, the less I said. We ran errands. She introduced me to shop owners and people she knew on the street. I returned polite hellos but said little else. Though I avoided conversation, I didn't refrain from examining the stores and the people in them. We stopped into half a dozen mom-and-pop shops: the butcher, the fish monger, a veggie and fruit market, a newsagent, a cheese and dairy store, and a bakery. The shops, all smaller than our sitting room, were attended by a cadre of talkers. They pointed out the day's specials, announced items arriving soon, prattled on about the weather, handed sweets to children, and wrapped purchased goods in brown paper or slid them into hand-sized paper bags.

The spectacle was captivating and so unlike supermarket shopping back home; there were no grocery carts, no cash register lines, and no officious attendants. My eyes were drawn to the window displays and gorgeous layouts inside the shops. Nothing was merely stocked. Every item was carefully placed and chromatically dazzling. I was content, happy to watch everything and let the ambiance soak in.

I didn't share my observations with Mum. I wasn't used to sharing my thoughts, so I found her stream of questions intrusive. She repeatedly pulled me away from where I wanted to be—deep inside my head.

"Something wrong?" she asked.

"Just tired," I said.

After dinner, I retreated to my bedroom. She knocked. "Come join us in the sitting room."

"I have to study. Art history test on Friday."

"The boys are doing homework, too. They won't bother you."

"In a bit."

"Tea will be on soon." She meant dinner, not brown water.

I had no intention of moving until she called me for tea.

Laying on my bed, staring at the ceiling, I welcomed the quiet of my bedroom. Outside, I heard a muffled "meh mehh." *The sheep must be in the south paddock.* A magpie was singing close by. Its song, a warbly giggle, prevailed over the clamor down the hall: Mum was telling the boys off for bickering. Listening to the magpie's shanty, I closed my eyes and let my mind wander, reflecting on the day. My first day was better than a dream. *It'd been absolutely friggin' glorious.*

Blocking all but the magpie's song, I recalled the eager looks people gave me and how they wanted to meet me, be with me, make friends with me. I laughed quietly, believing I'd fooled them. *They had no idea who they were courting. Thank God.*

I reconsidered my no-host-sister status and concluded that it hadn't mattered. Annabelle and Faith volunteered for the position. Besides, it was better this way. Pam shared a bedroom with Mariah, and I had this one all to myself. Devouring my good fortune like a fine meal, I reflected on my classes. Visions of my teachers and classmates came and went, but it was the tit for tat with Headly that replayed over and over in my head.

"Holy shit!" I shouted to the magpie. "I shut him down."

"What's that?" Mum yelled.

"Nothing. Shooing a noisy magpie!"

Too excited to remain still, I jumped off the bed.

"Insane," I said, laughing.

Counter quips were not unfamiliar; I'd composed them before, when I imagined eviscerating Hunter and Steve. I'd never said them out loud, that is, until today, when something took hold of my mouth. Not me . . . not the old me. Mum dropped her off, but she didn't go to class, and I intended to keep it that way.

Giddy and drunk on my good fortune, I attempted a pirouette, lost control, and landed on my butt. I got up, laughing. "Catherine the Exchange Student attempts death defying—"

"Tea's on!" Mum yelled.

"Coming!"

Skipping down the hallway, I entered the dining room beaming, death-defying escapades swimming in my head.

"Must've been a good study session," Mum said.

"It was," I said.

I ruffled Sarah's curls, crouched down to eye level, and tapped her on the nose. "Most indubitably."

Chapter Twenty-Four

The Talk

The school bus creaked to a stop at the entrance to our driveway.

"Thank you!" I yelled, bouncing down the steps.

"Welcome. G'day," the driver answered without looking my way.

Waving absentmindedly, I agreed—*a good day indeed.* It was my one-month anniversary, exactly one month to the day that I walked down the airplane steps and inhaled New Zealand as if I'd found the *Secret Garden,* despite the gray tarmac that stretched out before me. The air was clean, imbued with promise and not a trace of mill town sulfur.

Replaying the moment, I inhaled the scents around me: gas, dust, grass, dung, and something sweet I couldn't place. I was surrounded by green and crowned by a clear sky, its blue as bright as a blue jay's breast. Eying the bus, I waited until the door whined shut and the wheels crunched gravel before breaking out in song like some starlet in a B-movie musical. I sang to the sheep on the hillside, the mangy crows and sleek magpies, and the graceful weeping willows, their limbs swaying to my off-key notes. Celebrating my most brilliant month, I shouted lyrics scrambled with unreachable stars, hopeless quests, unrightable wrongs, and heavenly causes.

A hawk circled above, searching for prey. I shouted to him and to God and to the cosmos. "Yes! Run where the brave dare not go, and reach that *frigging* star! Right you are, Don Quixote!"

Marching in step with the melody, I climbed our driveway, a steep gravel road. Before long, my lungs balked, and the hill claimed my breath. I spent the first of many breaks squinting at the sea beyond the hills where the harbor slept: no tankers in sight. Silvery blue sparkles danced on the horizon against the backdrop of Hawke's Bay. The bay's dominant feature—shaped like a fisher's hook—is visible from space. Cape Kidnappers sits at the tip of the hook, where the world's largest colony of gannets resides. Mum, who'd assumed the role of my personal travel guide, took me to see the gannet spectacle. There were so many birds that I couldn't see ground for miles. The grounds I now surveyed were dotted with sheep dung, mounds of round pellets like stacks of mini cannon balls.

Recuperating, I attempted a short-lived jig, the gravel shifting and spinning under my shoes. It was like dancing on marbles, and my right foot shot forward, tipping me off-balance, but I caught myself before falling face first. Relieved there were no witnesses to my idiocy, I moved on, placing one foot carefully in front of the other.

Ten minutes later, I bent down to catch my breath and counted the sheep pellets between my shoes.

Dad must've moved the flock to the back paddock.

My host family had thirty of the wooly beasts; they'd clearly done their business while crossing the driveway. The sheep were as round as rain barrels, but they weren't fat: just ready for shearing. Dad said I'd get to "'ave a go," maybe this weekend. He and Mum were intent on giving me an authentic country-life experience. Their efforts were working, but not as they'd planned. I liked the countryside; New Zealand's scenery was lush yet tranquil, as if painted with watercolors. The view from our house was captivating; I got lost within it while gazing dreamily between the house and the bay beyond. That was all the country-life experience I wanted. I didn't need the addition of messy, hands-on animal know-how my New Zealand parents were so keen to provide.

I certainly could have done without Misty. Mum, a die-hard horse-woman, was teaching me to ride like a good country girl. Mum and Dad bought me a horse, a pretty, dappled gray whose temperament mismatched her outer allure. She bit, stepped on my feet, kicked, and did her best to throw me off mid-gallop. Aiming for a ditch or fence, she'd stop short and drop her head, sending me somersaulting into the air and onto the ground. I hated Misty.

"Show her who's boss," Mum said. "Give her a good smack and hold the reins tight." The miserable animal knew I was terrified of her: she knew she was boss. I feigned a busy schedule so I didn't have to ride, but Mum insisted: "Poppycock. She needs exercising."

I looked up the drive, took a deep breath, and marched on slowly, my steps more deliberate. Misty was in the south paddock. Her gray frame was expanding; she wasn't getting enough exercise. Mum would expect me to go riding. The weather was perfect, and Misty's spreading girth wouldn't have gone unnoticed by Mum or Dad.

"Not today," I grumbled, envisioning another tumble in the mud.

My calves were on fire from the hike up the hill. Thankfully, the last thirty feet were flat. I smelled vanilla and cinnamon. Mum was baking. Walking under the arbor overgrown with vines and passion fruit, I couldn't resist fingering the wrinkly purple balls. Slime dripped from a rotting fruit overhead. I picked it and threw it on the lawn. The birds would finish it. I wasn't a fan of the fruit, but it was scrumptious over pavlova smothered with cream, a New Zealand delicacy named for a Russian ballerina—the meringue emulates her tutu.

Opening the kitchen door, my ears were assailed by a keyboard barrage. Mark was pounding on the keys, a sign he was fed up.

"Good grief. Not helping," Mum scolded. "Try the progression again, and slow down. You're rushing." She paused. "You know the notes," she added, her voice a touch warmer.

He began again, the notes forming recognizable music. They were coming from the sitting room. Just eleven, Mark was the lead organist at our church; not a bona fide prodigy, but pretty close.

The younger boys, Greg and Ricky, played in the front yard. I could see them through the expansive kitchen window and hear their muffled words and shrieks of delight or outrage, especially Greg's cutting, high-pitched cackle. Sarah sat at the kitchen table coloring, mostly scribbling, on a sheet of paper, but I could detect the makings of a house. Debbie, only two, sat in a high chair squishing crackers between her fingers, eyes focused on the outcome. Only Mum was allowed to feed Debbie, who was round and on a strict diet. I only saw flaxen curls, faraway blue eyes, and baby fat. She had a history of very poor nutrition, evidenced by baby teeth filled with cavities. Mum and Dad were trying to adopt her, but her history was complicated, and the process was problematic. It might not happen. She came for visits—family auditions.

Mum was at the sink scrubbing potatoes. Roasted potatoes for dinner—*Yum!*—soft in the middle, crunchy on the outside.

"Well? . . . Go on, how was it?" she asked.

I mouthed her words before she said them. Her greeting was as predictable as ice in Greenland.

When she picked me up on that first day of school, I didn't know what to say or what she wanted. Weeks later, I still didn't know. No one had ever asked me about my day or inquired, "Penny for your thoughts," when I didn't answer. Mostly, I shrugged off her questions with a forced smile. Our chitchat—her chit, with me not chatting—persisted for two weeks, then I got *the talk*.

"I've not been blessed with sixteen years to figure you out," Mum reprimanded me. "You have to help . . . share what's going on. You're not a lodger. You're a member of the family. . . . You have to participate." She paused, waiting for my reaction. I stared back, not knowing what to say. "A query about your day," she continued, "deserves something in return."

Dodging, I offered a remorseful shrug and looked away.

"All right, I'll start. Debbie and I met Gran in town. She's feeling a bit poorly—tummy bug. So, no visit this Saturday. Now, it's your turn." She waited. I had one hundred answers in my head, but nothing came out. My eyes darted around the room, searching for somewhere to land other than her eyes.

"Right," she said, undeterred. "How about school? What's different from your school in the States?"

"Uniforms," I said. She wanted more, her eyes burrowing into me, through me. "The classes are segregated by ability. Back home, everyone is together, except for in honors classes." She waited patiently. A softening around her cheeks and eyes encouraged me to go on. "Teaching is different. At home, we're expected to participate in discussion, we're graded on it. Here, you have to listen and copy down what the teacher says."

The words came, and sentences formed, one connecting to another and spluttering out like a clogged faucet. Then gradually, as the blockage cleared, my words flowed more smoothly. "Some stuff is the same, like the length of our skirts." I kept going, doing most of the talking while she bridged silences with questions.

I'd given competent speeches and handled interviews with ease, but I'd never had a conversation about me. It was now our ritual. I wasn't keen on this new custom, not at first, but then I found myself disappointed when I came home and she was out running errands. I would listen for the car to pull up and meet her at the door, waiting in anticipation for our talk. Before long, I, too, initiated our sessions. The ease of doing so baffled me, but I chose not to examine why. I didn't want to jinx it.

I tousled Debbie's curls, took a seat at the table, and said, "*Kia ora.*"

"*Tena koe.* Your pronunciation is capital," she said. "Good day?"

"Most in-du-bi-ta-bly!"

We talked while she prepared a lamb roast and showed me how to score and season it. I watched her arms and hands move in a measured dance, massaging garlic into scored slits.

The cooker—what Americans call the oven—was on, and the kitchen was toasty but not uncomfortable, thanks to the open windows. Her soft chatter was like music, and I kept it going using skills I learned from her, injecting the odd question and answering hers. Bewitched by the rhythmic strokes of her hands, the movement of her lips, and our easy banter, I sunk into the chair, not wanting to be anywhere else.

Mum didn't talk about her background. Dad was adopted. She'd forewarned me that I shouldn't ask about his background. I suspected that was why Mum never talked about her childhood or relatives, except for Gran. Gran was Mum's stepmom, and they were close from what I could see. Her parents were not in the picture; I assumed they'd passed away. Mum went to a private girls' boarding school—a ritzy one—from a young age. I guessed boarding had something to do with her domestic situation, but I didn't know. Maybe her parents or Gran simply wanted the best for her.

Unlike my own mom, Mum relished being a homemaker. I never saw her flustered by the weight of household tasks. Both Mum and Mom tackled chores with furor, buzzing around the house, but Mom wore a face curdled with frustration. Mum also enjoyed being a mother. Her children were her life. Parenting was deliberate: she dedicated time for each child, cultivating unique paths for each one; things they ought to do to learn and grow and be their best. Mom had eight children and little time for such an approach—seat-of-the-pants chaos ruled. In many ways, we were on our own, a common reality for children in a large family.

After dinner, we retired to the living room, a family custom. Nights were now chilly, and Dad had a first-class fire going: our only source of heat. Its red and amber flames reflected on our dark TV. Dad was reading the paper, the muscles in his forearm flexing when he turned a page or tapped his pipe, loosening the tobacco. When he wasn't talking, the pipe dangled from his lower lip. He spent his days traipsing over hills and measuring and mapping coordinates. I spent one exhaustive day shadowing him as he worked, demonstrating what it meant to be a land surveyor and what it would take to acquire his athletic frame. One day was enough for me. Greg loved traversing the hills with Dad. Greg'll probably be a surveyor, too—not Mark though. We shared a dislike for physical exertion.

Mum snored, her knitting inert on her lap, a ball of twine between her feet. She could fall asleep anywhere, any time. I once saw her nod off at a party. She was standing in a corner snoozing until a concerned neighbor, fearing she'd fall, dispensed a gentle nudge. Mum came to life and joined the conversation as if she'd never left it.

The boys were doing their homework: Ricky at Mum's feet, Greg near the fire, and Mark on a chair beside Dad. Paging through a picture book, Sarah sat on the sofa next to Mum. Debbie was back with CYF (Department of Child, Youth and Family Services). She wasn't allowed to stay overnight, a bitter pill for Mum. I wasn't sure what the delay was; Debbie had been visiting for months without incident. Mum didn't know either. She worried about Debbie's adoptable status, worried that the mother might change her mind or might not relinquish her parental rights. I wondered if CYF had second thoughts about Mum and Dad and their ability to address Debbie's needs—she'd be the fifth child. Would she get the attention she needed? If asked, I'd testify with zero doubts: Debbie would.

Art history notes sat unattended on my lap, my mind meandering. Egyptian statues, pottery, and amulets circled round and round in my brain. An image of an ancient kiln had my nose analyzing the sitting room aromas: wood, ash, and sweet tobacco. And despite the stirrings of six people—Mum's occasional snorts, Greg's intermittent groans over a math problem, the clicking of Dad's teeth on his pipe, and Ricky's fidgeting, his toes brushing the wool rug—the room possessed a distracting stillness. Every night was the same, but I was still not used to it. I had no memory of this kind of stillness, not in my parents' bedroom behind a locked door, not alone in the church, not anywhere. No matter how quiet, I could always hear it, smell it, taste it: my fear. I could never relax and let my guard down.

It was ungodly different here. Recalling family time back home, I struggled to remember intimate details as I could here, except for maybe the acrid smell of Dad's cigarette. Family harmony only revealed itself during movie time; Dad chose the movie and no one was allowed to speak. I thought of summer picnics, my siblings dashing for the best piece of fried chicken, and the baseball games afterward. There was a form of harmony; it was louder, messier, but mostly jovial. And I took part, though only by standing far-off in right field, avoiding Steve, the baseball, and pining for the game to end.

It took me a while to adjust to the ways of my new family. I underestimated the differences from day one and proceeded as if they were minor. My first instincts drove me to familiar territory: Sarah, a replacement for John Patrick. But Mum intervened: "No favorites, and she doesn't need looking after. That's my job."

I was floored.

What does she mean it's not my job?

Second mom was my job; it had been since as long as I could remember. I was perplexed and angry—not with her, but with Mom. How often had I wanted to say, "It's your job!" and how sweet it would have been to call her out, reclaim my childhood, and be a kid again?

I stared at Mum, speechless.

She nudged me toward the boys. Resigned, I focused on them, deploying my sisterly moxie: teasing, tickling, and roughhouse playing. Mum and Dad's responses were quick and harsh; I was to stop immediately. "Teasing is bullying. Tickling is torture. Roughhousing always ends in tears." I was dumbfounded. Teasing and tickling were how my family showed affection, and roughhousing was *our* play. We treasured tickles. Tears fell when fists were drawn, not when tickling occurred.

What now? I didn't know what to do. Adept in autocracy—giving orders and keeping underlings in line—I didn't fit in.

I fought joining in, not knowing how to do it. I could perform looks-good-on-a-résumé stunts, but this was different. Searching for clues, I observed Mum and Dad and noticed that at times, simply being around was enough: show up and tune in. After a while, I copied them. It was getting easier. Finally, one week I was pretty good: I attended Greg and Ricky's school fêtes and showed interest; played cricket, running between wickets without chasing or mock tackling; decamped from a favorite spot on the beach to bodysurf with the boys; and resisted the urge to jump up and tease or tickle during our evening huddles by the fire. Showing up was easy, but paying active attention was hard—hard to fake.

Basking in the glow of the living room fire, I was unaware of the onset of the seismic shift within me, unaware that the warmth I was embracing wasn't coming from the fire. I wanted to join in, to be one with these people, to be a full-fledged member. The internal terror that blocked me from doing so was slowly ebbing, each outreach unlocking another layer of defense.

A sudden whimsy overtook me, an urge to record the moment. I closed my book and inspected the room, logging the tiniest details for memory: Greg's stubborn cowlick, the rich chocolate-brown streaks in Ricky's hair, Mum's sleeping face, Mark's frown with the crevice that formed between his eyes, the dip in Dad's lip where his pipe lodged, and Sarah's determined fingers pointing to words she couldn't read. The couch needed new springs, the piano needed polishing, and the fire needed more wood; it was dying. I got up, but Greg beat me to it, grabbing the poker to stir the embers. The fire popped and sizzled louder and louder, waking Mum. Her head jerked to the right then bolted straight up. She yawned and stretched her arms the length of the sofa.

"Who wants tea?" she asked while yawning.

Eyes brightened around the room.

"Yes, please," Dad said.

"Me, too," Mark added, eyes glued to his book.

"Please," Ricky said, his *please* more a *thank you.*

"Biscuits, too, please! . . . Ta," Greg said, stoking the embers.

"I'll get it!" I offered, jumping up.

Chapter Twenty-Five

Back to Front

THE AUDITORIUM SMELLED OF WOOD AND CHLORINE. I SAT TO the right of center stage on a metal chair, thighs stiff against its frigid surface, my kneecaps knocking like cymbals bashed together by a rabid monkey. I grabbed my knees, but my elbows started quivering, goosing my ribs. The doors opened. Students filed in. My feet joined in, bouncing up and down, tap-dancing in my shoes.

The hall was empty when I first climbed the stage steps. Breeze blocks, maple floors, and tiny windows kept it cool despite the heat outside, but the accumulation of bodies was warming it up—or was I the only one sweating?

I'd been dreading this day. *I'm not ready.*

Headmaster Turner stood at the lectern with his back to me, his silhouette reminiscent of Rockwell's painting *The Connoisseur*, which depicts a man standing in front of an abstract painting, his back the cryptic clue to his deliberation. Was he confused by the drip painting? In awe? Meditating? Waiting for someone? Like the man in the picture, Headmaster Turner folded his hands behind his back, but he was eying more than six hundred students and teachers. I would, too. I was up next. My stomach curdled, the butterflies now displaced by fiery hornets.

Cyclone Mary wasn't this scary.

I'd dreamed of this presentation since that first AFS dinner when I pretended to be an exchange student. In my dream world, I wore a cowgirl outfit. Costumed students from around the world sat to my right and left. I'd authored thousands of versions of presentations since, but none had a large crowd, no cadre of exchange student supporters, and me dressed in a flimsy gingham frock.

The headmaster and I were the headliners. Last-minute arrivals scrambled for seats. Once the stragglers sat down, he raised his hands, resting them on the podium.

"Good morning." His voice was an octave deeper than when he'd told me where to sit.

"Good morning." Students and teachers responded in ear-popping unison. At my high school, he'd have received a limp response from brown nosers and nascent first-years.

He reiterated the school rules on parking—locals were complaining—then moved on to a list of *important* announcements. My stage fright ballooned with each passing second. I stopped listening and watched the crowd. The students were astonishingly serene: no fidgeting, no looking around, and no wisecracks passed to neighbors. Would they give me the same courtesy? I looked for a friendly face in the back row, thought better of it, and decided to focus on the wall. My voice would have to carry over hundreds of heads to reach it; there was no microphone.

Eyes fixed on the wall, I repeated my opening statement over and over in my head. If I could manage one sentence without freezing, without tripping over my own tongue, I'd be okay. I concentrated on that one sentence, not the headmaster, not the student body, and not the dozen treacherous steps to the podium.

"Catherine?" The headmaster was staring at me, waving his hand as if I needed waking.

Jumping up, I raced to the podium. "Thank you." I waited for him to sit down before turning my back to him.

"First of all, I'm from Washington state, not Washington DC."
Cripes, I should have said hello.

Laughter echoed, bouncing off the walls. *Guess it doesn't matter.*

"Washington state is three thousand miles from DC."

More laughter—*I'm killing it!*

"DC is for politicians. Washington state is the land of lumberjacks."

The crowd laughed again, but their response was somewhat stunted. I moved on, sharing tidbits about my family, my town, and fun experiences that had occurred since my arrival, closing with New Zealand's mighty UV rays and my evening sunburn.

The students clapped. I sat down. The headmaster took the podium and delivered the closing remarks. I didn't notice he hadn't thanked me or commented on my speech. My head was spinning happy thoughts accompanied by bastardized "Impossible Dream" lyrics. *I did it! I did it. I reached that cursed star. Holy shit!*

The crowd dispersed. Annabelle and Faith waited for me. I raced up, expecting a "congratulations," or "well done!" but they were surprisingly quiet.

"Why did you put Headmaster Turner on the spot?" Annabelle asked, her eyes searching mine.

"What do you mean on the spot?" I was baffled. The look on her face scared me.

"You caught him out in front of the whole school!" Faith admonished. Her face was Annabelle's: appalled, disappointed, waiting for an explanation. The hornets returned, tormenting my stomach, crawling up my throat. I swallowed hard. Something had gone terribly wrong.

"I don't know what you're talking about. What exactly did I do?"

"You kept going on about Washington," Annabelle said, arms crossed tightly under her breasts.

"Why is that a problem?"

"You wouldn't let it go. It made him look stupid."

"Stupid? How?"

"Saying you were from DC isn't a—"

"Wait, he said I was from DC?"

"When he introduced you," Annabelle said, eying me suspiciously.

"Oh, no! I didn't hear him. I was practicing my speech." *Crap!*

"You really didn't hear him?" No longer appalled, Annabelle looked worried. "Bugger! You have to apologize."

I spun around and ran to the office. "I have to talk to the headmaster." The receptionist glared at me. *She was there.* I begged, "Just one minute— I'll be quick." His door was open—he must have heard. She flashed a look his way. *What if he won't see me?*

She waved me in.

He didn't look up, but he knew I was standing at attention, waiting. Pen in hand and bent over a document, he continued reading. After an icy minute, he moved it aside and uttered a perturbed, "Yes?" His eyes fixed on the discarded paper.

"Headmaster Turner, I didn't hear you introduce me." Talking fast and sputtering, I managed to say, "I was rehearsing my opening sentence, afraid I was going to freeze up. I never would've gone on about DC if I'd heard you say I was from there." He looked up. I fought the urge to look away. "I'm so sorry."

"You didn't hear me?" His eyes bored into me as if looking for clues, deciphering my intentions. "Very well. You better get to class."

He doesn't believe me.

Even if he did believe me, the damage was done: I'd embarrassed him in front of the entire student body, teachers, and staff. My small circle of new friends understood my mistake, but others thought it was intentional, including my teachers who gave me the cold shoulder. The last time I was castigated at school, I was seven and whipped by a nun. This time the hosing was subtle, but it burned deeper.

Determined to redeem myself, I was nice, available, helpful, and positive. After an arctic month, I won over all but one teacher. Thankfully, Mr. Reid's icy vibes seemed to be thawing, but the chill between me and Headmaster Turner persisted. Another month elapsed, and my faux pas was ancient history to all except Headmaster Turner.

I avoided him.

New Zealanders have a term for my affliction: *back to front.*

I was living in an upside-down world. At my old school, my grades were good, and the teachers liked me. I preferred their company to peers, and I avoided social immersion, eschewing popular hangouts. I loathed clubs, sports, and getting involved. I wasn't socially inept—I just didn't *want* to be social. I did what I needed to do, just enough to demonstrate exchange-student finesse on my application. Here, I was friends with everyone, a bona fide social butterfly flitting from group to group; except I didn't flit, they came to me. I was never without company, whether I was at lunch, shuffling between classes, or on the bus. I was one of the popular kids without having to earn the rank. High achievers were the big shots here, not bouncy cheerleaders or jocks in letterman jackets. Social strata hinged on academics. I was on the verge of failing.

Students were assigned to a form class, similar to a homeroom, but a form class was aggregated according to academic achievement: first class included the top performers, and bottom class, the strugglers. Prefects— much like student council members but with more cachet and author- ity—were at the top of the food chain. They treated me like an honorary member, the only non-prefect allowed in the prefect room, but if they had seen my mediocre grades, they'd probably have blocked the door.

My forte was the essay; I always could count on an A when taking an essay-weighted exam. Here, all tests were in essay format, but I didn't know how to write a New Zealand essay. Teaching methods here were beyond my comprehension. I didn't understand what the teachers wanted. Stu- dents sat mute in class, copying every word the teacher spouted. Notebooks were graded for accuracy and thoroughness; seemingly graded for our abil- ity to transcribe. We were completely dependent on what the teachers fed us, and nobody asked questions—teachers or students. I found the sys- tem ludicrous. Were they prepping us to be secretaries? My tests were one wipeout after another. Worse than eating sand, I was choking on failure. I studied hard and knew the material, but it didn't make any difference.

Panic set in a week ago, when Mr. Reid returned a spectacularly failed paper. Disgust percolated across his brow when he dropped it on my desk. He likely assumed I was coasting, spending my year free of GCE pressures. He wasn't the only one who thought I was going through the motions academically and didn't need the GCE. A few students pro- tested, accusing me of biasing the results and "lifting GCEs from New Zealanders." They didn't know about my recurring nightmare: a long day flipping burgers at McDonald's followed by night school to earn my high school diploma.

If it weren't for my fear of flipping burgers, all would be peachy. Academics aside, life couldn't be better; I even enjoyed extracurricular activities. A sport and a club—loathsome *have-to*s back home—were my favorite parts of school. I never missed a Māori club meeting or a bad- minton practice. A serious sport in New Zealand, badminton was played at dizzying speed, and I was good. I don't know who she was, but when the shuttlecock closed in, a badminton wiz slipped into my gym uniform and smashed a perfect backhand lob, clear shot, drive shot, or drop shot. Once in a while, I even beat Headly, our team champion.

Māori club brightened the worst of days, like when I blew a test or was homesick after receiving a letter from the States. The club and Mrs. Rātana were the perfect foil to academic setbacks and fueled my penchant for fantasy. Her stories and legends were as far-fetched and ingenious as Greek mythology and lots more fun to learn. Māori folk tales graced my dreams: riding a whale with Paikea, helping Māui fish the North Island out of the sea, separating the earth and sky with Tāne's help. During the day, Māori words and phrases enriched my vocabulary: *arohaina mai* (sorry), *kei te aroha au ki a koe* (I love you), *haere atu* (leave me alone), and *āwhina* (help!).

Mrs. Rātana taught us Māori dances: chants accompanied by rhythmic movements, bold steps, posture shifts, and pivoting—Māori do not hula—and how to twirl *poi*s, balls connected to a string and spun, up, across, and over the body. I'd avoided dancing in public or wiggling my body at all except in the privacy of my bedroom, but not here. I practiced at school and at home. Hand movements were especially tricky, and the *poi*s fought back, whacking me in the face and bashing my chest, arms, back, and thighs, but I carried on nonetheless. When Mrs. Rātana danced, her hands trembled like hummingbird wings, her body rocked, and her every gesture was mesmerizing. When I danced, my hands mimicked a thrashing fish out of water, not the least bit attractive or threatening when performing one of the many challenge dances.

Mom and all my siblings wrote. She probably insisted. Letters written by Greg, Joe, and Barry were the most difficult to read with a dry eye. I'd picture them at the kitchen table carefully holding their pencils, searching for words they could spell, pressing the pencils on paper, erasing mistakes, hiding the smudges and holes from Mom, and triumphantly placing a stamp on the finished product. They mostly wrote about sports: a stunning catch, a home run, a league championship—games I'd missed. Thanks to badminton, I could write back about a sport, which was a first.

Previously empty, my calendar was filled with after-school activities: exchange student engagements, family commitments, and weekend parties. I could have used a social secretary. The extra twin bed was in constant use. I had many girlfriends: Pam, Annabelle, Faith, Rosemary, Ria, and Chris. We did mundane silly girlfriend stuff I'd never done before, like gabbing about boys, sharing clothes, clowning around, playing practical jokes on each other, and spending time together. Pam invited me to her parties, as did other local exchange students, and my Māori buddies invited me to festivals and *hāngī* feasts. I performed with them at *wharenui* meeting houses, dancing (flailing and *poi*-bashing my body) in the front row—flat out happy to be in the front row.

Back home, when I entered unfamiliar territory, I'd watch and choose my words carefully before speaking. Here, my vernacular was loose, charged with words alien to my own ears. New Zealand phrases and slang messed with my word choices. I loved the playfulness of the lingo; it was loaded with slang. Mum cornered a library of ditties: *do a runner* (take off without doing something), *pack a sad* (throw a tantrum), *what are ya* (friendly insult), *bit of a dag* (hard case), *take the dog for a walk* (go to the toilet). I didn't repeat them—they felt silly coming out of my mouth—but I did pick up many words, and I used familiar ones differently, like *chips* for *fries* and *crisps* for *chips*. Some stuck, residing in my vocabulary long after leaving New Zealand.

Best of all—and first-class amazing—a potential boyfriend was prowling. Headly stopped goading me and started treating me nicely. He sauntered over one day at lunch, plopped himself on a desk next to me and asked, "So, what 'ave you seen of New Zealand, eh?" Initially, I mistook his query as a derisive challenge. I paused before answering, looking for clues to his goal. His lanky body was tense, the tone of his voice less assured than usual. I decided the question was simply a conversation starter, not a debate, and the only topic he could come up with that didn't concern Vietnam. I told him about Auckland, a trip to Rotorua with Mum, hiking in the bush, bathing in thermal pools, trips to the beach, and outings near Hawke's Bay. He listened, and when he spoke, he did so without talking over me.

Thereafter, he made a habit of joining me for lunch. My friends noticed. We huddled afterward, sizing him up, speculating what his next move might be. Before long, Headly and I were bantering in the schoolyard, rehashing literary classics, ranking breakthrough rock albums, and discussing the fundamentals of badminton, rugby, cricket, and the parliamentary system. He couldn't bring himself to completely drop Vietnam, but our rumbles were unlike the bull sessions I remembered back home, where discourse burned. Fierce debates between Steve and Dad on Vietnam, China, Nixon, drugs, college demonstrations, the draft, and Black Power ended in shouting matches. I hated these altercations of one-upmanship that went nowhere.

It was different with Headly. I thrived on our tango of words. Our skirmishes were a race-cum-chase, and I didn't mind getting caught. I wanted to get caught. Maddening and bombastic, he was at the same time shy and utterly captivating. I found myself stealing chances to look his way and counting the minutes until lunch. I'd never had a boyfriend and never been kissed: decking Jeff had killed my chances with him. I had a crush on Ray, the dark-haired boy with those chocolate eyes, once I realized he wasn't Hunter's double, but by then it was too late; he'd paired off with someone else. Back home, I went to high school dances but never danced. I was invisible. Not so, here.

Headly and I were the perfect match: the sought-after bloke and the foreign exchange student, just like the king and queen of prom back home. Daydreaming, I pictured the two of us in fancy dress with prom king and queen sashes over our shoulders and crowns on our heads. Watching his lips, I ached to kiss them and wished he'd stop jabbering and *do* something.

With an almost boyfriend, a slew of real friends, an unending list of parties, and my spinning *poi*s and hummingbird fingers, Bob's your uncle—except for my grades. I loved this upside-down world and couldn't bear the thought of ever leaving.

Chapter Twenty-Six

A Real Boyfriend

I MARVELED AT MY PREDICAMENT, A SUBLIME AND LAUGHABLE wonder: *Headly, my boyfriend.* It was a truth as unreal as flying through the jungle picking mangos for a late-night supper. How was it possible, me an exchange student, me in New Zealand, and me with a boyfriend? Being with *him* and not seven thousand miles away avoiding Hunter and Steve triggered a desire to break into one of Sister Brendan's Irish jigs.

I felt taller, like Alice, but without the magic wafer. I took a deep breath, inhaling the aroma of Headly's room. It stank: apparently his Mum didn't open the windows like mine did come rain or shine. Discarded clothes, dust, and a half-eaten apple marked his turf. Towers of books lined the walls, reaching toward the ceiling: a quasi-library with a substantial Russian lit section. The room was devoid of decoration; no band posters or Hollywood starlets beamed from the walls. Only books, clothes, and idle shoes peeked out from under the bed. A stream of light breached the solitary window, rescuing the cramped space from claustrophobia.

He stood in front of his prized collection of Russian novels. The columns of books were reminiscent of precarious Dr. Seuss dwellings. His blue-black hair brushed over his collar, barely adhering to school code. A black T-shirt and trousers fused to his body, a fashion preference during after-school hours. I watched him pontificate, his mouth moving in earnest about a book and author I'd never heard of. His thin body jerked awkwardly out of sync with the dull flow of words rolling off his tongue. An image of a stickman cartoon on overdrive popped into my head. Stealthily eying him—I didn't want to appear too eager—I wondered if his erudite prose was original or lifted from the inside cover of his precious book.

I wanted to be the precious one. Begrudging him the book, I wanted him to kiss me, to lock his fingers with mine, to hold me. I willed him to put the book down and imagined touching those dancing cheeks seesawing with each word he uttered. *Sixteen and never been kissed. I'm sitting on his bed!* Why wasn't he sitting next to me? Why wasn't he running his fingers through my hair like lovers in the movies? Why was I not fighting him off? Maybe he was afraid his Mum might pop in with tea and biscuits.

"You've never read any of the great Russian authors, writers of the human soul?"

I stared at him blankly. *What did he say?*

"Tolstoy? Nabokov? Chekhov? Dostoevsky? Gogol? Lermontov? Solzhenitsyn?"

Tolstoy was familiar, but I remembered him from history class, not English: he'd had something to do with the Russian Revolution.

He tried again. "*Crime and Punishment? Anna Karenina? War and Peace?*"

"I started *War and Peace,* but I didn't finish it."

"What was the last book you finished?"

Unwilling to admit it was *Gone with the Wind,* I sought out English reading lists stored in my brain, searching for a book he'd approve of.

"*Catcher in the Rye,*" I offered.

I would've included the author's name, but it escaped me.

"Ah . . . Salinger, full of teenage angst and rebellion. I prefer the layered beauty of the Russian prose." Composing his next line, he looked above me and out the window.

I liked watching him recite as if on stage, but eventually it became tiresome. Every sentence spilling from his mouth was important, earnest, or grave, often all three. I followed his lips; they were taking on a life of their own, like goldfish nibbling fish feed. When he got excited, a piranha came to mind, as did Tarzan, who only possessed twenty-odd words in his vocabulary. Sitting alone on the bed, I ached for his version of a Tarzan *ungawa*, and I imagined Headly yodeling instead of prattling on about Russian angst. In Headly's opinion, the books I knew and could confidently discuss were common: popular best sellers, transporting the viewer to foreign lands and through outlandish adventures, ones that didn't dwell on the fragility of my soul.

His attention veered to his favorite Russian classic, *One Day in the Life of Ivan Denisovich*. The trancelike hum of his voice and the warm sun streaming on my back had my mind drifting and my body aching to lie down on his bed and let the warmth embrace me, since he wasn't about to.

I bathed in boyfriend-luck—*I had one!*—musing about our upcoming Auckland trip. We were going as a couple. My stomach did the bunny hop and my face flamed, a knee-jerk reaction whenever the trip entered my thoughts. Two students from every high school were chosen to attend a United Nations youth conference in Auckland. Headly was one of the two from my school. I was going because of my exchange student status; I was invited to everything. We'd be traveling on the same bus and staying at a UN-designated hostel.

Headly and I avoided eye contact when Headmaster Turner warned us about inappropriate behavior. "Students caught with alcohol or drugs or found in a room other than their own will be expelled." The trip was metamorphosing into a dangerous enterprise. If expelled, would they send me home?

Maybe I shouldn't go.

Sudden concern shifted my eyes to the floor. Headly noticed and stopped talking. Looking up, I smiled at him. Assuming I approved of something he'd said, Headly nodded back and continued orating about poor Ivan—so many words per breath I wondered why Headly wasn't a dull shade of blue. His hands joined the conversation.

I thought of us sitting next to each other on the bus, his hands and lips inches away. I imagined scooting up to him, the two of us taking up only half of the seat, my hand resting on his lap, his hand over my shoulder . . .

At three o'clock sharp, the bus pulled up in front of the school. A dozen teenagers were already aboard, all a chatter. George Harrison's "My Sweet Lord" blared from a transistor radio. I followed Headly to a bench five rows in on the left side, an inconspicuous spot—the back would be far too obvious—and slid in next to the window. The hot vinyl seat burned, sticking to my legs. I jiggled them up and down amid a chorus of high-pitched squeaks and then sat on my hands.

"Everyone, in their seats! No walking or standing in the aisle!" yelled the bus driver, an ordinary-looking bloke in a gray uniform and matching cap.

A legion of hands synchronized like members of a band pushed the windows open, sending gusts of air over our heads and down the aisle. The breeze was welcome despite its chilly edge. Headly and I were the target of catcalls, goo-goo eyes, and winks. With a Cheshire cat smile, he welcomed the attention. I wore a straight face, broadcasting confidence with a tinge of the possessiveness I'd witnessed on cheerleaders' faces back home when claiming their dates. I readied for his advances, the divine purpose of an out-of-town trip.

I expected him to shimmy up against me, but he didn't. *What was he waiting for?* I shifted over closer to him. He didn't pause his monologue, just kept on shooting off words. Too nervous to decipher them, I nodded, smiled, and waited for him to make a move. My hand was barely touching his leg. I so wanted to place it on his lap, but I was wary of making another advance he might ignore.

Finally, in mid-sentence, he leaned over and kissed me. I shivered when his lips touched mine. We didn't smash noses or teeth as I was afraid we might. His lips were soft, and I wanted more of them.

What is it about being lip on lip with someone other than family?

My only reference was the movies, those slow zoomed-in shots with the actors' lips barely touching, holding the moment, and then meeting, the actors' bodies collapsing into each other and swooning as if drugged.

But his kiss didn't linger, didn't pause to explore. We did not swoon. He dispensed a succession of short quick pecks like a chicken searching for seed. Though he was the only boy I'd ever kissed, I suspected his execution was flawed, even pathetic, but it still thrilled. He pulled back, took a breath, and renewed his one-way conversation. I sensed the time-out was a relief for him. He'd fulfilled his duty and satisfied the blokes whistling and jeering in the back of the bus.

It would be our last kiss.

The night before we left for Auckland, Pam and I were informed by our local AFS representative that we could not stay at the hostel. We billeted with host families. I stayed with a Māori family; their middle daughter, Jenny, was my age. She didn't attend the conference, but she joined us afterward, as did Pam's host, Anna. Day one's theme was *race*, focused on South Africa. Day two was *disarmament*, focused on American intervention. Both days were heated. Day two's debate carried on through dinner. Headly, Ian (the other candidate from my school), Jane (representing a school in Auckland), Pam, Anna, Jenny, and I went out for pizza. Headly was in good form, admonishing American imperialism without addressing the two Americans at the table. It was all for Jane.

My eyes were glued to the two of them, his delivery painfully familiar: pompous yet intimate. Jane laughed—eyes wide, teeth bright—as if he were a comedian from *Saturday Night Live*. Her miniskirt exposed thin legs. Buttery locks covered her shoulders. When we got up to leave, she balanced on platform shoes, then rocked on her heels and faked a tumble. Grabbing his arms and shoulders, she teetered mere inches in front of him. Reaching out to steady her, his hands brushed down her back.

"He's a prick, also a prig," Pam said, directing her comment to me, while speaking loud enough so he could hear. I hadn't realized she was behind me.

Heat rose on the back of my neck. I knew my face burned bright; I was horrified that Pam had witnessed my humiliation. Jenny was watching, too. I'd told Jenny all about Headly, and now wished I hadn't. Her eyes darted from Headly to Jane to me, studying my reaction. Jenny was an easy read; she was embarrassed for me.

"Come on, this is boring," Pam said, slipping off her shoes.

She took off running. Jenny and I followed. We spent the evening traipsing unsupervised around Auckland, pub crawling. There was a legal drinking age, but no one seemed to be constrained by it. Children of all ages were welcome in bars, and if you looked to be in your mid-teens, you were served. I discovered rum and coke—a lot of it that night.

I was a no-show for the rest of the convention. I wasn't going to watch Headly slobber over Jane. Jenny had a better idea. We visited her grandmother, Tupana, at a *pah*, a Māori settlement. Her grandmother was born and raised there. She'd never had any interest in living with *Pākehās* (white New Zealanders). She spoke no English and had a face tattoo on her chin. Blue swirly lines flowed from her indigo lips to the base of her chin. Ancient looking and stooped, she rose to her feet when we entered her home. She gave Jenny a *hongi* greeting: pressing noses together. I was familiar with the custom, having witnessed it at Māori club performances, but this would be my first *hongi* hello. Tupana was a head shorter than me. I had to bend way down, or we would have missed noses. She pressed hers against mine. Neither of us breathed, but I could smell her and her breath. It was nice. She closed her eyes and held our *hongi*, the greeting more intimate than an embrace. I forgot about Headly, at least in her presence.

Our visit was impromptu, but word spread, and within the hour a festival materialized. Distant family members arrived, as did friends and community leaders. Gobs of food appeared from nowhere. Young children sang and danced; even the littlest ones were *poi* pros. Elderly women chanted, their consummate hands trembling hummingbird wings. Not to be outdone, the men lined up. Two groups faced each other. A war cry pierced the *pah*, then another, which was followed by rhythmic shouting and stomping and slapping as the men challenged each other, performing the *haka*. No sooner had they finished than a group of four grabbed long *patu*s and started weapon dancing. An older gentleman and his son were brilliant, but the other pair was terrible and spent the better part of the dance laughing and shouting "ouch" and "oops" when a *patu* accidentally smacked a tender body part.

The *pah* visit was more than enough to lighten my mood, but Jenny thought a party was just the thing I needed. Like the *pah*, her house filled in no time at all. I recognized a few young people from the *pah*, but most of the partygoers were kids from her school. They all clutched a beer, her dad's homemade brew. It seemed every dad in the nation made beer, including mine. "The French love their wine, and this country loves its beer, especially homemade," I thought, ready to try another. And I'd tasted rotgut, but this was good. And strong.

"Jeremy, this is Catherine. She's a Yank," Jenny said, introducing me to another of her friends.

Jeremy was six-foot-twoish with Tarzan shoulders, mammoth hands, and a curly blond mane too thick for combs. Strategic strands framed his hazel eyes where gold flecks twinkled in time with the curls bouncing on his forehead. He was like an Adonis and was a naughty gift—*thank you, Jenny*—to mend my bruised ego.

The living room was crowded; people sat on every available chair or on the floor, and danced or traipsed from the kitchen to the sitting room to outside. Jeremy grabbed a chair after its occupants stepped out for a smoke. Unlike Headly, he was lusty—ravenous—and didn't waste a second in case a chaperone might burst through the door and thwart his plans. His hands searched eagerly, fingers disarming my bra more nimbly than I could. Two days ago, I'd nuzzled a chicken pecker, now I was cruising with an octopus-man, fluttering from titillated to terrified.

There's another pair of hands under that sweater.

I pushed him off, adjusted myself, and headed for the door. He apologized, persuading me to stay. We spent the next hour kissing until my mouth hurt and the skin around my lips turned raw.

On the bus ride back to Hawke's Bay, I sat alone and stared out the window, ignoring the awkward glances and hushed whispers. I didn't care about the end of Headly and me—Pam was right, he was a prick and a bore, and the memory of his chicken pecks made my skin crawl—but I worried that my magic had vanished, the fairy dust had dried up, and Headly's rejection was proof of my ordinariness.

All had been going so swimmingly. I should have stuck with being everyone's friend. Now it was all ruined because of a stupid boy. Everyone would soon know about Headly and the thin-limbed flirt and my disappearance on the last two days of the trip. He'd brag for sure, and there was a witness to back him up: Ian. One lousy trip was all it took to reveal the truth. I wasn't someone great, someone cool, or someone fabulous after all.

I ate more than I should at dinner and stared at my plate or the wall behind Dad. I responded to questions but asked none, and I chewed over tomorrow's arrival instead of my food. Gnawing over imagined encounters, each more poisonous than the last, I retreated to my room in a panic. Razor-sharp stares from the past assailed me, opening old wounds, obliterating rational thought. I couldn't bear it, the contempt, pity, loathing. Too embarrassed to confide in Mum, I sweated alone, pacing between the bed and the closet.

If I'd told Mum everything, I could have vented about Headly, but he was not the issue. I knew at some level Hunter and his abuse was the source of my agitation, but I couldn't articulate how; and even if I'd found the words, shame prevented me from sharing. So contrary to who I wanted to be and who I was shaping myself to be, I buried those memories and locked them in a file labeled "Done," a place I refused to go, even for Mum.

I couldn't sleep. The brutal stares from the past demonized my new friends and school, mutating into a version of St. Rose without hallways. Lying under the covers, I heard giggles. Images flashed in and out of focus, newly formed cliques making a show of blacklisting me. Last week I was ants-in-your-pants boyfriend crazy, eager to show *us* off and flashing our couple status at school and on the bus. *What a fool!*

One o'clock passed, then two thirty. Sometime later I drifted off, only to be woken by a pair of magpies who would not stop yapping. I got up, shut the window, and slumped back into bed, dogged by the magpies' giggle-fluting. They, too, were laughing, taunting me.

"Shut up!"

I dressed, styled my hair in braids, spoke as little as possible over breakfast, and stared out the window all the way to school. Filing off the bus, I looked for a deserted route to take, but the campus was too open:

no obvious detours. I should have been more diligent early on and discovered hiding places and clandestine routes to class. *Too late now.* I pushed my shoulders back, sucked in my gut, and engaged a honed poker face.

Word spread fast. I was swarmed ten feet from my first period classroom. The popular girls pushed forward; they'd gotten an earful from someone. I braced for an onslaught of mean-girl taunts designed to take me—fancy-pants exchange student—down a notch or two. They all had an opinion, and each delivery was heartfelt, but not what I'd prepared for.

"I can't believe it."

"The sod."

"He's not worth it."

I'd seen this play before but never as a cast member. In the hallways back home, I'd witnessed the earnest girlfriend scrum. This time, I was center stage.

They hadn't figured it out, didn't know I was a smoke-and-mirrors VIP, a nobody dressed up with an exchange-student moniker. My spirits went from downtrodden and defeated, to delirious.

Catherine the Exchange Student lives on!

Chapter Twenty-Seven

Cheater

I PULLED OFF MY BOOTS AND SHOVED THEM AGAINST THE MUD-room wall.

Mum looked up from her ironing. "What happened?"

"She threw me again."

Misty had careened to a sudden stop at the edge of a ditch and ran off, leaving me face-deep in mud. "Same trick, but this time she bucked."

"Bucked? Really? Sure she wasn't pigrunning?"

When a horse kicks its back legs up while running, it's called pigrunning.

"It felt like being thrown."

Mum's super-sized eyes narrowed. "We'll see about that. Come with me."

She unplugged the iron, removed her apron, and put on her wellies: no time to fetch riding boots.

I thought I was done for the day. Grumbling and ranting a soliloquy of curses, I put my boots back on and chased after Mum. She was headed for the garage and Misty's saddle. Her stride was twice mine, and the gravel under her boots crackled grinding into the dirt. Had Misty been close by the sound would have scared her off.

Mum grabbed Misty's saddle and a riding crop. I never used the mini whip, fearing it would rankle the vile beast, making her bite, kick, and stomp all the more. I fetched Misty's bridle and caught up with Mum who was opening the paddock gate. We found Misty where she'd left me sprawled in the mud. Her gray coat looked near white in the sunlight. Head down, nose to a lush crop of grass, she munched lazily, unaware of Mum's wrath and what was coming. Misty always took off when I approached, but

Mum rounded her up without effort. Holding firmly to her mane, she fastened the bridle, tossed on the saddle, used her knee to give Misty a good belly-thumping—the mare habitually overextended her stomach, effecting a loose fit that was unsafe for riding—and tightened the straps.

Misty was done for: her ears pricked up, and a sudden get-up-and-go spark in her eyes indicated she knew it.

"Time for a lesson, you cheeky sod," Mum barked.

Mum pulled the bridle tight, forcing the pony to look her way. Face-to-face, she treated Misty like a disobedient child, Mum's voice harsh, assured, forceful. Misty was getting *a talking to,* an expression Mum used before scolding the boys. Misty resisted, resorting to biting and stomping. Mum jerked the bridle, the bit grating on Misty's mouth. Deploying the full force of her body like a mallet, Mum slammed against Misty's side.

Mum's next move surprised me. She mounted the mare. Misty's eyes widened. Holding her head high, Misty wailed, mustering a gnarled whinny. Big Red, Mum's horse, was twice Misty's size. Mum's boots hung well below Misty's belly, and the saddle was swallowed by Mum's frame. I imagined Misty's back giving way, the animal forever swaybacked. My anger turned to guilt, my hatred into pity, and I turned away.

Mum proceeded to run Misty through a series of riding maneuvers—walking forward, backward, in circles, over low logs, around the perimeter, and into 'a ditch and back out—again and again. Mum executed abrupt transitions and subtle ones. Misty surrendered. Mum dismounted. Misty kept her head down, eyes to the ground.

"Up you go."

I had no choice after Mum's performance.

"Hold her mouth tight. Show her you won't stand for any nonsense."

Misty behaved like an angel. She dared not misbehave. Mum was in the paddock the whole time, watching.

"Did your test results come back?" Mum asked as I entered the kitchen after a quick change. She'd put the ironing away and was starting dinner.

"Not yet. He's taking his sweet time." Mr. Reid normally returned our tests within two days. It'd been over a week.

"I'm sure—"

"I know . . . she'll be right." *She'll be right* is slang for "whatever's wrong will be okay in the end."

Mum smiled. "Don't get your knickers in a twist."

"I'm not, just nervous."

"Cuppa tea?"

I was always anxious when waiting for my test results, but I was more so this time. After my last abysmal score, I'd borrowed previous exam papers from a classmate who'd earned high marks. I hoped her tests would somehow clarify what I was doing wrong. They were an eye-opener and were not what I expected. There was no structure to her answers; no beginning, middle, and end as I was taught, no point of view. Essay after essay was the same: a regurgitation of Mr. Reid's lectures. She'd aced her tests by virtue of a formidable memory and perfect transcription. That, I could do. I took good notes and copied down everything Mr. Reid said, no matter how trivial. On the day of the test, I vomited it all back: no structure, no analysis, just his drivel.

Waiting for the results was clawing away at my confidence. Was my analysis amiss? Was I blind to some brilliance buried in my classmate's answers? I'd tried everything else. The new approach had to work, or I wasn't graduating.

Mum set the teapot on the kitchen table and a plate of McVitie's digestives, a semi-sweet cookie with dark chocolate on the underside. I found them dry and tasteless at first, but they'd become a favorite. Low in calories, they helped curb my appetite. I'd gained back the eight pounds a month ago. According to Mum's scales, I was up an additional six pounds: fourteen pounds total in two months. Worrying over my grades had me overeating. My waistline was swelling as fast as Misty's barrel—the correct word for a horse's belly according to Mum's country schooling.

"Package arrived today, a good-sized one." Mum drowned her tea with milk.

A package from home meant presents for everyone; Christmas without the anxiety. The box was larger than previous ones; it was nearly two feet wide, and the right-hand corner was covered in a bevy of stamps. Mum carefully cut them off for Greg, who had an impressive collection thanks to my family and Gran, Mum's stepmom. Whoever wrapped it had gone overboard with the tape: layer upon layer coated all sides, requiring a carving knife to open it.

After dinner, I played Santa, handing out the gifts. Mom had packed three baseball caps, a recipe book authored by her sorority, a toy horse, and a pamphlet on the history of Cowlitz County. Dad always sent a tape, and he did not disappoint. On previous ones, he'd recorded birthdays, holidays, sports events, and my siblings' babble when he managed to ambush them. I never heard Mom's voice; as promised, she refused to talk into the mic. Greg, Ricky, and Mark tried on their caps, Mum flipped through the cookbook, Dad checked the facts and figures of my hometown, and Sarah trotted her horse up and over her legs.

Mark turned on the tape. John Patrick was singing "Jeremiah was a Bullfrog," a hit song on the radio. He only knew the first stanza and belted bullfrog croaks after each line. Ricky and Greg cracked up, and Sarah giggled, joining in on the chorus. Mum's involuntary belly laugh filled the room, as infectious as John Patrick's recital. Convulsing with laughter, tears ran down my face. I wiped them away. I missed John Patrick terribly, wanted to reach through the tape and grab him, cuddle him, smell him, and cover him with kisses—but I still didn't want to go home. I wanted him here with me.

Joe and Barry's laugh and Mary's giggles provided the background to John Patrick's performance. I envisioned them in the living room or around the kitchen table. We were in the sitting room; the fire had been recently lit, so the room was still cool. Greg stoked the fire with wrapping paper.

Suddenly, the flames exploded.

"Enough!" Dad rushed over and dispersed the paper.

My real dad's voice filled the room, his voice deep, clear, and contagious. He was telling a story—he loved his stories—this one was about the Nutty Narrows Bridge, a miniature expansion built for squirrels. The sound of his voice heightened my guilt and churned my stomach, twisting it ever tighter. I was a terrible daughter. A terrible big sister. I'd done everything I could possibly do to get away, but listening to their chatter, their laughter, and John's singing, I ached to be there, sit around the table, and join the party; but not stay. I wanted to pop in and pop out, landing right back here.

I don't wanna go back.

I pondered how different it was to be here than to be with my real family. I sensed it wasn't only the absence of lists and predatory insults, though that was pretty darn fabulous.

What was it?

Words confounded me, and then it clicked: it was *easy* to be here with my New Zealand family. I was at ease, as if I'd stood at attention for a dozen years and the gods that be said, "At ease, soldier," and I exhaled. The air was safe to breathe.

Why would I want to leave? *It's perfect here.*

The tests were stacked on Mr. Reid's desk. This was it. It was all I could do to sit still in my seat; it was like waiting for a birthday gift and praying it'd be that bike you wished for. He slapped the test on my desk, the force of it like a gust of wind in my face.

"What do you make of this?" he said, scowling.

I looked at the score: thirty-two out of thirty-five, a near perfect mark. I lit up like a Christmas tree.

Bloody hell . . . I did it. I did it!

At first, I thought Mr. Reid was messing with me, his way of celebrating my victory. Any minute, he'd crack a smile, pat me on the back, say, "Good on ya! Well done!"

"It's not possible. How did you do it?"

I stared at him, blank-faced. Everyone was watching.

"Not believable, not with your other scores. How did you do it?"

He thinks I cheated.

He crossed his arms, waiting for my response, my confession. The room was silent except for the air blowing out of his nose. All eyes were on me, burning into my skin.

They think I cheated.

"You can explain it to Headmaster Turner," he said, snatching the test from my desk.

I felt the army of eyes studying me. The few who expressed sympathy wrestled with their suspicions. The rest decreed me guilty.

After class, Mr. Reid stomped ahead as if in a race, a race to the gallows. This was a nightmare. *Please, God, wake me up.*

The receptionist sent us in without delay. Mr. Reid, huffing and puffing, could have blown the office down. I took the blows and stood there expressionless, wondering how and why I was there.

Headmaster Turner was enjoying the hosing. There was a sparkle in his eyes—my comeuppance.

"Explain yourself," Headmaster Turner said.

I drew a blank. *What would they believe?*

"Well?"

I'd never cheated. No one back home would think me capable of it.

"It's different, like you said. I didn't know what I was doing wrong, so I borrowed old tests and studied them."

They glared, waiting for me to tell the truth.

I continued, "How could I cheat on an essay question?"

"It doesn't add up," Mr. Reid said, addressing the headmaster as if expecting him to step in and drop the gavel on my New Zealand year.

"Mr. Reid has a point. The variance in your scores is suspicious." He turned to Mr. Reid, "Let's see how she does on the next one."

I joined my next class and couldn't concentrate: the looks on my history classmates' faces haunted me. I struggled to follow Mr. Taylor's lecture and later, Mr. Campbell's. I wrote down every word, but when I reviewed my notes, they made no sense.

"What's wrong?" Mum always knew when something was up.

I didn't answer, couldn't.

"Set yourself down."

I took my usual spot at the kitchen table, but my words were grounded on another planet, a vile one. We should be celebrating. She likes good news; she's always over-the-top delighted.

Mum brought me a cup of tea and sat down beside me. "When you're ready."

We sat quietly and drank our tea, tears dripping into my cup. She passed tissues and shooed the boys away when they wandered in looking for snacks. I wiped my face, blew my nose, and started to talk, but I just cried all the more.

"They think I cheated."

"Who does?"

"Mr. Reid and the headmaster."

"Hogwash!"

Mum's response was immediate, followed by a long pause; she was the master of pauses, each one a hug. Mum slipped back into her chair. "Start from the beginning."

I told her everything: the classroom castigation, Headmaster Turner's reaction, the slander, and the fact that I didn't want to go back. "Maybe I could transfer to Pam's school."

"Hold on a minute. We're not going to let this fly. Bugger that." Mum never used that word. "I'm going to make a little visit tomorrow." She was furious, determined to do a Misty on Mr. Reid and Headmaster Turner.

I looked at her with eyes freshly teared, but these tears didn't flow from sadness or distress. She was prepared to go to war for me. No one had ever done that before. Mum, my Mahuika goddess of fire. *Together we'll burn 'em.*

Smiling, I hugged her. "Thank you."

Her offer and her embrace calmed me, like a babe to the tit.

"It won't make any difference. The only way I can prove I didn't cheat is to ace the next test."

"Let's have a look at that paper."

I pulled it from my stack of notebooks and handed it over. "Mr. Reid wants it back tomorrow."

"Does he now?"

She scanned the paper, then delved deeper into the questions. "Brilliant! We have to celebrate. How 'bout we go for Chinese?"

The dinner was divine. I ordered my favorite dessert: banana fritters topped with ice cream. The following morning, I told Mum that she didn't have to come to school, that I was fine and would prove them wrong with each impending test. She agreed, but I had a hunch she'd call Headmaster Turner for a *wee chat.*

I descended the driveway with care. My shoulder and left hip smarted from yesterday's tumble into the ditch. Walking gingerly, I prepared myself for school. Once off the bus, I knew the scarlet letter C would flash across my chest and remain there until I aced the next test. The pressing requirement to do so made my hands sweat. I wiped them on my uniform.

I was smiling: none of it mattered. I felt light, sublime, yet befuddled. I didn't know what to make of this outburst of emotions, especially considering the big C and the impending efforts I'd have to make to dispel it. I would eventually realize that it had everything to do with Mum's reaction. She'd believed in me, had my back, and was ready to fight for me.

With my shoulders back and my head high, I emerged from the bus, ready to take on any and all naysayers. I walked with a brisk pace and, once in class, acted as if nothing was awry, and it worked: no one mentioned the history fiasco or my moral shortcomings. Morning passed quickly, too quickly. History called. My head spun. My stomach hurt. I didn't want to face him, not today, not ever. I took a deep breath, imagined Mum's "Hogwash!" and entered history. It was gruesome—all eyes were on me—and it was dead quiet. I wanted to run, then I noticed Mr. Reid. He was avoiding eye contact, especially with me. I don't know what Mum did, and I never asked her, but she must have made an impression. He was clearly embarrassed and tongue-tied. He collected himself, cleared his throat, and began today's lecture. His eyes bore into the back wall; they could have peeled paint off it. I wanted an apology but accepted his discomfort as a win. Mum's win. I planned to rub his nose in it with another nearly perfect score.

Chapter Twenty-Eight
A Country Life

WELLIES SCRAPED AGAINST MY CALVES, BURNING MY SKIN RAW. The early morning air was brisk and damp but did not penetrate my thick wool sweater and school blazer. Coats were rare here, as if the country were allergic to them, except for the waxed jackets wealthy wannabe farmers wore. In winter, wool jumpers were the go-to garments, even in rainy conditions. Lanolin-rich fiber kept the rain out and softened my skin, but I couldn't get used to the itch.

I struggled with two buckets, one weighted with milk, the other filled to the brim with scraps. Nicholas's formula slushed near the top, daring to escape. The scent of milk and leftover slop mingled with dung threatened the loss of my breakfast. I stopped breathing through my nose. The fresh cow piles were Nicholas Nickleby's handiwork. He was my new calf: very new—unweaned in fact. Mum bought him for me in an attempt to ensure I experienced a *rounded* country life beyond afternoon pony rides. I had a piglet, too, Hogsnort Rupert. I named him after a New Zealand band. I pinched Nicholas's name from a Dickens serial, *The Adventures of Nicholas Nickleby*. I liked how the twosome sounded: Nicholas Nickleby and his brother, Hogsnort Rupert.

My babies.

I was in a hurry but walked slowly. Milk sloshed about, splashing onto my wellies and the ground. It was nice of Mum to think of me, but I didn't appreciate getting up half an hour earlier to feed my two youngsters. It was not a quick process. I couldn't drop Nicholas's bucket and leave; he didn't know how to drink from a bucket. I was teaching him.

"Good morning, Nicholas."

Baby-mooing, he was waiting for me, his nose pushing through the fence of his pen. Too young to graze in the paddock—he didn't know grass was food—he relied on me, his substitute mum.

"Hungry?"

His eyes were like pools of maple syrup. On sunny days, I could see my reflection in them. I scratched him behind the ears as if he were a dog and smoothed the soft fur on his face. Rubbing the curls between his nose and eyes was like kneading a rug over cement: a thin coat over an iron-hard skull.

"Such a good boy," I said, slipping my fingers into his mouth.

He suckled. Strong cyclical thrusts forced my fingers against the rim of his mouth. I could feel every ridge. Slowly, so as not to scare him, I lowered his mouth into the bucket. The maneuver was flawless, my best attempt so far. Bent over with my fingers in his mouth and milk up my arm, I steadied the pail a good twenty minutes while he suckled. Leftover dregs remained on the bottom, unreachable. In time, he would learn to lick the bucket clean.

"Good boy, Nick. See you later."

I gave him one last pat and rushed over to Hogsnort. Pissed I didn't feed him first, Hogsnort was squealing loud enough to wake the dead.

"Okay, okay, okay! Shut it, you little glutton."

I patted the top of his head—but he was too busy eating to notice—grabbed the buckets, raced to the house, washed my hands and the buckets, put on my school shoes, and bolted down the driveway.

I was soon back in the kitchen. "I missed the bus."

"Again?" Mum shook her head, her brows raised.

I'd missed it yesterday, too.

Farm life didn't come naturally, but Mum wasn't deterred. She regularly sought out new opportunities to induct me. Exasperated by her diligence, I wondered if she'd concluded my future was in agriculture since my grades didn't auger a university placement. Her latest initiative was an arranged weekend at a working farm, the Drummond farm: a *serious* farm according to Greg. The Drummonds had a daughter, Wendy, who was also an exchange student. She was going to New York in September. I liked the Drummonds, and the idea of working on a farm during lambing season sounded cool—cuddling lambs, bottle-feeding orphans—enchanting, and less messy than finger-feeding Nicholas. Greg, the bona fide clodhopper in our family, would take care of Nicholas and Hogsnort while I was away.

Mum dropped me off at the Drummonds'. A Land Rover was parked in the driveway with the engine running. A slight bloke with thin, flaxen hair waited by the truck. I guessed he was about five years older than me. Wendy bounced out of the house, happy to see me and ready to go. They both wore thick jumpers made from natural brown wool. Standing side by side, they looked like a pair of two-legged sheep that'd been recently shorn. I had on my thickest jumper. In an hour's time, I'd wish for a pull-over with the weight of a T-shirt.

"Cheers! Just in time," Wendy said, grabbing my overnight bag. "We're off. Lambing, you know." I didn't know but nodded. She pointed to the guy alongside the truck. "This is Tony."

"Morning," he said, looking at my tennis shoes. "Those won't do. Wendy, get her some wellies."

Wendy ran back inside with my bag and returned with a pair of wellies. They were too big. An extra sock would've made a difference, but Tony and Wendy were already in the truck. He drove slowly over a cattle stop, turned onto a gravel path, and headed into a vast pasture. It seemed to go on forever; I could detect no fences in the distance. When the gravel disappeared, he continued on, going up and over the hills. We left tracks in our wake, flattening the grass and coating it with mud. Everywhere I looked, wooly creatures chomped grass. Dragging their lambs along, ewes ambled for sweeter fare, seemingly unaware that their youngsters suckled beneath them. Occasionally, a pair of lambs played on their own, but most were too young. It was early in the season.

The truck shimmied and jerked. I held tightly to a sidebar with one hand while the other was braced against the back of the front seat. Bouncing made conversation difficult, plus we were separated by high-reaching seats; I could see only the top of Wendy's head. It was dreamy except for the shimmy. I didn't know where we were going or why, and with no expectation to interact—they were silent, eyes facing the front—I allowed my mind to wander. Twenty minutes, maybe more, passed.

"We's here," Tony said, stopping at the edge of a gorge.

He got out, offered zero instructions, and marched into the gorge. Wendy and I followed. He led us down a thin path covered in sheep pellets. It was tough going. I reached for rocks to steady myself, but they were wet and slippery. Turning around, he pointed to the path, "Made by the sheep." He wasn't much of a talker. I think he only spoke because Mrs. Drummond told him to.

We walked and climbed up and down the rocky gorge. Tony traversed the hills like a four-hoofed climber. He was fast and way out ahead. Occasionally, he stopped, not for my benefit but to search the hills. I took a break when he did and looked the direction he was searching, but I saw only more rocks and sheep. We spent hours wandering, climbing up to the top then down again, as we made our way through the gorge.

I was exhausted, hot, and sweating profusely. I ached to strip, lie down on the grass, and let the brisk air cool me. The lambs dotting the country-side no longer looked cute, and I'd stopped ogling the scenery. I counted the pellets at my feet and swore profusely under my breath. This was not what I expected . . . a crazed hiking expedition? My anger rose with each step. I was mad at Mum, the Drummonds, silent Tony, the sheep, and myself for agreeing to come.

"Over there!" Tony yelled, pointing across the gorge. I couldn't make out what he was pointing to. "She's at the bottom."

"It's a ewe in labor. She's having trouble," Wendy said.

Unlike me, she wasn't out of breath, obviously used to these awful afternoon strolls. I looked again and spotted a white wooly patch on the bottom of the gorge. Tony was walking toward her. When Wendy and I reached the ewe, he was huddled over her and had figured out the problem, a breech birth.

"It's all right," Tony said to the ewe, his voice a soft rumble. She bayed, wrestling, trying to get away from his inquiring hands. "Hold her under the arms," he shouted, positioning the ewe between my legs.

I grabbed her and laced my arms under her front legs then locked them around her hard belly. Two tiny feet were hanging between her hind legs. Tony reached inside the ewe under the baby's hooves. The ewe fought back. Her head smacked against my chin. I bit my tongue. Tony twisted and pulled the lamb. The ewe screamed, her bony arms jabbing into mine.

"She'll die if we don't get it out," Tony said, looking at me. "Lamb's already dead."

Finally, the lamb was extracted, its body flat without air, covered with blood and slime, and no bigger than my forearm. The ewe stood up, jumped away from us, and lumbered off, her legs wobbling as if she were drunk.

"She'll be fine. Okay for next season." He left the lamb for the buzzards.

"The ewe's more important than the lamb," Wendy explained. "She'll have many lambs; she's young."

We were looking for ewes in trouble. *Why didn't they say so when we started?*

No longer clueless, I searched for white specks on the ground. The next one we found was walking with a tiny head between its legs. The expired lamb was stuck, its shoulders too big for the ewe to pass on her own. We saved this ewe and the next. The search, triage, and midwifery maneuvers were thrilling but increasingly depressing—all these dead babies. Tony and Wendy focused on the ewes and were unmoved by the lambs we left for the buzzards. I understood but became disheartened when lamb after lamb failed to breathe. Earlier on, climbing up and over the hills, I was ready for the day to end, but now I didn't want to leave, not until we had a successful birth.

The next mother-at-risk also struggled with a breech birth, but she was early on in labor. The lamb was alive, and Tony managed to turn it. It was plumper than the others but wasn't breathing. Tony cleared the lamb's nose and mouth, shook its chest, and was about to blow into its mouth when the little fellow mewed. I gasped in delight. Tony laid the lamb next to its mother, and we backed off.

"I think we can call it a day," Tony said, flashing a toothy grin.

"Too right!" I said, laughing. They both responded with heavy laughter.

I climbed up the hill with a huge smile, taking back my earlier curses.

Tony dropped us off in front of the house. Opening the door, my nose was bombarded with the smell of yeast and strawberries. It was bread-baking day. Fresh loaves covered the counter.

"We freeze most of them for the week's use," Mrs. Drummond said. She handed me a fresh slice covered with her homemade strawberry jam. "Go stand by the fire and warm up. Tea will be ready soon."

"Can I help?"

"No need. I'm nearly there. Wendy will help finish up."

The jam and bread melted in my mouth like homespun ice cream. My back to the fire and front facing the kitchen, I watched them work. Wendy and her mother spoke quietly and moved effortlessly around each other, a familiar dance between individuals who danced often. Mr. Drummond came in from the fields. His skin was ruddy, his hair sandy and sparse on top. He had a taut body, unlike Mrs. Drummond's; she did not traverse the hills. He nodded to me, lit a pipe—a quirk seemingly essential for New Zealand men of a certain age—and sat down on a cushy chair opposite the fire.

"I hear ya saved our ewes . . . and a wee one," he said, waving his pipe at me.

"Too right we did," I said, smiling.

He grinned, grabbed the evening paper, and started reading.

I returned his grin. *Too right,* slang for *absolutely,* was one of those phrases I'd adopted as my own. I felt like a quasi-local when I used it, and New Zealanders found it amusing when I did, which I also liked.

My legs were sore. The fire eased the stiffness and warmed my body. I felt ever so satisfied: I'd saved lives!

The day's exertion amplified my appetite; I was famished. My stomach rumbled, and saliva rose in my mouth, incited by the bountiful aromas coming from the kitchen. I helped Wendy carry out the food and resisted digging in until Mr. Drummond finished saying grace. Everything tasted good, and I ate with abandon—two helpings of steamed pudding!—despite having vowed to eat like a mouse over the weekend.

After dinner, everyone parked in the sitting room by the fire. A wooden spinning wheel and large bag of wool nudged the sofa. Mrs. Drummond motioned me over and demonstrated how to operate the wheel, explaining different spinning techniques. She told me tales of spinning and the history of New Zealand spinning wheels. I was familiar with *Sleeping Beauty's* wheel but not the portable Thumbelina wheel made by the *Sleeping Beauty* company founded in Auckland. I spent the evening spinning, a vexing exercise that produced a measly ball of yarn only two inches in diameter. Washed but not bleached, the wool sweated lanolin. My hands were as soft as a baby's bottom, but my first specimen was diabolical and unusable in my mind, some sections as thin as thread, others thick and clumpy.

I showed it to Mrs. Drummond. She grinned. "It won't matter once you knit it. The uneven parts will merge together. You'll see." I wasn't so sure.

The following day, I milked a cow and sheared a sheep. The poor thing looked tortured: there were nicks on her belly and under her arms. Another evening in front of the fire produced a wool hat. Mrs. Drummond was right; the wool merged beautifully, and my hat looked splendid. Departing, I thanked her for everything, expressing how fortunate I was to experience New Zealand farming firsthand. I was so effusive, she decided to repeat the experience, inviting all the exchange students in the vicinity.

Three weeks later, six lucky candidates arrived at Drummond Farm. Pam and I would be the only ones staying the night. The atmosphere was unlike my previous day-in-the-life-of-a-farmer stay. Docking weekend was celebratory, crazy, and more like a carnival. Extra crews were on hand, plus a professional shearing squad. The sheep were rounded up by Tony and two farmhands riding motorbikes. Mr. Drummond's sheepdogs performed the close-in work, nipping at the legs of itinerant sheep.

Hundreds of ewes and lambs were herded into an enclosure and separated into different pens. Their cries of protest hung over us, unrelenting.

We were assigned to the lambs. There were four stations: docking (severing tails to prevent fly-induced parasitic infections), banding (castrating with an elastic band), tagging (applying ear identification tabs), and flocking (vaccination). We would take turns. My first job was to catch the little buggers and take them to station one. It wasn't hard. The pen was so crowded that all I had to do was bend down and grab. I carried my first victim to the docking station, flipped it over to determine its sex, slid him into the docking cradle, and held him down. Tony took a hot iron and pressed it onto my lamb's tail an inch from its bum. The lamb cried, the iron sizzled, and the smell of burning meat overpowered. I would get used to it. The tail dropped to the ground. Tony held the iron on the open wound, cauterizing it. I moved my sizzled lamb to station two—banding. A ranch hand unfamiliar to me picked up a plier-like tool, attached a thick rubber band to its tip, and slipped the band over the lamb's testicles.

"The band stops blood flow," he explained. "They'll fall off in a matter of weeks." I pictured shriveled testicles scattered over the fields like sheep pellets, but bigger. "Doesn't hurt 'em."

Off to the next station: Mr. Drummond clamped a tag to the lamb's ear. Lastly, my little guy was immunized against a slew of scary diseases.

I mastered every station but preferred the last one—the least mercenary. The day was brilliant, like attending an interactive state fair. As if in competition, we rushed from station to station, eager to doctor the most lambs and counting the number we'd docked or banded. We dined on Mrs. Drummond's goodies and quenched our thirst with Mr. Drummond's beer. But I was glad when they all went home, when it was only Pam, me, and the Drummonds sitting by the fire.

I took another stab at spinning. Mrs. Drummond saved the wool from the sheep I'd shorn. I was making another hat, but this time every step, from the sheep's back to the finished product, was rendered by me.

The room was homey like I remembered. The scent of pipe tobacco and burning wood was familiar, as were the last traces of dinner and Earl Grey tea, but it wasn't as peaceful as my last visit. Mr. Drummond hunkered in the same chair, a pipe between his lips, reading the paper.

Mrs. Drummond sat in her chair, a worn yet cuddly-comfy armchair, and flipped through a magazine. Pam appropriated the rocking chair; Wendy, the sofa. Both were knitting. The family engaged as before: Mr. Drummond's voice was as deep and soft, and the mother-daughter banter was just as speckled with the occasional cackle—in a good way—from Mrs. Drummond. Nonetheless, something was off, preventing the room from settling and reaching that sweet spot where shared intimacy thrived without breaching personal boundaries.

The difference was Pam. She fidgeted and chattered about nothing in particular, purging silence like a bothersome fly.

She didn't like quiet.

I could not stop watching her, but I heard little of what she said. There was something about the moment, something I needed to pay attention to, but I couldn't parse what it was. Her knitting needles clicked in sync with her banter. Counting the clicks under my breath, I had one of those aha moments. I sat up with a start. The yarn in my lap dropped to the floor, and the spinning wheel slowed to a stop. I knew what it was, and it wasn't complicated; not a brainteaser or a shocking revelation.

I like the quiet.

I'd reveled in the day's chaos: the rapport between strangers, and the kinship with my friends; but I was just as happy sitting by the fire doing nothing at all, maybe more so. A preference for private spaces had been my norm prior to New Zealand, a choice shaped by growing up in a house of ten where space was limited. And I was always looking for space to hide from Steve at home and Hunter at school.

Stirred, my mind awhirl, I continued watching Pam and Wendy. They chatted amiably, their knitting needles tapping, swaying, and prancing like my thoughts. I was a child again, alone, walking, exploring, conversing with ants, and flirting with bees. Feeling the presence of my younger self was strange, but I embraced her, collecting the magical gifts she bestowed as if I were hitching a ride on a hairy bumble bee. In the moment, I realized aloneness wasn't feeble, singular, or a mere device for escapism. Solitude was a gift, a legitimate choice.

Chapter Twenty-Nine
Cinderella

I ACED MY NEXT HISTORY TEST, THE ONE AFTER, AND THE ONE after that. When Mr. Reid returned our exams, he dropped mine on my desk and walked on as if it were unoccupied. Regurgitating facts and figures bereft of opinion worked for all my subjects. I stopped worrying about passing, but the encroaching GCE exams kept me sober and diligent.

My calendar was as busy as ever. Weekdays began with farm chores and ended with homework. Now that I was an adept speaker, AFS engagements tripled. I presented at local events (the Lions Club, the Rotary Club, my siblings' schools, regional secondary schools, and AFS meetings), took part in an unending string of school activities (badminton competitions, Māori club performances, debates, parties, and sleepovers), and attended family endeavors (cricket and rugby matches, music recitals, church fetes, pony clubs, carnivals, and beach outings).

Even school breaks were packed with nonstop activity. The school year was divided into four terms commencing in January and running through mid-December, with a two-week break between the first three terms and a six-week summer break. I spent the first school holiday camping with my family on the bank of an almost deserted lake. The trout were as big as salmon and were delicious cooked over the campfire. I spent the next break touring the South Island with my exchange student colleagues, performing our quasi-talent show at every stop.

Pam and I made a deal before the trip to intervene on each other's behalf to help us stick to our diets, promising to use physical force if necessary and grabbing and tossing high-caloric fare before it reached our mouths. The oath was toast before we landed on the South Island.

Our first stop was Wellington (on the southern tip of the North Island), the capital of New Zealand and the home of parliament. We sat in on a session and, thereafter, met the prime minister for lunch. The spread was deluxe, the cream cakes divine. It was imperative to be polite—we represented the United States of America after all—mustn't decline the prime minister's hospitality; that would be rude. We weren't rude, then or later. Every stop along the way begat a feast, sometimes more than once a day. Pam and I were very polite, indulging as if every meal were a once-a-year Thanksgiving binge. I gained ten pounds, eighteen in total since Cyclone Mary.

I wasn't the only one battling the scales: all but one exchange student piled on the average twenty pounds we were warned about. Our sole outlier, Chris, lost thirty pounds, having spent her first three months in the hospital with granular fever. She missed first term and might not graduate with her high school class, but she looked great. I wanted to look like her—hungry.

That first week, when I lost eight pounds, I imagined going home two sizes smaller, walking down the gangplank wearing the latest fashions—a decorative belt adorning my svelte waist, a miniskirt exposing slender legs, my arms lithe at my sides—unrecognizable, like Cinderella at the ball. That wasn't going to happen. I needed a fairy godmother working overtime, performing magic on my body as well as my clothes—none of which fit—and I needed her now.

Like Cinderella, I was going to the ball (three balls in fact): two end-of-year school balls, mine and Pam's, and a royal ball. Princess Alexandra, granddaughter of King George V, was in New Zealand on the Queen's business. The entire town was abuzz. Tickets were hard to come by, but Mum and Dad managed four. Dad nabbed two because he ran a business: the royal visit's primary purpose was to enhance trade. Mum got the other two like everyone else, by standing in line. I would be going with a family friend, Patrick, who was a few years older than me. Gran was making both mine and Mum's gowns. I had to lose the ten pounds or, better yet, a stone (New Zealanders measured weight in stones, a unit of fourteen pounds); otherwise, my dress would require a mountain of fabric.

"Our fitting's next Saturday," Mum said. "Gran's coming at three thirty."

"Great," I said, sarcasm souring my tongue.

Gran was an excellent seamstress, but I needed a fairy godmother's touch.

"Try not to give her the silent treatment," Mum said for the umpteenth time.

"I don't mean to. She makes me nervous."

Gran was a stepmother, not a fairy godmother, and she scared me. Small to Mum's tall but with thrice the energy, Gran was a drill sergeant, brazen and sharp. My mouth refused to open around her, which riled her to no end.

"It's her way. She won't bite."

I envisioned yipping dogs nipping at my ankles, their owners alleging, "All bark—won't bite."

"Snack? I sliced up some veggies." Mum carried over a plate of carrots, celery, cottage cheese, and Swedish crispbread that tasted like burnt cardboard.

After the South Island trip, I resorted to fasting. Mum ignored my absence at the table for two days, then insisted I eat. A pattern evolved: two-day fast, two-day gorge, repeat. Mum stepped in. She proposed a sensible diet, one we'd tackle together.

"Any apples?" I asked, looking at the meager vegetables.

I gnawed on the phony bread and crunched apple slices and carrots to free my teeth of the bread's dusty grains.

"What about your hair?" Mum asked. "An updo maybe?"

"I'm not sure, but I think I'd like to wear it up."

"I'll set you up at my salon."

"What about you?"

With her mouth full and two fingers balancing a celery stick smothered with cottage cheese, she managed a garbled, "Mine's too short, what could they do?"

"You should come, too; get a trim and a comb-out. Please?"

Mum lost ten pounds that first week. I lost three. When Gran arrived for our fitting, I refused to look at the tape measure and could think of nothing to say to her. She tugged and pulled at my body. I remained mute. She brought a full-length mirror. I avoided looking at it. Since third grade, I'd endured a contentious relationship with scales and mirrors. Neither could be trusted, especially mirrors; each and every one was an arcade twin, warping my body shorter and wider, exaggerating every flaw.

Gran tugged harder. "Fabric's not very giving, but it's comely."

It was beautiful, shimmery, and the color of spring hyacinths, just shy of violet. Gran's comment was an invite, but I didn't respond. I had things to say, but my mouth wouldn't cooperate. Mum came to my rescue, acquainting Gran on every minuscule endeavor the boys and Sarah had accomplished since her last visit. The intervention was obvious; Gran was noticeably the wiser. I appreciated Mum's effort but ignored both of them. Animal taunts and old nicknames thundered in my head. All I could think about was a pretty dress on an ugly *cow*.

On the morning of the royal ball, Mum and I faced the scales. She stepped up first.

"Two-stone-two!" She was ecstatic.

A thirty-pound loss was not tantamount to slim on Mum—her clothes draped loose at the waist, but she appeared just as broad when viewed from the front—though you wouldn't have known it. Cutting loose a celebratory dance, she shimmied like a chorus girl.

My turn. Praying for a stone, I slowly stepped on the scales. "Ten pounds."

"Smashing! Come on, that's brilliant," Mum said, noticing I wasn't dancing. "Mind you, I had . . . still do, have a lot more to lose," she said, reassuring me. I managed a half smile in return.

Gran did a beautiful job tailoring the dress to my figure; no bulges even before the weight loss. The gown encompassed two layers: a violet underlay topped with a leaf-embroidered translucent shift. The dress draped to the floor and had an empire waist, three-quarter length sleeves, and velvet trim. Standing in front of the mirror, I examined the dress and me in it, scrutinizing every angle. It looked nice, not a size eight nice—but nice all the same.

Mum wore a two-piece gown: a sleek black skirt and a glittery gold top that highlighted her dark hair and brown eyes. She dazzled.

Jac and Gus would approve.

We both felt airy: if not Cinderella herself, a close cousin. Dad was equally handsome in tux and tails.

He smiled from ear to ear. "I'm the luckiest chap going to the ball, by far! Gorgeous . . . the two of you." His eyes were true, and I believed him. "Come on, give us a twirl."

I obliged, and my dress cooperated, swirling as regal as its color. Neither Mum nor Dad offered advice to "stand taller, push your shoulders back, and suck in your gut," so I'd look slimmer, better, more presentable. They thought I looked pretty, and so did I.

"Smashing!" Greg said.

Mark, Ricky, and Sarah showered all three of us with compliments. Their faces were bright, and so was mine. Gran primped and tucked, smoothing our outfits, and took pictures. She used an entire roll trying to capture a few snaps sans children.

Patrick was dashing in his tux, too, but was very shy. He hardly said a word in the car. Mum and Dad chatted up front. I sat as still as possible, not wanting to crease my dress or mess my hair. Patrick looked straight ahead. I looked out the window. Thankfully, this was no ordinary dance, or I would've been counting the minutes to its end. He was going to be no fun.

We approached the last few blocks to Napier's finest theater. Limousines and Rolls-Royce sedans lined the streets. Having deposited their auspicious patrons, suit-clad drivers leaned against fancy vehicles, smoking and waiting. They'd have a long wait—we arrived an hour before the official start. A crowd blocked the theater entrance. Everyone dressed to the nines in exquisite gowns, expensive jewelry, top hats, and tuxes with penguin tails.

Once inside, Mum found our table. Despite her size, she'd darted through the crowd, maneuvering like Tinkerbell. We were right in the middle. Perfect.

"Wee cracker!" Mum said, super pleased, "we'll see everything from here."

"For sure," Dad said, helping Mum to her seat.

Patrick mimicked Dad but shoved my chair instead of nudging it, causing the legs to screech against the wooden floor, but nobody noticed: a roar of voices covered our faux pas. Mum's eyes danced around the room and Dad attempted to wake Patrick while I inhaled the room, a night of nights I wanted to remember whether I danced with a prince or not. The scene was more magical than the starry-eyed balls I saw watching Disney movies as a child. . . . And this was real.

Mum had insisted I take ballroom dancing lessons, but someone should have sent Patrick, too. We didn't dance; we shuffled, his shoes hitting mine and vice versa. Dad cut in, rescuing me. We waltzed almost as smoothly as he did with Mum. After two dances, Dad circled back to our table, deposited me, and whirled off with Mum. I was watching them when the orchestra stopped playing and everyone stood up. The music shifted into marching band mode. "God Save the Queen," echoed off the walls. I stood on tiptoes like everyone else, looked left and right, and whispered, "Where is she? Where is she? Do you see her?"

I got a glimpse of a tiara and then an ear graced with dark hair. Finally, the crowd parted, and Princess Alexandra floated toward me. She was beautiful, a vision of old-school royalty: tall and regal, hair thick and bejeweled with diamonds, comely figure adorned in a traditional gown.

Cinderella bedazzled Napier, and I waltzed right alongside her.

After dinner, the princess and her husband, Sir Angus Ogilvy, mingled. He was the more gregarious partner. I watched him work the room, charming the ladies and engaging the men in serious discourse. At one point, he was so close I heard him discussing New Zealand farming.

I imagined sashaying over, adding my two cents on inhumane docking methods, and Sir Angus siding with me because my argument was so very convincing.

He's coming over here!

Mum held her breath. "I think he's coming to our table," she whispered, a bit too loudly.

The *Sir* sat down, right next to Dad!

I was speechless. Sir Angus shook hands with Dad and asked him about work. They talked surveying. Sir Angus knew a lot about surveying or was an adept pretender. Dad changed subjects: "Catherine, here, is an exchange student from the States."

"How exciting," Sir Angus said, staring at me, waiting for a response.

I froze.

"Whereabouts in America?"

I opened my mouth, said hello, and told him about my hometown. Me and Sir Angus had a chat.

The school balls were not glamorous, but they were lively, festive, and fun. Mine was the better of the two. Pam and I double-dated, accompanied by different dates for each ball. She chose the guys. As luck would have it, Pam, who was boy crazy, ended up at an all-girls school. Pam and I swapped schools for a week. Regional school exchanges were a local exchange student tradition and was a godsend for Pam. She made the most of her coed stint, entrancing the prefect boys, pairing up with one during the week, and, subsequently, dating all the cute ones. Her current beau was Gary. I went to Pam's school ball with Gary's friend Brian, who was also a prefect and friend of mine. For my school ball, I went with Tim, another friend of Gary's. He was older and attending university.

I wore the same dress but did not go to the hairstylist—no bouffant updo with cascading ringlets. Brian was awkward, like Patrick, but Tim and I got along fabulously. We chatted in the car on the way to the dance. I didn't care if my dress wrinkled; I sat facing him and let my body sink into the seat. There were no klutzy breaks in our conversation or excruciating silences.

The hall was packed. Annabelle and Faith rushed over. We formed a girl scrum, jabbering about dresses and dates, while Tim took off to get drinks and chat with his mates. When the band started, Tim pulled me onto the dance floor. We danced as if we'd taken lessons together—no bruised toes. Whether we danced slowly or quickly, it didn't matter. We rocked.

Someone tapped me on the shoulder. I turned around, giggling. *How formal, but the bloke's got it wrong. He should be tapping Tim's shoulder.* My giggle vanished the second I identified who it was. Headmaster Turner stood with his hand out, a no-hard-feelings look on his face.

I took his hand and placed my other hand on his shoulder. It felt odd, but I didn't stiffen when his free hand rested on my lower back. We danced a sort-of waltz to a slow rock tune. I waited for him to speak.

"So . . . what parts of New Zealand have you visited? Did you get to the South Island?"

I thought of Headly and our first amicable conversation.

"Yes, I did, over winter break. It's true what they say. It's breathtaking. Made it all the way to Invercargill and Slope Point."

We talked geography: names and places he'd seen, I'd seen and what I should see. At first, my words came out wooden: I was holding out for an apology about his role in labeling me a cheat, but I let it go somewhere in the middle of our dance. I was a different person than that frightened girl who accidentally disparaged him nearly a year ago. I didn't need his apology or approval. When the music stopped, we parted graciously, our chapter closed.

I wrote home two entire pages about the royal ball, followed by a letter describing the school balls. Several weeks passed, but no letters arrived in the post—nothing about *The Ball.*

Three letters finally came on the same day, despite being posted days apart. I tore into them, excited to hear what my family thought. The letters were from Mom, Barry, and Joe. They wrote in awe and asked scads of questions. Was Sir Angus Ogilvy a knight? Did he carry a sword? Did the princess arrive by coach? Did I really waltz? The boys followed their questions with Halloween drawings, scrawled images depicting the costumes they'd worn. Under the drawings, they described the scary houses they'd visited, the size of their candy hoard, and how long they expected it to last.

It had been my job to take the younger boys trick-or-treating. Mary took them this year. Halloween pumpkins and visions of dancing skeletons stuck in my head. *I missed Halloween.*

My feelings stumbled, smashing into each other. I felt guilty for not being there and sad I had missed out on the birthdays, sports victories, vacations, and holidays. I thought of last year's Halloween: helping the boys make their costumes, walking them door to door, holding John Patrick, clutching Greg's hand when we approached a scary house, watching Mom and Dad suit up in their costumes—mummies wrapped in torn sheets—and promising I'd check all the candy before letting the kids partake.

Afflicted with a bad case of absence-makes-the-heart-grow-fonder, even minor and vexing incidents ripened into precious events. Mary was voted yell queen (head cheerleader) at St. Rose. Had I been home, I would have been jealous; but, reading her letter, I felt only delight. I missed helping the boys make Easter eggs, missed cooking up dishes that widened their eyes, missed playing cards with Tom, missed the birthday parties and making the birthday cakes (each one expressly designed for the birthday honoree), missed going to the park, and missed seeing the boys play baseball; how they ran bases and swung bats so differently and yet so alike.

Most perplexing of all, I missed Mom. Her letters disarmed me, each one chipping away at the resentment I harbored against her for making me her maid and babysitter, for quashing all hopes of just being a kid, for not protecting me, for not hugging me. I pictured my mother's face. Two images emerged: in one, her facial muscles are taut, and she is about to yell or just did; in the other, she's smiling, and laugh lines punctuate her features, crinkling her eyes and nose. The fraught face was the one I knew best. The smiley face was for friends, customers at work, or strangers on the street. What struck me most, as I read her letters, was the lurking sense of calm in them. No matter how hard I tried, I could not remember calm in her stance or on her face. But it was there in her letters. There was also love; I couldn't deny it. She wrote only of everyday occurrences, but she included me, as if I were still there, as if she wanted me there. She included me not as her maid, her babysitter, or her ally, but as me—her daughter.

> We all sure do miss you // There are so many things you did we all just took for granted. Now I really know how many things you did. I was frantic last night trying to help all the boys with their homework. They had to write riddles, and you are so good at those things. Also, the bath and hair washing! The little boys probably won't get a bath or their hair washed untill you get back!! ...

I wondered if she, too, found it easier to love from a distance . . . to love me?

It wasn't only family letters that turned me into emotional mush. One of my AFS duties was writing letters to friends, teachers, city leaders, and other AFS members. A few ended up in the newspaper. My table-of-eight friends sent both collective and solo letters. The pages were filled with school activities I had zero interest in. I didn't care about homecoming decorations or how many touchdowns the team scored. But the tone of their letters unnerved me. The words on the page were written as if to a true friend rather than to someone who'd appropriated their circle for cover.

Letters, both when writing and reading them, did not instill in me a desire to go home. I found the whole process disorienting, perplexing, and scary; the distance between us, more than seven thousand miles, was comforting. They were writing to the girl who left, the one I ran away from. They didn't know me, not this me. How could they? The letters I sent home detailed my New Zealand life—everyday occurrences, notable adventures, and the makings of a day, a week, a month—but not the scent of being here, not the intimacy, the flesh and blood of it. They hadn't waltzed in my shoes at a royal ball, or inhaled the aroma of tea while discussing parliamentary customs with a prime minister, or felt the energy of a crowd enthralled by your every word, or felt what it was like to suddenly become someone great, someone cool, someone fabulous: to see yourself differently in the eyes of other people.

The last act of my year was approaching like a slow-moving storm. How had time passed so quickly? Eying my reflection in the mirror, I looked like the Michelin Man. Reentry dread had driven me to the refrigerator, cupboards, candy aisle, tea shops, and bakeries. I'd regained my precious ten pounds. My jeans didn't snap. My T-shirts were stretched out of shape. Stuffed into my summer uniform, the gingham frock looked and felt like a sausage skin.

I was meant to go home model-skinny with my family and friends in awe, but the end was nearing, and I was fatter still. I pictured them gaping at my frame and dismissing all I'd done as if my year had been eviscerated, erased like Cinderella's finery at the stroke of midnight.

Chapter Thirty

Father Time

"BYE, AND THANKS," I SAID, WAVING TO THE BUS DRIVER AS HE pulled away.

It would be the last time I said goodbye. *Another last, a month of lasts.* I wasn't fond of this driver or his bus, but I felt a deep longing watching the bus disappear. The ride to school and back was long, bumpy, and noisy, yet I stood somber, gazing as if a passionate affair had come to an end.

Thinking about *lasts* was depressing. Mum suggested focusing on irritants I wouldn't miss. We played a little game; every annoyance awarded a rating. Mr. Reid was a first-class *last*—he would not be missed.

Looking up our steep driveway, I shouted, "Bloody last climb, thank you very much!"

Six sheep blocked the gate. "Shoo. Out of the way. Move it!"

I pushed the gate against their wooly behinds. Three took no notice, but the others eyed me as if I were an annoying flea. Shoving the leaden gate, I managed to clear an opening big enough to squeeze through.

Reflecting on my last day of school lifted my mood, and the going-home blues melted away. I ran at the sheep, laughing as they scattered and yelling, "I did it! I did it! I bloody well did it!" not caring whether anyone was in earshot. *Bloody* was a favorite New Zealand swear word, one inherited from Britain. Mild and not that offensive, it was oh so useful: bloody hell, bloody well, bloody to anything added extra impact. I would miss using it among people who appreciated its adroitness.

It was a brilliant day. My goodbye presentation was dead-on perfect. I had them eating out of my hands, laughing on cue, and thunderously clapping at the end. I heard Headmaster Turner laughing. He even complimented my performance, saluting me in front of the entire student body. *That was de-li-cious.*

And, hallelujah, I passed my GCE exams. I couldn't wait to tell Mum.

I grabbed a stick and charged the sheep, pretending to fence with them. "Olé, ya wooly buggers! Take that!"

My stick sword sank a good four inches into the sheep's wool. Withdrawing, I pulled out a ball of it. Tossing the weapon, I ran up the hill, my arms held out like Maria in *The Sound of Music*.

"Zip-a-dee-doo-dah, zip-a-dee-ay. . . . What a *beautiful* day. I'm going to graduate!"

Exam week was brutal, and so was studying, but it was all worth it: five GCEs and three UEs (University Entrance). UE credit was awarded to students achieving high GCE scores, thus bypassing the exam requirement. I had three: art history, English, and history.

"Yes, Mr. Reid, a UE in History! Ha! Chew on that!"

Out of breath, I carried on up the hill at a slower pace. Halfway up, I spotted Misty.

"No offense, girl, but I'm not gonna miss you. I'd rather take another GCE—"

Three days ago, the she-devil tried to break my toe. I was buckling her saddle, and she stomped on my foot and wouldn't let up. Screaming, cursing, and shoving her made zero difference. I was stuck and at a loss until I remembered to pull on her mouthpiece. It worked.

My toes still smarted. I searched for Nicholas; I knew I would miss him. There was no sign of him. *He must be in the North paddock.* Beyond the hills, I could see the rugged cliffs abutting Hawke's Bay. Gran's house sat atop one. I wondered what she was up to, afternoon tea most probably. *She did have good biscuits.* To my surprise, I was going to miss her; nobody does cantankerous like Gran. She'd make a good character actress, particularly if she played Katherine Hepburn as a crotchety old lady—an endearing crotchety old lady once you got to know her.

The sky was pale, dulled by the direct heat of the sun. I took off my glasses and wiped the sweat between my nose and across my forehead. Sweat dripped down my back and between my thighs.

"No more kewpie-doll frocks!" I shouted while prying the sweat-soaked smock from my back. Mum was donating the abomination—next year's hand-me-down—but I was keeping my winter uniform as a souvenir.

With a pep in my step, I set off again; I couldn't wait to tell Mum about my exams.

After one break and then another, I reached the house and ran inside, but all was quiet. She wasn't home—nobody was. My stomach growled. Back to dieting, I hadn't eaten much all day. I dropped my things on the kitchen table and went searching for snacks. Finding nothing of interest in the cupboards and no fruit in the bowl, I shimmied over to the fridge.

Mum must be shopping.

I opened the refrigerator, froze in motion—one hand in midair—and screamed. The refrigerator fan moaned, and so did I. Eyes wide, my mind in shock, I couldn't believe what I was seeing. Hogsnort's head was in the fridge. He was looking back at me.

HOGSNORT!

His face was the color of frozen fat. Tiny lines of fresh blood ran down one cheek. His eyes were cloudy, but his ears pricked forward as they always did. His nose was still pink, and it pointed accusingly at me, as if I'd swung the ax. I slammed the refrigerator door and ran out of the kitchen and right into Mum.

"Why didn't you tell me about Hogsnort?"

"Don't be silly. You knew he wasn't a pet."

"You could have warned me. I came home to find his head in the fridge! I've been feeding him since he was a baby."

"You *and* the boys," she reminded me. I often avoided slop-feeding. Greg had taken over most of Hogsnort's feedings.

"Doesn't matter. I practically fainted. Couldn't you have at least wrapped him up?"

"No reason to bust a gut," she said, depositing the bags on the counter. I fired a look of outrage, but she countered with, "He'll make a luscious Christmas ham."

"God, no! I'm not having any."

"Suit yourself."

I stomped out of the kitchen. Too pissed about Hogsnort to tell her my news, I groused for an hour in my bedroom until I couldn't stand it any longer. I had to tell her. I told Mum everything. Plus, I yearned for the highlight of my day, our afternoon chat. When I got my results, I'd pictured myself running into the kitchen and firing off my scores, her face ablaze with delight. I didn't know whether to blame Hogsnort or her for our tiff. I didn't like or dislike Hogsnort, but finding his head in the fridge was horror-movie creepy.

She could've warned me.

I returned to the kitchen, huffing and puffing down the hallway.

"Better?" Mum asked.

"Not really." I glared at her. "But I have some news."

She stopped what she was doing. During the prolonged wait for my results, she was my rock, and when her eyes caught mine, I realized she knew I had my exam results. "Go on," she said calmly.

"Well," I began, playing cagey and suppressing a grin.

"Come on, don't make me beg."

"Passed them all!"

"Crikey! Knew it."

I fell into her arms, a bear hug like no other.

"Three UEs, too: art history, English, and history!"

"Blow me down! No cooking tonight, we're going out."

She called Dad and held the phone out to me, but I shook my head, "You tell him."

I watched her light up. A stranger might've mistaken her enthusiasm for a triumph of her own.

I did not eat the Christmas ham, but the steamed pudding and brandy sauce were out of this world. My serving included a hidden coin, a good luck omen for the new year. The dessert was but one of many differences between Christmas here and back home: we wore shorts instead of coats; the news captions exposed Santa surfing and sailing in swim trunks; our Christmas tree was not buried in gifts, though we each received a few well-considered presents; Christmas crackers were a place-setting essential; and I'd cooked many a Christmas dinner but had never before been on a first-name basis with the main course.

It was a cheerful day, intoxicatingly free of tension. No fuss. No hassles. No bickering. No presents returned.

After Christmas, we went to the beach. Another *last* that brought me to tears during the long drive, while lying awake at night in my bed, and intermittently throughout the day. I bodysurfed without one wipeout, swam and sunbathed without getting a sunburn, and welcomed a string of friends: some just for the day, some camping out in our yard for days. I would miss all things *beach*, except *pāua* (abalone) fishing. Energized by the calendar and with my last days approaching, Dad was determined to do a country-life campaign focused on coastal living, starting with diving for dinner.

Pāua hunting sounded brilliant. I might have declined Dad's offer had I known about the bruises I'd collect on my knees, elbows, hips, and ribs, but probably not; a solo adventure with Dad was hard to pass up. *Pāua* were delicious to eat, and their shells were a prized material used by Māori to make jewelry and adorn sculptures. They live on rocky coasts, where they attach themselves like cement to the rocks. Hunting them required diving skills, a knife, a net, goggles, and guts. When I agreed to go, I didn't know about the knife or *guts*.

A knife and net dangled from Dad's waist, and goggles protected his eyes. I was slathered in sunscreen and also possessed a knife, a net, and a pair of goggles—my gadgets the only parity with Dad. He dove in, passing right through a giant wave. I waded out timidly.

"Dive!" Dad yelled.

Afraid of a wipeout, I resisted until the water reached my chest and there was no other option but to swim for the rocks where he was waiting. Dad explained the process, "Uproot 'em off the rocks, and drop 'em in your net. Watch out for the waves."

He disappeared under the water. I ducked my head under and watched him pry off an oversized specimen. He dumped it in his net and tackled another. Spotting a rock covered with the little monsters, I dove for it but never made it. A wave seized me, throwing me against the rocks and pummeling my arm and shoulder. Another wave smashed me against a different rock formation, one further away from the beach. I tried to grab on, but the slippery surface and clusters of sharp shells made it impossible. I grabbed seaweed and embraced rocky outcrops, shells, and anything that would keep me from bashing against the rocks or being carried farther out to sea. I made no further attempt to collect *Pāua*. Afraid to let go, I held on to branches of kelp and used my feet to push off from the rocks. I caught bruises while Dad filled both his and my net. *Pāua* hunting topped my will-not-miss list. They were tasty roasted over the fire, but if I ever wanted them again, I'd buy them or, better yet, order them in a restaurant.

New Year's spawned crowds of partiers; our little beach was private no more. We and an array of friends and strangers launched Dad's latest batch of home brew. We sang and drank around a bonfire, the flames rising a good eight feet. Pam was with us, and, true to form, she brought a beau for me. He was cute and a master at making out, but I spent most of the evening with Mum and Dad—right where I wanted to be.

When midnight rang, we drank champagne and sang "God Save the Queen" followed by "Auld Lang Syne." I never understood the fixation over the Queen—she wasn't even a Kiwi—yet "God Save the Queen" was played more frequently than their own national anthem. As for "Auld Lang Syne," it fit my going-home blues best.

The crackle of dry wood competed with the circle of beer-satiated crooners. People, mere shadows in the dark, danced around the fire, faces glowing in the fire light. I memorized the expressions of the people I knew. Mark focused intently on the lyrics, Greg performed a war dance of his own making, Mum sang loudly and, at times, off-key, Dad's lips trembled every time the pitch swelled, and Pam had her eyes on a stranger. My voice cracked every time the chorus came round: "Should auld acquaintance be forgot."

I don't know how many times my voice cracked—these people knew a lot of verses—but when the last verse ended and people embraced, cheering and hollering in the New Year, Mum leaned over and whispered, "You won't be forgotten."

Chapter Thirty-One

Homecoming

LAMBS PLUMP ON SWEET GRASS AND UNAWARE OF WHAT WAS coming frolicked under tender weeping willows. By month's end, only their mums would dot the hills—naked mums baying for their young, packaged for Sunday dinner. Leaning against the fence separating the manicured lawn and the paddock, I noted how neatly the sheep tended the fields; they clipped the grass more uniformly than Dad's mower. Dew and spider webs snared the sun's morning rays. The sky was cloudless. A translucent contour of the moon perched above the horizon. Doleful I would not see this view or the bay beyond again, I imprinted it in my mind, hoping it would never fade.

It was time to go.

I didn't say goodbye to Misty but did traipse down the South paddock to pet Nicholas's curly forelock. He, too, would be gone next year: steaks for the table.

Looking up, I imagined seeing the night sky, one so different from its northern cousin. The southern Milky Way was exactly like the pictures I'd seen in science books: star soup. While at the beach that first month, Dad had shown me how to locate the Southern Cross.

When will I search for it again?

Walking toward the house—*my home*—I drew a picture of it in my mind, coloring every detail: reddish bricks, white trim, lace curtains, and purple passion fruit.

I roamed inside, stopping intermittently to store moments that had transpired: evenings in the sitting room, chats in the kitchen, my place at the dining table, Christmas dinner, my good luck coin, and singing birthday tributes and "God Save the Queen." The kitchen table, where I sat with Mum every day after school, now looked ordinary. I wished I could take it with me. I eyed the refrigerator, Hogsnort's final resting place, and remembered Mum's retort: "No reason to bust a gut." I managed a smile. Latent aromas from Dad's pipe, smoldering embers, Earl Grey tea, coffee, toast, and yeast haunted me. Dormant sounds whispered in my ears: Mark on the piano, bagpipes whining on the record player, shrieking magpies, Mum snoring, and Mum laughing.

I stared at my Wellington boots slotted next to Mum's. *They'd be Sarah's someday.*

Perusing my bedroom, I recalled that first day: "Give 'er some peace," Mum had said, smiling, the boys poised in the doorway. Back home, my room was sparsely decorated; there were only a few choice items on the walls. I'd wallpapered this room with memorabilia from AFS trips, school exchanges, and family adventures. Stripped away, the room now felt empty. The walls would need plastering and paint. When she saw them, Mum was aghast, but she didn't say anything.

A whirlwind of times spent engulfed me. Brushing off tears, I moved on, documenting minuscule details of my New Zealand home, from the airborne dust to the way the house creaked. My mind was overwhelmed with a cocktail of sadness and fear, the emotions too biting and novel to make sense of. I never thought I'd be mourning the loss of these people, the hosts and keepers of the home I lived in; I never thought they'd come to be my family, that I would let them in, that I would become one with them.

Mum and Dad were outside, waiting. I closed the kitchen door, walked under the arbor one last time, stroked a wrinkly passion fruit, and made my way to the car. The boys and Sarah were already inside. Mum stood by the car. Dad was at the back, lifting my suitcase into the trunk. Stuffed and bulky, it was difficult for him to maneuver it. If not for the flexible fabric, it wouldn't have closed.

After more than an hour, our journey mostly silent, we arrived at the airport. My eyes were drawn to Pam's voice before I saw her, flanked by her host family. A frenzied mob awaited at the Air New Zealand ticket counter: my mob. We knew each other well, but this was the first time I'd seen my colleagues with their host families, everyone savoring every minute before separation. Most likely, we would never see our families again—the US is a long way from New Zealand—and after we arrived in San Francisco and went our separate ways, it was doubtful we'd see each other again either.

We continued to the gate where I said my goodbyes to Mum and Dad and my siblings—my second family. We promised to write, to send tapes, but I wouldn't see them again, or if I did, it wouldn't be the same. Not wanting to let go, I hung on to each hug, especially with Mum. *Who would I talk to now?*

"Cheers, love; it will be fine," she said. I wasn't so sure.

I had a window seat and planned to track the islands until they disappeared. Searching the terminal windows, hoping to see my family, I saw only shadowy blobs. I imagined the forms were them and returned waves though I knew they couldn't see me.

The giddy mood of my fellow exchange students across and up the aisle was confusing but helped elevate my mood. I felt sorry for the stewardess who tried but failed to get my friends to stay in their seats. This was our last party together, and several kids were determined to make the most of it. Friendly and coaxing at first, the stewardess resorted to exasperated threats.

I wasn't the only one conflicted about going home. No one wanted the year to end, but their escalating chatter revealed a desire to return to old haunts: rejoin a sports team, edit the school newspaper, go to a game, get ready for prom. My internal dialogue deviated considerably. I bristled when contemplating the chaotic lair I was returning to, each recollection competing with memories of afternoons and weekends spent with my New Zealand family where it had seemed so easy . . . so safe.

A veil of loneliness ensnared me, my mind crammed with serial images of airport reunions: loved ones running with arms reaching out and collapsing into joyous embraces, and young children and girlfriends lifted into the air, faces ecstatic, gleeful, and loving. I envisioned my family jumping with excitement at the airport, all poised in midair, and me not moving at the arrival gate, my feet rooted as if buried in concrete.

Fourteen hours later, by way of Fiji and Hawaii, Pam and I said goodbye in San Francisco. We made a pact to see each other in the near future, maybe after graduation. Boarding the plane to Portland—my final stretch and only one hour away—I thought of Mom scurrying about the kitchen, cleaning up and yelling for everyone to get ready, "We can't be late! And put on something decent." The image aroused both comfort and dread.

The hour-long flight dragged. I never felt lonelier, and I fought off tears. My neighbor didn't seem to notice, which was an improvement over the outgoing trip's *Playboy* pervert.

"Ladies and gentlemen, on your left is Mount Hood," the pilot announced. "Gorgeous views to the right and left. Clear skies over Portland don't happen every day."

The mountain filled my window frame, its majesty demanding attention. Heavy with snow, it reigned over the terrain. Where the snow ended, cedars blanketed the landscape right to the shore of the Columbia River, their tips like crayons jammed in a box, each point a shade of dark green. Far off in the distance, I could make out Mount St. Helens, Mount Rainier, and Mount Baker. A flurry of emotions rushed through me: excitement, apprehension, joy, warmth. I was taken aback by the kinship I suddenly felt for this place and the people waiting below. I was home. Ant-sized cars passed on the freeway. I imagined my family in one of them. *They were probably late.*

I collected my bag—loaded with memories, clothes, and gifts—and proceeded through customs. Following a convoy of travelers, I exited the international gate and scanned the crowd, searching faces, looking for my people. Not seeing them, I panicked.

They're not here.

At last, I saw them, four towheads, three gingers, and two proud parents smiling a delicious cocktail of delight, love, pride, and, in my parents' eyes, relief. My pace quickened. I stopped just short of barreling into them. John Patrick wrapped his arms tightly around my legs. The others pushed and shoved playfully, sparring to bestow a welcome-home hug. Mom and Dad gently nudged their way into the fray, their embraces lingering and their grips calm, deliberate, and intimate. Engulfed by their hellos, I let go, releasing my fears.

On the drive home, John Patrick sat on my lap, covering my face with kisses. He expected some in return, but I pulled back, not knowing what to do. His affection was overwhelming and scary— a channel to my old self— and despite resisting, my barriers mounted. I didn't want to be sucked back into that universe.

If only I could dive into my bag and throw it back onto the plane.

Questions erupted. So many eager eyes and expectant faces; so loud. I drew a blank, which one should I answer? My stomach stiffened. I couldn't breathe, as if I were bound by a vintage corset, the laces pulling ever tighter.

Once home, I floundered, unable to settle in. Nothing was the same. Steve was a college student. Attending LCC (Lower Community College), he still lived at home, but he was different, the magnitude of his evolution mind-boggling. We never spoke of our former rivalry or the bullying, not then, not ever. His eyes told me everything: "It happened. It's over. I'm sorry. Forgive me. Let's move on. Can we start anew?" Just one look had expressed what seemed like our entire lifetime together.

I was mystified.

Tom, my closest sibling, was a mega popular high schooler. He was having a brilliant year: like my exchange-student year but without the traveling. The one person I could've sought out was unavailable, busy, and, in my mind, unable to help. How could he understand what it was like to flip from being a no one to a someone and back to a no one?

Once the carefree bouncy girl I envied, Mary had taken over my role as babysitter and mother's helper around the house. Barry, Joe, and Greg had replaced Steve and Tom on the baseball field and the basketball court, coalescing into a mighty threesome and carving out a new space within our tribe.

I didn't know where I fit.

And most alarming of all, my parents were different parents. New norms replaced the belt and the wooden spoon. Now there were conversations, time-outs, and motivation. Soap was still generously deployed for language violations—especially when the f-bomb slipped—which was a welcome confirmation that I was in the right house. What's more, watching Mom parent John Patrick baffled me to no end; my John Patrick whom I'd cared for.

I used to collect him after school from the neighbor lady across the street. She had a little boy near John Patrick's age, a seemingly perfect babysitting option while I was at school and Mom was working. Now he spent his days at the store with Mom. I disapproved. It didn't seem right. While working at the store, I watched him play alone, racing Matchbox sports cars, and demanded to know why.

"He doesn't have anyone to play with. Why doesn't he go to the babysitter anymore?"

"He was miserable. He's happy here."

"He wasn't miserable before."

"Well, that changed. You left, the boys were at school all day, and I was working. He was lonely, unconsolably sad. He told me he hated being the youngest. *Everybody leaves you,* his words."

Engulfed with guilt, I said nothing more. John Patrick's distress wasn't only due to my absence, but I'd hurt him while having my perfect year. Guilt wasn't all I felt. I heard another voice while listening to him play with a race car, an ugly scream coming from my gut.

Why weren't you there for me, Mom? Where were you when I needed you?

She'd heard *him.* She'd listened to *him.* And she'd stepped in. She was there for him.

Located alongside her desk was an area set aside for him, awash with a collection of his toys. I unpacked a new shipment of clothes and watched him play in a makeshift fort made from my emptied boxes. He was happy. Mom sat at her desk, tallying numbers. I scanned her face. It was a face

I only remembered seeing when she was with her friends—calm, poised, happy. I realized in that moment that John Patrick had a different mother.

Mom and Dad were sixteen when they met. They married three days after her eighteenth birthday, when she was of legal age. Eleven months later, Steve was born; eleven months after that, I was born—one month shy of her twentieth birthday. She was thirty-three when John was born. My parents were now thirty-seven and partners in business.

I was completely flummoxed. I didn't know her. I didn't want to believe it, but I had to admit her transformation hadn't happened in one year. All I'd wanted was for her to be strong, to stand up to Dad, and to be lively, spry, and playful. But when she did show signs of change, when she got that first job (long before John Patrick was born), and when she looked more assured, I was not happy for her. My resentment rose with her newfound independence, an independence that meant less freedom for me. I was still angry, but while watching her with John Patrick, it was harder and harder to hold onto my rage.

I examined her face, drawing it in my mind and capturing every nuance as if she were a stranger. I didn't know this woman.

I turned my gaze to Dad, who was also in the room; he was on the phone at his desk. I didn't know him either. The three of them were a happy little unit. I was the outlier.

Who the hell was I supposed to be?

Chapter Thirty-Two
Catching Up

I'D WORKED MYSELF INTO A TIZZY THINKING THE EXTRA POUNDS on my frame was the forbidding threat to going home; but it wasn't, though people did notice. I watched their eyes drift from my face to my body, appraising, judging, castigating. It stung, despite no one saying a word about the weight, not even Steve. He held his eyes aloft, preventing them from wandering, as if habit would intercede.

Fortunately, once there were no cream cakes and outlandish spreads, the weight dropped off, and, before long, I was wearing my pre-New Zealand clothes. The real predicament was being around people who looked at me but saw only the girl who left. I didn't know how to climb back into her skin. I didn't want to nor knew how not to.

Being alone was easier. My favorite time was between home and school.

It was Monday morning, the beginning of another baffling week. It had rained the night before. I kept to the sidewalk, avoiding puddles. If not for the muddy trail, I would've taken the lakeside path, which was down and under two bridges, dreamy passages promising alternative worlds beyond the shadows. I missed my New Zealand home. It was summer there and early morning (twenty-two hours from now, or tomorrow minus one hundred and twenty minutes). The sun would be advancing on the horizon like watercolors across paper. Mum and Dad would be stirring, the boys and Sarah still snoozing.

I'd left the house early—John Patrick was still in his pajamas, and the boys were fighting over toast—so I could take my time, soak up the scenery, and let my thoughts wander. For a blissful thirty minutes, I didn't have to fake how wonderful it was to be back or subdue the alleged British accent I'd acquired. "I didn't go to Britain," I insisted. It made no difference.

My inner voice was now an American-Kiwi-Māori mix full of New Zealand phrases I struggled to not use. I'd absorbed the rhythmic cadence of their sentences, my voice swinging high and low as if riding a wave. On my morning walk to school and afternoon saunter home, I didn't agonize over what I said or how I said it. Sometimes I spoke aloud, spewing whatever slang or curse word was on my tongue, desperate to let go.

I was plodding and would be late if I didn't get a move on. "Crikey, you're going to miss the bus," I imagined Mum yelling.

"I'm coming," I shouted, but only the trees heard me.

Back in New Zealand, Mark, Greg, and Ricky would soon don their school uniforms: gray shorts, a short-sleeved shirt, and a tie. Dad would wear shorts, too, with a suit jacket and knee socks. Grinning at the silliness of his ensemble, I remember thinking it was more suitable for a child's uniform, but I never said so. If I could see him again, I wouldn't secretly laugh at his knobby knees. Mum favored sundresses; she always wore them, except when riding. Flashbacks of Misty, me plowing over her head, invaded my happy thoughts and precipitated an evaluation of my platform shoes: useless for riding, but the toes were factory-strong, perfect for protecting my toes from Misty's hooves.

Sorry, Misty. I don't miss you.

I stopped to wipe off my glasses. The air was wet, like walking through a fine spray; the hillsides were cloaked in clouds. Entrapped cedars appeared gauzy-gray, but the town itself was green, carpeted with lush grass. But there were no sheep or cattle grazing, and the paper mill made everything smell of rotten eggs instead of that familiar whiff of dung. I still liked mornings like this, but now they were different. I was different. The gray was inviting; it gave no expectations as a New Zealand blue sky did. And the mornings were quieter: as if the mist had made off with the clatter. Even the nearby squabble of geese seemed muted, and I could hear myself, choose the conversation, and think only of trees and mist and home without feeling guilty—without deferring to the old me.

The high school chaos—banging lockers, strangers, and, especially, old friends I didn't know whether to duck or embrace—assailed me, even though nothing ugly had happened here. I'd walked these hallways for some two-and-a-half years, nearly five hundred days without incident, while expecting catastrophe: something heinous around every corner. Not a mean word was said to me, yet I could feel her, this terrified shadow, trailing me, clawing to get inside and reclaim her territory.

I plied my way through the lunch crowd, took my seat at the table of eight, and assumed my former demeanor—there but not there. I was biding time. The moment I arrived on US soil, I began planning to leave. Soon I'd be gone, out of here, and off to Seattle, a first-year at the University of Washington. Once there, I would let loose and be who I wanted to be: among strangers. I could taste those early days in New Zealand, when I operated on my own terms, free of baggage, and I wanted them back. I knew New Zealand wasn't perfect: adjusting to my new family hadn't come easily; I'd been branded a cheat; my first boyfriend jilted me; I'd deplored the school system, and I'd spent eleven months terrified of the GCE exams. I'd been a feeble country girl, and I'd forever hesitate when opening a refrigerator for fear of Hogsnort's eyes reproaching me. But none of those downsides mattered now. I'd felt whole there, aware and able to deal with anything that came my way, and I ached to return or to run away and start over.

I'd embraced my old ways for weeks, fading into the background. Now I was stuck, mired in my own quicksand. I hadn't minded, until today. Mum's words were needling me, as if she were sitting next to me, scolding, "This will not do." My friends were immersed in prom planning. I didn't care about the prom theme, but I pretended to be enthused. Their presence bedeviled me. Three years on, and I didn't really know a single person sitting at my table of eight.

One of those we-need-to-talk sessions spurred by Mum, who was fed up with my detachment, spun about in my head. "A gift and a curse," she'd said. "Watchers see the minutia the rest of us miss." Parceling a warning, she'd added, "It can be a comfortable place, roaming around in your own world. . . . And lonely." She'd been in story mode that day as we sat at the kitchen table for our afternoon ritual. I missed that ritual and tried to recollect our conversations. They were beginning to dim, but not this one. She'd evoked an Indian proverb of blind men examining an elephant that illustrates the folly of trusting a singular point of view. Individually, each blind man detected a different object—a wall, a spear, a snake, a tree trunk, a fan—depending on their location around the elephant. None realized it was an elephant. At the time, I'd kept a straight face and rejected her reasoning while taking note of everything she said.

Now her words rang in my ears. She was right about loneliness but only half right about the meaning of the elephant story. I now realized that watching without engaging didn't give rise to a richer perspective. I'd been watchful but hadn't paid attention. I was a poor witness to everyone's story, especially my own. My world had become small; like the blind men, I saw only a fraction of what was before me.

I looked around the table. "Eight elephants," I thought, "all a mystery." Barb was laughing her across-town laugh. People said she had a belly laugh. They were all wrong; she laughed from her throat. Her eyes were small, and her thick bangs laid straight, undisturbed despite her laughter. Concentrating on her gestures, like the slight changes in the lines around her mouth and the crinkles about her eyes, I searched for clues to this person I thought I knew.

Did she laugh as freely in her own home?

Her face contorted by a monstrous mouth and flashing green eyes, Barb threw me a quizzical look. Embarrassed, I looked away, puzzled by the odd vision. *I should have some inkling about Barb's world.* What was she like at home, with strangers, or when alone? I moved on to Carmen, then to Lynne, and then to the others around the table. Dreaming up outlandish personas and backstories, I inspected their faces when they were quiet or animated. When I ran out of specimens to observe, I turned the lens on myself. *I wasted so much time hiding.*

I missed Mum. Seeking her advice, I imagined the two of us sitting at the kitchen table and chatting, her eyes dive-in-deep accessible, kind, and patient. I knew she would not stand for my in-between state. If the table of eight were Down Under, I'd be commenting on my friend's ideas and jumping in—willingly—with my own, even when I didn't care about the topic. I was a participant over there. I was present.

I knew how to do it. What was I waiting for?

The thirst for a new audience, one that didn't know me, consumed me. Yet looking around the table, I felt like a cheat by not giving them a chance. Something inside me flared, and I shuddered. This time the big C fit. This time, I really was cheating.

"Let go," I heard Mum say.

On my walk home, I thought about the blind men's elephant and imagined my family as a herd crowded in front of the TV, trunks entangled, massive bums warping the walls outward. The vision was only partly funny; deep down at the very center of my bones, fear and unease stirred. If I walked away now, I'd be walking away from them. I was raised a Catholic. Family was always front and center—the Holy Family and my own—a belief that had been ingrained in me since my first mindful Christmas and the first day a newborn sibling was placed in my lap. I'd resisted being a part of my family, fighting against its righteous pull from the pulpit, the nuns, and my parents. It wasn't a conscious choice to keep everyone at bay, not at first, but simply a survival response: flight. School was not safe; home was not safe; nowhere was safe. I fought back the only way I knew how; I retreated inwardly to the one person I could trust: me. With time, I became the great disappearer of foe, ally, and, unwittingly, myself. Until New Zealand. Until I was a bona fide member of a family—not a pseudo parent or a perfect daughter.

I knew Mum would scoff at my reticence: "That was then. Now is now; give them a chance." She'd taught me what a family could be: full, supportive, and joyful. Now, I wanted my family, I wanted to treasure each annoying member, and I knew that if I left them now, I'd lose my chance to rewrite a future with them. I knew what I had to do. I took a deep breath before opening the door. I walked inside, my steps now lighter but stronger.

John Patrick was home, sitting on the floor playing with Lincoln Logs. Mom and Dad had hired a gal to run the front of the store. She opened in the morning and closed at night, allowing Mom to come home early. He jumped up when he saw me. "Catherine! Want to build a farm with me?"

"Sure do." I lifted him up, and we twirled. The two of us laughed, me from deep in my belly. He was getting big, but not too big for piggyback rides and up-in-the-air hugs.

We built a one-room house, a tower, a barn, and several fenced enclosures. John Patrick placed animals (which had all been appropriated from other games) of varying sizes into the pens. The sheep towered over the horses, as did a rooster, and a tiger stood in for a menacing cougar. The boys were playing nearby, racing Matchbox cars. I observed them as I'd watched my table-of-eight friends. I could describe the boys, sketch a close likeness, but I knew nothing of their worlds, their joys, their trials, or their dreams. How could I? I hadn't paid attention.

I waited until dinner was finished, the dishes were dried and put away, and my siblings went downstairs to watch TV. Mom and Dad were in the living room reading the paper, enjoying their quiet time at the end of the day.

"Got a minute?" I asked.

They looked up from their papers, eyes wide with curiosity, knowing by the tone of my voice something was up.

"I've decided to go to LCC, get my associate's degree, and then transfer to UW."

"I thought you couldn't wait to leave?" Mom asked, unveiling unspoken exasperation and hurt.

I'd never mentioned wanting to leave, but it was obvious she knew and had held her tongue. Another truth I'd missed: she'd been watching and paying attention. I, on the other hand, hadn't noticed she was hurting.

"I can complete most of my pre-med prerequisites here. It would be cheaper—a third of the tuition and no lodging for two years. I was hoping to stay here, if that's all right."

"I'm all for cheaper, but what about your plans to move to Seattle and UW?" Dad wasn't buying my argument either. He waited, the paper now folded on his lap.

I'd succumbed to the travel bug on the flight out to New Zealand. Now as emblematic as my red hair, I knew travel was in my future—new cities, new countries, new friends—but it could wait.

"I'll still go, just later." My mouth went dry. I knew what I wanted to say, but a coherent explanation was as elusive as the glass of water I was suddenly thirsty for.

Mom and Dad sat still, waiting.

"I missed a lot in the past year. John Patrick's grown so much; the boys, too. Besides, I just got back. Leaving again, so soon, would be hard on John Patrick."

Mom's eyes widened. I couldn't tell whether she was surprised or bewildered. She looked over at Dad. He was taken aback, but I could tell neither would challenge my decision.

"I don't have a lot of time left with the family. This will give me two years before I move out for good." The phrase *with the family* hung in the air, odd and awkward, but not wrong.

I'd done it: stated my intentions aloud. There was no going back. Relieved and in need of oxygen—I'd been holding my breath—I inhaled slowly and deeply. Mom and Dad were still staring, their mouths open.

I wanted to tell them I'd noticed how their manner toward my younger siblings had changed, how supportive they now were, and how they now gave the kids their full attention. I wanted to say I understood that they were both so young when I had needed them, that there were so many of us, that they'd done their best, and that I'd changed, too. I wanted to say so many things, to tell them that I loved them and that things would be different from now on.

Not wanting to hurt or ambush them, I held my tongue. It didn't seem necessary to explain. I'd outgrown the hunger for it.

Instead, I said, "I have a lot of catching up to do."

Acknowledgments

THIS BOOK WOULD NOT HAVE BEEN POSSIBLE IF NOT FOR THE gracious support of my mother and siblings. All were available for my calls, no matter how vague my requests for information. Our memories were not always the same. There were times when multiple versions of a story surfaced. Late night or early morning discussions sorted out the varied takeaways of common exploits, enriching my understanding. Sadly, my father passed while writing this book. I and my siblings often remarked, "Dad would know," when no one else could remember. In his absence, Steve was my go-to for those early memories, memories that had become family legends that only the two of us could recall firsthand. And a special thanks to Steve. This book is not about him, but about bullying, in which he played a part. He could have spurned my requests for help, but he did not, a testament to his character.

I'd like to thank my husband, who was the first to read every chapter and each completed draft. Also, to my daughters Kyra and Megan, both talented writers who offered succinct and thoughtful advice. I will be forever indebted to the Algonquin Writers Group. The first time I publicly read my work was during a group session. The members listened keenly and afforded kind, practical, and upbeat feedback. They continued to do so during the following months and subsequent four years it took to complete the project. A special call out to my beta readers, Brad and Michelle Mathis, Megan Sullivan, Chris Bell, and Kevin Ottem-Fox. Brad and Michelle deftly lead our writing group and agreed to be beta readers for multiple draft manuscripts. And much gratitude to Kevin Ottem-Fox, who read every version and encouraged me to "dig deeper." The book would not be the book it is without his sage advice.

Three editors have worked on this book in its varying stages: Linda Carbone, Erica Manfred, and Jasmine Marrott. Linda tackled the book in its earliest format, when the manuscript was muddled and unfocused. Erica helped shape the next phase, bringing it all home. Jasmine, from WiDo Publishing, steered *Chasing Tarzan* to print. All three made me a better writer.

Lastly, I'd like to thank my mother and my New Zealand mum. Without them, I would not be the person I am today.

Supplemental Thoughts from the Author

MY GREATEST FEAR WHEN TEN YEARS OLD WAS ENDING UP LIKE that woman pictured on our Old Maid deck of cards: alone and ugly. Neither happened. This year, I welcomed my twenty-fifth year of marriage to a man I trust, love dearly, and respect. He is my go-to person, the first to view a new artwork or writing project, and the one I look to for guidance on personal issues and parental matters concerning our children. I did go on to the University of Washington and graduate. Later, I sought out postgraduate studies in Chicago and London. And, yes, travel became a core element of my life, one of many gifts fostered during my year in New Zealand. I've lived and worked in numerous countries, and I've endeavored to expose our children to the diverse people and landscapes of our planet. But it has not always been easy. It was naive to assume one year in New Zealand would erase years of unrelenting abuse. Nearly a decade of conditioning had bred a jaundiced internal voice that reigned for many years into adulthood. Thankfully, my parents were there for me. Moreover, I knew what being whole felt like—my New Zealand year—a blueprint I relied on and pursued until it became my norm and remained so.

The long-term effects of bullying are real. Research findings, regardless of their genesis, are remarkably similar: adults who were victims of bullying are more likely to suffer from depression, relationship problems, substance abuse, stress-related shorter life spans, and suicide; bullies who were also bullied, are susceptible to the same problems as their victims, plus they are more likely to be incarcerated; on the other hand, bullies who were not bullied have a higher risk of antisocial behavior and are likely to continue bullying into adulthood.

Despite the potential long-term aftereffects, those who've suffered bullying do not have to be defined by the abuse. Studies show that when a child has a trusted advocate, the impact of bullying can be diminished. I know firsthand that having a champion, someone who believes in you, stands up for you, and validates that you're worthy of love and deserving of nothing less, makes all the difference. While writing this book, I discovered many vigilant angels: the lovely Miss Jo; Mr. Holbrook, who honored me with my first insult-free nickname; Debbie Moon, who was not a friend but left a formidable mark; my brother Tom, whose eyes told me it would be okay; my parents, who watched as best as they could and took in more than I knew; and my New Zealand mum, who saw through me, acknowledged the wounded girl within, and helped me see who I could be, who I already was.

To my readers, know you have the potential to change a child's trajectory, and to those who have suffered bullying, know that this was abuse, and you are a survivor.

About the Author

Catherine Forster honed her powers of observation early on, and later applied them to artistic endeavors. Although it didn't happen overnight, she discovered that seeing and hearing a bit more than the average person can be beneficial. As an artist, her work has exhibited in museums and galleries across the United States and abroad. Her experimental films have won accolades and awards in more than thirty international film festivals, from Sao Paulo to Berlin, Los Angeles to Rome, London to Romania. Through her work, she explores the dynamics of girlhood, notions of identity, and the role technology plays in our relationship with nature.

In her capacity as an independent curator, she founded LiveBox, an eight-year project that introduced new media arts to communities at a time when few knew what media arts was. For the past four years she has been a member of the curatorial team for the Experiments In Cinema Film Festival held annually in Albuquerque, New Mexico. She received a Masters of Fine Arts from the School of the Art Institute of Chicago, a Masters of Business from

the London Business School, and a fellowship in writing from the Vermont Studio Center. She is also included in the Brooklyn Art Museum's Elizabeth A. Sackler Center for Feminist Art.

Ingram Content Group UK Ltd.
Milton Keynes UK
UKHW021952080523
421401UK00015B/881